Children in the Taiwanese fishing comn
drawn, consciously and unconsciously, to
their participation in schooling, family life
about 'virtuous mothers', share 'meaningl ... . other villagers, visit the
altars of 'divining children' and participate in 'dangerous' god-strengthening
rituals. In particular, they learn about the family-based cycle of reciprocity, and the
tension between this and commitment to the nation. Charles Stafford's study of
childhood in this community (with additional material from northeastern mainland
China) explores absorbing issues related to nurturance, education, family, kinship
and society in its analysis of how children learn, or do not learn, to identify
themselves as both familial and Chinese.

Cambridge Studies in Social and Cultural Anthropology

97

THE ROADS OF CHINESE CHILDHOOD

Cambridge Studies in Social and Cultural Anthropology

Editorial Board
Ernest Gellner, University of Cambridge
Jack Goody, University of Cambridge
Stephen Gudeman, University of Minnesota, Minneapolis
Michael Herzfeld, Harvard University
Jonathan Parry, London School of Economics and Political Sciences

The monograph series Cambridge Studies in Social and Cultural Anthropology publishes analytical ethnographies, comparative works and contributions to theory. All combine an expert and critical command of ethnography and a sophisticated engagement with current theoretical debates.

A list of books in the series will be found at the end of the volume.

THE ROADS OF CHINESE CHILDHOOD

Learning and identification in Angang

CHARLES STAFFORD
University of Cambridge

CAMBRIDGE UNIVERSITY PRESS
Cambridge, New York, Melbourne, Madrid, Cape Town, Singapore, São Paulo

Cambridge University Press
The Edinburgh Building, Cambridge CB2 2RU, UK

Published in the United States of America by Cambridge University Press, New York

www.cambridge.org
Information on this title: www.cambridge.org/9780521465748

© Cambridge University Press 1995

This publication is in copyright. Subject to statutory exception
and to the provisions of relevant collective licensing agreements,
no reproduction of any part may take place without
the written permission of Cambridge University Press.

First published 1995
This digitally printed first paperback version 2006

A catalogue record for this publication is available from the British Library

Library of Congress Cataloguing in Publication data
Stafford, Charles.
The roads of Chinese childhood: learning and identification in
Angang / Charles Stafford.
   p. cm. – (Cambridge studies in social and cultural
anthropology: 97)
Includes bibliographical references.
ISBN 0 521 46574 5 (hardback)
1. Children–Taiwan–Angang–Social life and customs.
2. Children–Taiwan–Angang–Family relationships.   3. Child
psychology–Taiwan–Angang.   4. Children–China–Manchuria–Social
life and customs.   5. Children–China–Manchuria–Family
relationships.   6. Child psychology–China–Manchuria.   7. Kinship–
Taiwan–Angang.   8. Kinship–China–Manchuria.   9. Angang (Taiwan)–
Social life and customs.   10. Manchuria (China)–Social life and
customs.   I. Title.   II. Series.
GN635.C5S73   1995
305.23'051–dc20   94-35660 CIP

ISBN-13 978-0-521-46574-8 hardback
ISBN-10 0-521-46574-5 hardback

ISBN-13 978-0-521-02656-7 paperback
ISBN-10 0-521-02656-3 paperback

For Jean-Jacques

Contents

List of illustrations	*page* xi
Preface	xiii
Acknowledgements	xv

Part 1 Background

	Introduction	3
1	Two roads	17

Part 2 Angang

2	Ghosts are not connexions	33
3	The proper way of being a person	56
4	Textbook mothers and frugal children	69
5	Red envelopes and the cycle of *yang*	79
6	Going forward bravely	112
7	Divining children	122
8	Dangerous rituals	144
9	Conclusion	166

Part 3 Epilogue

10	Notes on childhood in northeastern China	175

Notes	186
Glossary	196
References	205
Index	211

Illustrations

1	Girl playing in a courtyard next to stove for burning offerings (Angang)	*page* 20
2	Girl wearing protective *xianghuo* (Angang)	23
3	Houses (Angang)	36
4	Preparing food for offerings (Angang)	85
5	Military service cadets at Angang Middle School	116
6	Chiang Kai-shek Memorial (Taipei)	119
7	Altar with images of gods and offerings of food and money	129
8	Sister and brother (northeastern China)	178
9	The *manzhousui* celebration for a boy (northeastern China)	181

Preface

The Chinese idiom *zuo ma guan hua*, 'viewing the flowers from horseback,' is used to describe superficial or hurried observations, and the conclusions they give rise to. Said with reference to anthropology, *zuo ma guan hua* would be a particularly telling criticism, because so much of life in China is rightly felt to reside beneath the surface, to be complex and hidden from view. But of course any perspective, 'from horseback' or otherwise, has strengths and weaknesses.

What follows is an account of childhood and learning based on fieldwork in the Taiwanese fishing community of Angang (with additional material from northeastern China). Rather than investigating in depth one aspect of the lives of children there, I have tried to hold many things in view: schools, families, money, food, spirit mediums, rituals and so on. Some may feel that this is an excellent example of 'viewing flowers from horseback'. Each of these subjects could easily fill a book, and many have been discussed in greater detail by others (I will direct readers to this literature). But I wanted to present my own wide-ranging, if incomplete, account of childhood in Angang; and hopefully in doing so to show some connexions which others may not have seen.

Before beginning, however, I should raise several important issues, and ask readers to bear them in mind. First, Angang is in many ways not typical of Taiwan, much less of mainland China. It is an unusually isolated fishing community, with its own unique histories and traditions. Many of these are, of course, linked to broader patterns of Taiwanese and Chinese culture and history. But my rendering of childhood in Angang should not be taken as a model of childhood anywhere else.

Second, readers should be aware that the text includes Chinese terms in both Hokkien and Mandarin. This will not be obvious except in the glossary, where the system of transliteration is explained, and the dialect of each term is indicated. But the question of language is very important to many people in Taiwan, and has political implications (as does the notion that Taiwan exemplifies China). Although the official language is Mandarin, and almost everyone in Angang is able to speak it, villagers usually speak Hokkien as they go about their daily lives. Mandarin is the language of schooling, and children and young people often use it amongst themselves (and usually did so when explaining things to me). This bilinguality raises questions of great complexity which are not explored here.

Third, I should stress that my account often deals with notions of what *should* happen, rather than detailed accounts of what does happen. For instance, the conviction that 'children should support their ageing parents' is certainly widely held in Angang. It is also easy to provide examples of it being put into practice, because many children do in fact support their parents in some way. Readers should bear in mind, however, that closer examination reveals many ambiguities surrounding such traditions. An account which focuses on representations may easily produce an overly conservative and static view of things.

The final and perhaps most crucial point concerns gender. Margery Wolf has noted that: 'Gender differences in personhood and the construction of the self in Chinese society are a much neglected topic. Much of the research either asserts that there are no differences ... or ignores gender completely ... by default taking the male self to be the Chinese self' (1990:429). In many ways, the lives of young girls and boys in Angang are quite similar; and especially in this way: they mostly encounter the same representations (in school and in the community) as they grow up. They usually read the same texts, observe the same rituals, eat the same 'meaningful' foods, and so on. They often appear to be treated in more or less the same way by the adults around them. But the apparent sameness in what children see and do is misleading, for the representations themselves often proclaim profound and irreducible differences between daughters and sons, mothers and fathers, wives and husbands. It is not so much that girls and boys learn differently, rather that they learn difference. The issue of gender is, in this way, and as will become obvious, immanent in the experience of childhood.

Acknowledgements

Fieldwork was conducted in Angang (a rural township consisting of several villages) during 1987–9. (In order to protect the privacy of informants, all place and personal names have been changed.) I first lived for several months with teachers at the Angang middle school (*zhongxue*), and then moved to the village of Beicun, where I lived with a local family for the remainder of my stay. I am very grateful to the many friends in Angang whose lives I undoubtedly disrupted, but who showed me unfailing warmth and generosity. I have not repaid their kindness, but I hope they would not be too disappointed by my account of their community.

During my stay in Taiwan, I was affiliated with the Institute of Ethnography at the Academia Sinica; I am particularly grateful to Lin Mei-rong, Huang Ying-kuei and Huang Hsuan-wei of the Institute for their help and assistance. Funding was received from the Taiwan History Field Research Project (Luce Foundation), the Wenner-Gren Foundation, and the Central Research Fund (University of London). The fieldwork was part of my doctoral studies at the London School of Economics, and I am indebted to many people there. The research was supervised by Maurice Bloch, and I am especially grateful for his help and encouragement over the years in spite of my manifest thickness.

During the preparation of this manuscript, and during more recent visits to northeastern China, I held a Chiang Ching-kuo Fellowship at the Faculty of Oriental Studies, Cambridge University. I especially thank David McMullen for his kind assistance during that time. I am also indebted to Stuart Thompson (of the School of Oriental and African Studies) and Stephan Feuchtwang (of the City University); they have given generous help, and the influence of their work will be clear in what follows. Finally I must thank my family and many friends, especially Rita Astuti and Janet Carsten, for their love and support.

PART 1

BACKGROUND

Introduction

This book is about education. However, forgetting that for a moment, imagine a situation in which children already knew most of what they are *taught*, having learnt it while it was *not* being taught to them. In which case, a book about education would become a complicated thing to write. Everything that presented itself as educational would have to be understood as something else again.

Angang is a fishing community, a rural township (*xiang*) in southeastern Taiwan, and a place in which formal education seems of obvious importance, a central concern of daily life. Clamorous student rituals echo off the surrounding hills and down onto the villages, children spend entire days in school-related tasks, and many adults follow with interest events inside the school compounds. At times, the daily and seasonal routines of the community seem as geared to the requirements of learning as they do to fishing, or to the complicated demands of the lunar calendar.

One morning in Angang I saw an elementary school student, the daughter of one of the richest men in a local village, pulling a cardboard box towards the kitchen of her family home. I asked where she was going and, with what seemed to be a look of satisfaction, she replied: *shao keben!*, 'To burn textbooks!' I wanted to know more, but she had no further comment on the subject, silently and unceremoniously placing her books in the stove. This calm act of incineration came soon after the end of the examination period, during which even very young students in Taiwan are exhorted by parents and by themselves to *chenggong*, 'succeed' in their exams. Perhaps she had had enough. Children and adults in Angang say *lu thak lu cheq!*, which roughly means 'The more you study, the more it makes you crazy!'[1] In any case, her textbooks were soon reduced to ashes. This evoked for me, if not for her, the many things in Angang which are burnt (*shao*), including incense (*xiang*), in order to be commended to gods and other spirits.² These offerings are made in various locations, including temples and domestic altars, but also, from time to time, in kitchen stoves.

As children in Angang could not help but know, Chinese food-related symbolism is highly elaborated. Division of a stove is symbolic of family division, and the kitchen is also the location for worshipping, and burning offerings to, Cau Kun, the Stove God.³ People in Angang do not emphasise this particular cult, but most kitchen walls bear a faded image of the God, and villagers know of his important role in the activities surrounding the lunar New Year. He is said to watch the home throughout the year, at the end of which he is sent to Heaven. Then people may for a time freely do the things they usually do not do, or at least should not be doing, such as gambling. Cau Kun meanwhile presents to the higher authorities an annual report, the harshness of which may be lightened in view of the offerings burnt in his honour, detailing the involvement of the family in good and bad affairs (*haoshi/huaishi*).

When is a child said to have withstood this divine scrutiny, to have been good (*hao*)? According to her parents, the girl who burnt her textbooks in the stove at the end of the school year was good, in part *because* she was a better-than-average student, based on her marks in competitive examinations. On this account she had been sent, for a time and at considerable expense, to study in the capital of the county (*xian*). The schools there are thought better than those in the countryside, and she had also been fortunate, as everyone agreed, to attend evening revision sessions at an expensive supplementary school (*buxiban*). As a twelve-year-old, she thus spent a large part of every day studying and re-studying the textbooks which she would later burn in the home of the Stove God. *Lu thak lu cheq!*

Western students of modern Taiwanese education (partly basing their analyses on readings of these textbooks) have been struck by what is most obviously 'Chinese' about it: the teaching of a version of traditional Chinese moral values. Reading the textbooks, it is certainly hard to ignore, for example, the emphasis given to *xiao*, filial obedience, and *zhong*, loyalty/ patriotism (see Wilson 1970, Martin 1975, Meyer 1988, Stafford 1992). But it is not clear that this moral emphasis (which, after all, forms only one part of Taiwanese education) is what stands out in the minds of students, teachers and parents in Angang. If it does not, it may be because it is more or less taken for granted (both the morality itself and the idea that moral instruction is a responsibility of schools). As one teacher told me when discussing middle school courses on ethics and morality, these topics are seen as 'easy to teach and to learn' (*haoxue, haojiao*). They are *changshi*, an expression usually translated as 'common sense', but which could also be rendered as 'ordinary knowledge'.[4]

One thing I hope to describe in this book is the extent to which the 'ordinary' morality of Taiwanese education is similar to, while not being the same as, the everyday morality of family life in Angang. An important difference between the school-based version and the community-based version is that the former is taught, in a direct and recognisable way, whereas the latter almost seems 'not to be taught'. The emphasis in schools on moral transmission is in contrast to a seeming lack of concern with moral *transmission* (as opposed to morality) in the family, and even in local religious practice. Children obviously learn from their parents in many ways, but explicit and public moralising is usually the business of schools, and is in some cases actually frowned upon in community life. I will later discuss the possibility that parental instruction takes place in private, but here I should at least mention that in Angang there is little scope for privacy. Although I lived for some months with the family of the girl who burnt her textbooks, I very rarely heard her mother and father directly discuss with her anything which might resemble *daode*, 'morality', in the classroom or textbook sense. On the other hand, I regularly heard them demand that she *thak cheq!*, 'read books!'

If people in Angang are not struck by the common-sensical morality of the educational system, what are they struck by? Certainly, among other things, by the competitiveness of it. Parents, teachers and children in Angang invariably comment on this (perhaps in part because their schools are very low in the Taiwanese hierarchy). With an eye to classroom rivalry, parents invest in the schooling of their children, and demand that they study. The reason commonly given for this is that parents expect, in line with traditional Chinese morality, that they will be 'respectfully supported' (*fengyang*) in retirement, and even in the after-life, by their children. It is in the interest of parents for their children to be as successful as possible, and educational achievement is seen as one of the most important and accessible paths to success. For this reason, the pressure driving the system is widely seen to come from parents, and not from the schools or the state; indeed, the supplementary classes attended by children in the cities are mostly illegal.

From the perspective of those involved in it, Taiwanese education is not then primarily concerned with the teaching of traditional Chinese moral values (such as filial obedience) because these are viewed as 'ordinary knowledge'. It may not, to them, even be primarily concerned with learning, in the strict sense, of *any* kind. By contrast, education *is* often described as if it were a competitive field, or a platform for success. This concern with school-based rivalry is, in turn, described as a product of the traditional morality of filial obedience. In other words, the content of the moral lessons which are so heavily transmitted in schools almost seems to be made redundant by the pragmatic concerns of a family-based morality which is 'not transmitted' (i.e. not explicitly) in the township. Instead, I will argue, children learn about this morality in other ways, for example through transfers of food and money, through participation in rituals, and so on.

Childhood in Angang is in part a shifting back and forth between these ways of learning. My description is therefore somewhat discontinuous, and it is far removed from an ethnography of education. Instead I will describe the frightening away of souls, textbook stories of girls who become good sons, the partaking of red turtles, teachers who are patterns, the self-mutilation of divining children, the dispensation of red envelopes, rituals of fire-walking and so on. I will suggest that children in Angang, as they encounter representations of childhood, have their attention drawn to certain things, including various forms of identification. At times, certain relationships and social connexions are pointed out, or highlighted, and *that*, inside and outside the school, forms a crucially important part of learning. This process is the theme of my book about Angang.

A Chinese version of education
It seems uncontroversial to say that 'education is important in Angang', or perhaps even throughout East Asia. But what does this statement mean? Education is an English word (from Latin terms meaning 'to raise' and 'to lead forth') and not a universal category. To ask 'What are the features of Chinese *education*?' is thus already to ask a biased question. Even using the Chinese term *jiaoyu*, 'education', which is used in expressions such as *jiaoyubu*, Ministry of Education, may be misleading. This is partly because the complexities of meaning behind the terms are difficult to condense into English.

Consider the following interconnexions between several Chinese expressions related to learning. (Bearing in mind that these are *pinyin* transcriptions of Mandarin pronunciations of Chinese characters.) *Jiaoyu* ('education') implies, as does the Latin root of education, 'raising or nurturing' (e.g., to *yu miao* is to 'cultivate seedlings'). *Jiao* itself means 'to educate', and is also used for 'religion' or 'doctrine' (e.g., in *fojiao*, Buddhism). *Jiao* is also used in one of the expressions for teacher: *jiaoshi*, 'teaching master'. A *shi* is a 'master', but also, in other contexts, an 'example, pattern, or model', an extended definition consistent with Chinese notions of learning (in which, e.g., students imitate the calligraphy of masters). The most common expression for teacher is *laoshi*, 'venerable master'. More simply, *lao* means 'old and experienced'. By contrast, the expression for student, *xuesheng*, means 'new to learning'; *sheng* can also mean 'to be born, to be uncooked, unripe, savage, untamed'. *Sheng* is also used in one of the respectful forms of address for male teachers (commonly used for men in general), *xiansheng*, which literally means 'born earlier'.

Of course, Chinese 'words about education' are actually *zi*, characters, and as such are quite different from English words.[5] For example, the left side of the character *jiao*, 'to educate', at least according to one commentator, is made up of strokes showing the 'influence' (of the master) over the 'disciple' (or 'son'). The right side of the character shows the master bearing a 'rod' (Wieger 1940:109,120). The strokes in *yu* (from *jiaoyu*, 'education') apparently mean 'to feed a child (or an animal), so that it becomes fleshy, strong, fat' (1940:235). The rather dramatic explanation given for the strokes in *xue*, 'to learn', is 'both hands of the master acting from above upon the darkness which covers the mind of the disciple' (1940:109).

These explanations may well be historically inaccurate but they are of the sort commonly used by students. What I am trying to emphasise here, rather than the etymology of specific characters, is a *potential*, and one which helps us to understand how culturally distinct a Chinese notion of 'education' might be. Return for a moment to the girl who burnt her textbooks. Throughout the year she copies various characters time and again, perhaps including the character *jiao*, while practising calligraphy (*shufa*). To what extent, if at all, does she internalise the connexion (regardless of etymology) between the characters for 'education' (*jiao*) and 'filial obedience' (*xiao*)? The left side of *jiao* could easily be mistaken for (and is often written the same as) the character *xiao*. *Xiao* ('filial obedience') very clearly is comprised of the strokes for *lao*, 'old' or 'senior', placed above the strokes for *zi*, 'son' ('descendants', 'seed'); as Karlgren puts it, the character shows 'son beneath old man' (Karlgren 1923:71).

Might a girl copying out these characters also learn principles seemingly embedded in them? One of these is hierarchy/seniority ('filial obedience' shows the elderly above their descendants; 'education' shows the influence of a master upon a son-disciple). Another principle is the significance attached to transmission (of kinship and doctrine) through men: both the descendants and the disciples are 'seed', i.e. 'sons'. It could be misleading to overstate the significance of these embedded meanings, which might not ever occur to a student. But the potential in the characters is one which does not exist in English, at least not in a remotely similar way. How much of the meaning of the Chinese character *jiao*, including its historical associations, could be translated by a single English word, 'education'? In our notion of education, how significant is calligraphy? For the tracing of characters is often described as if it were the definitive act of Chinese learning.

Learning as 'part of life'

But the difficulty here is not simply that of cultural variation in notions, or even systems, of education. The larger problem is that 'education', by any definition, is itself a strange way of classifying an area of social activity. This it shares with the category 'religion'.[6] Where is it to be located? In Taiwan the lives of children and young people seem dominated by universal, mandatory education, which takes place in clearly set off, modern institutions. These institutions seem, in many respects, to be Western in form and inspiration and, in other respects, to be recognisably Chinese. Is education what takes place in these *buildings*? Education (or *jiaoyu*) in Angang might be conceptualised as a classroom interaction, or as the content of lessons, or as the stories in textbooks. But textbooks are also written by people: perhaps one should study the histories of these writers? Or the histories of schoolgirls, or of parents who insist that their daughters should 'read books!' Education is not a discrete category, and someone trying to conceptualise it inevitably has their attention drawn to other difficult to define areas of social life: religion, kinship, economics and so on.

In an ethnographic setting where education was largely informal, and not organised by a Ministry of Education, this loose boundary is perhaps what would be expected. Learning would then be 'part of life'. For some reason it is more difficult to ignore the boundaries of schools once they have been established.[7] Many sociologists have, of course, questioned the point of simply studying the formal aspects of formal schooling. Instead they have framed their questions 'about education' very broadly, and have tried to understand Western schooling in a more general social and historical context (e.g., Durkheim 1972:203–18, Bernstein 1975, Willis 1977, Bourdieu & Passeron 1990).[8]

Anthropologists have, for their part, questioned the very distinction between formal (e.g. school-based) and informal learning, and questioned the way in which we apply the distinction. For instance, Akinnaso (1992) points out that learning in non-literate societies is at times quite formal, and argues that it is therefore mistaken to automatically associate the development of schools with the advent of literacy. Akinnaso thus provides examples of non-literate school-like institutions as evidence against the view that learning in non-literate societies is always informal, simply part of life. Borofsky (1987), in turn, describes Pukapukan learning as it takes place in various contexts, each with its own characteristics and levels of formality. He emphasises the importance of these contexts for the ways in which Pukapukan knowledge is not only passed on, but also approved and disapproved of, and thus made.[9]

So, while sociologists have said that formal Western education must be seen beyond the boundaries of schools, anthropologists have questioned the supposed unboundedness and informality of non-Western learning. This examination of the contrast between types of education is part of a much broader question: what are the implications of transmitting *knowledge* in an increasingly fixed, formalised, organised or institutionalised way? This is, in fact, a series of questions, which anthropologists have addressed from many perspectives. (For instance, in debates on the fixity of ritual, the formalisation of medical knowledge, the introduction of literacy, etc.)

Bourdieu has discussed the rise of educational institutions within the context of these broader questions. His notion of habitus includes a model of learning without institutions: if people have certain 'dispositions' (e.g., to react or behave in particular ways) it is because they have been *inculcated* with these dispositions. The word inculcation comes from a Latin term meaning 'to tread', and Bourdieu focuses especially on informal, pervasive, 'physical', unconscious, and non-verbal transmissions of knowledge. (I have already implied that children in Angang sometimes learn outside school in this way.) Bourdieu notes the immanence of this style of education in traditional societies, its location virtually everywhere and at all times, and contrasts this with formalised instruction:

So long as the work of education is not clearly institutionalized as a specific, autonomous practice, and it is a whole group and a whole symbolically structured environment, without specialized agents or specific moments, which exerts an anonymous, pervasive pedagogic action, the essential part of the *modus operandi* which defines practical mastery is transmitted in practice, in its practical state, without attaining the level of discourse. (1977:87)

One of the implications of this passage may *seem* to be that traditional informal education (through an 'anonymous, pervasive pedagogic action') is ultimately *replaced* by modern formal education (through 'specialised agents' and 'specific moments'). However, the contrast between these types of learning in a single location is, of course, one that anthropologists have often described, especially in colonial settings (and one that Bourdieu himself draws out, see below). Firth (1970), for example, stressed the difference between traditional Tikopian education and that brought by

Europeans. The former was continuous (temporally and socially), it was 'an activity of kinsfolk', and it was practical in that it arose 'from actual situations in daily life'. By contrast, European-style education was periodic, segregated from village life, taught by strangers, and not related to practical concerns (1970:75–6).[10] A somewhat similar contrast might be drawn between school and non-school learning in Angang.

But what is the *significance* of such a contrast? The style of transmission (e.g., the existence or expansion of formal schooling) might (or might not) influence how and what people learn, but also the social relations within which they live. That is, it might have both cognitive and political implications (cf. Bloch 1989:106–36). Bourdieu, for instance, describes the advent of formal education in traditional societies as introducing new forms of learning, but also as part of a broader shift in relations of power (1977:183–97). The actual impact of formal education in specific historical circumstances is a matter for analysis. For example, it has at times been externally imposed and specifically directed against local traditions with dramatic consequences (e.g., see Godelier 1986:191–224). Eickelman has argued (from a political perspective) that 'mass higher education in the Arab and Muslim worlds is reshaping conceptions of self, religion, nation and politics' (1992:643). But Bloch has argued (from a cognitive perspective) that in one Zafimaniry village 'neither writing nor schooling have made any significant difference to the basic organising principles governing the evaluation of knowledge' (Bloch 1993:106).

Cognition, representation and learning
In *Reproduction*, Bourdieu & Passeron (1990:1–68) have outlined two ways of transmitting knowledge.[11] The first is through 'the unconscious inculcation of principles'; the second is through the organised transmission of 'articulated and even formalized principles (explicit pedagogy)' (1990:46–7). The discussion which follows makes clear that the two modes of transmission (through 'unconscious inculcation' and through 'explicit pedagogy') overlap and that both may co-exist in one place and time. Because learning is irreversible, the unconscious development of a 'primary habitus' in childhood will shape the understanding of everything else that follows, including 'explicit pedagogy'. It is 'the basis for the formation of any other habitus' (1990:42).

Schools are one way of organising the transmission of knowledge, and there are other imaginable ways. The nature of the transmission (e.g., skilful, inept, written, unwritten, explicit, unconscious) might influence what is learnt, as might the way in which the knowledge itself is systematised. But learning does not stop and start simply because people set about *organising* the transmission of knowledge. If learning is seen through children, the boundary between school and non-school becomes confused. After all, the question of what people *learn* is, or at least should be, partly distinct from the question of what they are *taught* (Boyer 1993:34). From this perspective, children in Angang could be said to bring 'life' (i.e., what they have learnt) into the school, while outside they continue to learn in informal and somewhat formal ways.

However, as Bloch (1989) has noted, it is also clearly inadequate to say that people learn by simply absorbing whatever knowledge is there (be it formally transmitted or otherwise). Cognitive anthropologists have shown, among other things, that human learning is fundamentally interactive (i.e., not passive), and they have argued that most anthropological accounts of how people acquire concepts are psychologically implausible (Lave 1988, Lave & Wenger 1991, Toren 1990, Bloch 1991, Boyer 1993). How people actually *learn* (as opposed to how societies organise learning) is scarcely understood by anthropologists.

This book does not address questions of cognition, as such, because I do not have the material necessary for such an analysis. As Boyer points out in his discussion of cognition and religious symbolism, material to help us understand cognitive frameworks 'may not be within the range of ordinary anthropological fieldwork, and may require quasi-experimental methods' (Boyer 1993:33; see also Toren 1990, 1993). But I also do not wish to imply that children in Angang simply learn ready-made identities as they internalise cultural patterns. Instead, I want to outline certain things to which their attention *may* be drawn during childhood, and about which they produce *their own* representations. In order to do this I will borrow two ideas from cognitive anthropology, without claiming to have studied cognition, as such.

The first idea – 'drawing attention to' – is partly inspired by Sperber and Wilson (1986), and especially by their discussion of the 'cognitive environments' in which people think.[12] They attach particular importance to ostension, i.e. behaviour which shows (or says) something to someone (1986:38–54, passim). As their discussion makes clear, ostensive behaviour is a central feature of human communication and cognition. Sperber and Wilson focus primarily on spontaneous, intentional communication and behaviour (e.g., utterances and conversations between individuals) rather than on social contexts of the kind described in this book (e.g., participation in rituals). Although some form of ostension is undoubtedly present in all of these settings, it is worth stressing at the outset the considerable difference between the way in which a textbook, meal, ritual, etc., might 'draw attention', and the way in which an utterance might 'draw attention'. Also, much of my description centres on religious beliefs and attitudes, rather than 'factual assumptions', and these may involve special cognitive processes.[13] But here I use the notion of 'drawing attention to' simply as an aid to the description of various learning contexts. My hypothesis is that ostension is an important point of *intersection* between what is there to be learnt, and what children actually learn.

My second borrowing – 'widely-distributed representations' – comes from Sperber's discussion of psychology and anthropology (1985). In his essay, Sperber focuses on the distribution of representations within human populations, describing this in epidemiological terms. His approach has the advantage of evoking the very dense and complicated environment of representations in which humans learn. The account of Angang which follows focuses on one loosely defined subset of these: the representations which relate, in some way, to the identities of Chinese children. These are encountered inside and outside of school, and they potentially influence identification, i.e., the ways in which children think of themselves *socially*.

Chinese education, identification and 'roads'
Some elements of traditional Chinese culture seem to be *self-consciously* transmitted in a non-institutional or non-discursive way. For example, Schipper has described the 'formal' teaching and learning of Daoism as '*l'enseignement sans parole*' (1982:237–75), as something which is learnt in practice, and in particular as a process of learning with the body. What I will be describing of family-based morality in Angang is not limited to (although it does include important elements of) Daoism. Some of it could possibly be described as 'Confucian', a doctrine which is certainly not wordless. But even this parents in Angang seem to teach their children, or children learn for themselves, almost 'without words'. In any case, it will not be difficult to convince anthropologists that learning *outside of schools* in Angang is carried out through what Bourdieu calls the 'whole symbolically structured environment'. The difficulty is in describing the extent to which Chinese schools, even in their modern institutional forms, and even with their unique modes of teaching, are *inseparable* from that environment, and form a key part of it.

The social anthropology of China has largely (but by no means entirely) focused on studies of kinship and religion, an emphasis which is partly a matter of intellectual heritage.[14] Education has usually been only on the margins of these investigations, perhaps because it is an area of marginal interest within anthropology as a whole. Also, there have been good reasons for thinking of modern Chinese education as relatively disconnected from the Chinese cultural tradition, and even specifically directed against it. This is certainly the case in the People's Republic, where official policy has included attempts during the Cultural Revolution to bring an end, once and for all, to 'feudal thinking' and 'superstitious practices'.[15] The Nationalists (first on the mainland, and later on Taiwan) may seem to have been more conservative in this respect, for instance in their apparent veneration of Confucius. But their overall vision was decidedly radical, and they also sought to 'restructure the Chinese socio-political order' through education and discipline (Eastman et al. 1991:30–2). In both cases, formal schooling has been seen as an important catalyst for change, and educational institutions were arguably as 'Western' as they were 'Chinese'.

Marcel Granet, near the end of *The Religion of the Chinese People* (which was written in 1922), seemed to suggest that modern Chinese education would indeed transform and supplant certain traditional ideas:

Education begins to reach the humblest classes of society. It imbues them with the sentiments proper to a morality that has only human ends ... One has now only to be present at a ball game or when school empties out to ascertain that the fear no longer weighs upon [Chinese children] of not preserving the integrity of the bodies bequeathed to them by their parents. (1975:156)

Ironically, this traditional 'fear' from which education was meant to free Chinese children is an important part of Confucianism, and Confucianism is itself arguably 'a morality that has only human ends'. The morality of self-protection (out of duty to one's parents and ancestors) was taught as part of classical Chinese education. But, in Granet's formulation, an important difference between this traditional education and its modern equivalent was that it now reached 'the humblest classes of society' and transformed them. Chinese education had of course long been explicitly organised, institutionalised and centred on literacy. But knowledge which had been restricted to the élite would now be given to the masses.

While usually not directly discussing the impact of modern education, many other writers on Chinese religion have similarly stressed some form of contrast between élite and popular traditions (e.g., Ahern 1981a, Sangren 1987, Feuchtwang 1992). This has been variously described as a relationship between, on the one hand, the 'official', 'orthodox', 'élite', 'state' or 'imperial', and, on the other hand, the 'unofficial', 'unorthodox', 'popular' or 'local'. Because an official Chinese religion *did* exist, and because modern Chinese popular religion *does* involve the use of archaic imperial imagery, it is tempting to make rather dubious historical comparisons. (For example, to examine *contemporary* popular religion alongside *ancient* official institutions.) These comparisons make intuitive sense because the traditions studied by anthropologists at a local level in China often seem to be addressed to a 'something else' (e.g., orthodoxy, or official power). It is as if we know that this relationship is important, and that it has a history, but find it difficult to locate within one time-frame.[16]

For example, Sangren (1987) observes that local Taiwanese religion stands in a relationship with what he calls 'state legitimizing' ideology. This relationship is described as both oppositional and complementary, and is said to play an important role in social reproduction. The 'local' part of Sangren's analysis comes from a detailed account of ritual activity within a marketing community in modern Taiwan. By contrast, his analysis of the 'official' relies on two kinds of material: historical accounts from Imperial China (e.g., of philosophical battles between early Daoism and Confucianism, 1987:176ff) and recent examples of government meddling in local religion. The difficulty is that while the practices of 'folk religion' are described, and are historically situated, it is less clear what the modern version of 'the official' or of 'state legitimizing ideology' would be (if anything), unless it is simply the reaction of the government to popular religion. Sangren acknowledges that this presents a problem of method, awaiting further research on 'new forms of the state religion in Taiwan' (1987:11).

One way out of this position (which seems to leave official education strangely neglected) may be found in Stephan Feuchtwang's analysis of Chinese popular religion (1992). Feuchtwang tries to hold in mind the *metaphorical* nature of imperial and ancient imagery in modern religious practice. Perhaps more importantly, he stresses the *interconnexion* between various kinds of identification (marked by ritual occasions) within Chinese social life (1992:1–24). He describes a series of identifications which might be made by an individual in history: with the 'classical' (primarily centred on texts, and including Confucianism, Nationalism and Maoism), the 'familial' (e.g., the private occasions marking the Spring Festival) and the 'local' (e.g., the territorial cults of gods). His point is that the rituals conducted in these various spheres may set out certain 'historical identifications':

By historical identification, I mean that each one of these three kinds of occasion – the classical, the familial, and the local – marks out a dimension of time and a dimension of inclusion and exclusion. The time dimension is the rhythm of repetition and of (re)origination ... In addition to this temporal rhythm there is a dimension of inclusion and exclusion in the extent and scope of the ritual occasion, its name and what it celebrates, by which an individual can be identified with the occasion.　　　　　　　　　　　　　　　　　　　　　　　　　　　(1992:2–3)

Feuchtwang's study focuses on modern festivals and the cults of local gods (which, as it happens, he contrasts primarily with an imperial institution: the official calendar). But his model suggests the value of studying the entire set of potential identifications. And he also implies (by placing textual Chinese nationalism and communism within the 'classical' tradition), that education plays an important part in the whole. In Feuchtwang's model, education could be seen not as a modern institutionalised disruption of traditional culture, but instead as an important part of, and transformation of, the classical tradition.

But what does it mean to say that someone within this tradition has, or makes, an identification? Is identification a matter of recognition (seeing a connexion between oneself and others), or a matter of commitment (acting on such a connexion)? Is identification a process which we should think of as coming from an individual, or as located between persons? A person in Angang might have a relationship with someone else and describe it as 'having a connexion' (*you guanxi*). But such connexions, aside from existing, are as well produced and acknowledged (e.g., through sharing food). People also have very different levels of commitment to the different relationships around them, which shift over time. If an identification is defined as an acknowledged connexion, then the process of recognition is crucial. What is it that draws attention both to identifications (e.g., with families and other groups of people) and to their features (e.g., the way in which an identification should be expressed)?

The term *dao* (Hokkien *tou*) is of obvious importance in Chinese culture, and might help in this description. It means 'a way' or a doctrine, or, more literally, a path or road. As is well known, Daoism (*daojiao*) is simply 'the doctrine of the way'. But there are other examples: *xiaodao* is the Confucian 'path of filial obedience', and *daoli*, 'reason', literally means 'the ordered way'. This term (*daoli*) is often used in everyday speech to refer to that which is logical or wise; that which 'follows the ordered way', *you daoli*. This idiomatic interest in 'ways' or 'roads' is situated within a broader cultural concern with the movement of persons, forces, spirits and destinies; the ever-shifting map of natural and spiritual existence. For example, great attention is focused on sending people and spirits away, and greeting them back. Relationships between persons are often described as a moving 'back and forth' (*laiwang*). The notion of 'drawing attention to' might be seen in this context. As they grow up, children have their attention drawn to various roads, or 'ways of being', which lead to certain kinds of relationships. Some of these roads are explicit doctrines, such as 'the way', but others are fragmentary, mere glimpses of identifications, attachments to diverse communities.

1

Two roads

A list of the activities of children in Angang might begin as follows: attending school and avoiding it, being taken to and kept away from spirit medium altars, participating in and sleeping through rituals, eating symbolic food, symbolically eating food, and so on. In the course of these activities, children make and hear a number of statements about themselves and other children, and they also encounter ideas about and representations of childhood in general, for example when reading stories or walking through temples. But it is difficult to hold in mind the distinction between children and ideas about childhood. And how, in any case, would such a distinction be made? Could someone who thinks of herself as a Chinese child totally fail to see herself in a story about Chinese childhood? If she almost recognised herself, would I then say that she was bound to be influenced by the story? In which case, where would the representation end and the child begin? Might not even the vaguest act of recognition influence her process of becoming something other than a child?

But such an experience, in Angang, would not be restricted to the young, for childhood is celebrated in China, and representations abound. People in Angang, regardless of age, are often *reminded* of the significance accorded to children within traditional Chinese culture and modern Taiwanese society.[1] In this chapter I will outline, in part by using ethnography from outside Angang, several of these reminders: quite general Chinese ideas and practices related to children, such as the notion that their souls are unstable before and after birth, and the events which celebrate their survival. I will also outline the way in which the boundary of childhood seems at times to include the middle-aged and the elderly, and the process of 'socialisation' to include the dead.

Putting together these Chinese ways of conceptualising childhood, personhood and the life-cycle, setting them out in a row as I have done, might help delineate a popular theory of socialisation. Or, as I will argue, it might help show the partial absence of one. Certain of these ideas and practices imply that there is not so much a problem with Chinese children *becoming* something, as with them *remaining* something. The underlying assumption is that children are, were, and will forever be persons, located in a matrix of human relationships. The emphasis is therefore not on making them social, but instead on protecting a natural process and on emphasising certain forms of identification. However, this exists alongside another more 'Confucian' view of things, in which children are in the process of becoming persons, in part through learning and self-cultivation. These 'two roads', ways of moving through life, are not mutually exclusive, and they form the background for much of what follows.

I have set out the discussion under headings which approximate what I take to be 'widely distributed' sets of representations (e.g., 'the souls of children may be frightened away'). Roughly similar ideas are undoubtedly current in Angang. But I should stress that these headings are *my* approximations, based on fieldwork, and that they should not be read as a list of notions which children acquire. Instead, I am trying to map out some of the directions in which they may be drawn, as they create *their own* representations about themselves and their world.

(1) The souls of children may be frightened away; adults are less vulnerable to bad influences

In Angang, people say that if an infant or child is unusually bad-humoured, without apparently being ill, her soul may have been frightened away. She is said to have 'suffered the frights' (*siu kia*).[2] The belief that the souls (*linghun*) or the energies (*qi*) of children are not very firmly attached to their bodies is widespread, and rituals to cope with this frailty are among the most common in Chinese popular religion.[3] So that even people who do not *believe* in this vulnerability might nevertheless associate it with childhood. Rather than analysing the condition or its religious implications in detail, here I will simply describe its most salient features. Something as minor and as ordinary as a loud noise may bring on the frights, or it may be the result of something more extreme, such as being bitten by a dog. It commonly occurs upon encountering a ghost (*gui*), which is said naturally to be more likely to happen to children than to adults. Then a girl or boy may cry for a long time for no apparent reason.

Different steps may be taken to remedy the situation. For example, some parents give their children commercially produced medicines, such as *jingfeng san*, 'frights powder'. The child may also be taken to a spirit medium (*tang ki*), or to some other local person who understands what should be done. For example, an elderly man who lives along the sea-front in Angang knows how to read from the face, specifically from the veins around the temples, whether or not a child has been afflicted with this problem. He performs a ritual called 'gathering the frights' (*siu kia*), in which he burns spirit money and incense, and chants over the child while ringing a bell, blowing a horn and cracking a whip. This, he says, will release the child's soul from the frights.

The child might or might not be old enough to remember the experience later. A young man told me that once, when he was a boy, his mother had called in a *siu kia* expert. He could clearly recall the woman placing three sticks of incense in a bowl of rice, spewing rice wine out of her mouth, and chanting over him, before sprinkling wine on his body in order to 'suppress' (*ya*) the frights. Some villagers say that parents cannot perform a *siu kia* for their own children, but one woman explained to me that she occasionally did so. In her version, she would simply bow in front of a god's image with a bowl of water, throw the water into the air, run her finger around the inside of the bowl, place her finger in the child's mouth, and call out the child's name. If the child calmed down, the ritual had been a success, the soul had returned to the body.

Adults may also lose their souls, and may even have a *siu kia* performed (for instance, if they are unusually nervous) but it is much less common. As Schipper explains, adults, being stronger, are thought less vulnerable to 'pernicious influences'.[4] So these ideas about soul-loss might tell us something about a difference (between children and adults) and a process (that of becoming an adult). The ideas could be part of a popular theory in which children are not full persons. They are not *chengren* (adults, 'completed persons'), nor are they *chengshou* (mature, 'fully cooked'), and their souls are not securely located in their bodies. They remain in special need of protection (*hu*) and of strengthening (*bu*), and sometimes in need of having their souls called back into place.

(2) Children may play with firecrackers, and they should 'cross the fire' for protection

But how seriously do parents take the possibility of soul-loss, or other signs of vulnerability, in their children? And are all kinds of vulnerability the same? *Siu kia* is a common ritual, and everyone knows of the condition it is meant to address. But suffering the frights is considered a relatively minor problem, and one which is easily dealt with. Nor is it clear that the apparent

1 A girl playing in a courtyard next to the stove in which spirit money is burnt for the gods

concern, such as it is, related to soul-loss extends to other areas of parent–child relationships. Certainly, as I will describe later, parents do worry about the health of their children. And the textbooks on filial obedience I will discuss later clearly stress the anxiety which children's illnesses are meant to cause to their parents. For instance, in one a 'child' says: 'I encounter difficulties, fall ill; [my mother] is anxious, for my sake forgetting to sleep and eat (*wei wo fei qin wang can*).'

But it would be wrong to simply portray parents in Angang as nervous about or protective of their children. It is as if there is a cultural 'anxiety' which does not translate literally into practice. On the contrary, when I first arrived in Taiwan I was struck by what *I* took as parental indifference. One of my first fieldnotes (written in Taipei) goes as follows:

There seems to be a lack of concern about child safety ... very young children running between speeding cars, buses and especially motorcycles ... One of the most common sights is of an entire family – mother, father, and two or three children, including infants – hanging on to the family motorcycle for dear life as they move in and out of the traffic ... as if there is a certain fatalism.[5]

When I later visited Penghu (a chain of islands to the west of Taiwan) I was again struck by 'the extent to which children are allowed to wander around next to motorcycles, firecrackers, etc'. And when I eventually moved to Angang I again noticed with surprise that very young children were allowed to play with firecrackers. I once asked a local shopkeeper whether it didn't concern her to sell firecrackers to children who might be harmed by them. She laughed at my censorious question, and said 'You're afraid of death!' (*ni pa si!*).

Looking only at these two notions ('children's souls are vulnerable' and 'children may play with firecrackers') one might suppose that parents are concerned about what happens to a child's soul and are less concerned about what happens to a child's body. But this would be to project onto the material a non-Chinese conception of the body, and of the meaning of 'physical' action. (Here recall Granet: the 'fear' among Chinese children of 'not preserving the integrity of the bodies bequeathed to them by their parents'.) In China, the body is an inseparable aspect of the moral person, and much of the ritual activity in Angang, especially that surrounding spirit medium cults, is carried out specifically to 'protect the body-persons' (*hushen*) of children.[6] This time-consuming and expensive commitment is said to be undertaken for children's spiritual well-being *and* for their physical health, two fundamentally indivisible things.

When parents in Angang do protect their children from (every kind of) harm through rituals, it sometimes comes in a form that might not be expected. For example, in the violent *kng put* (god-carrying) ritual, to be discussed later, villagers (primarily adults) carry a god's image (*shen xiang*) for many hours. This activity is said to strengthen the deity. At the end of the day, villagers walk through fire protected by the newly strengthened god, saying that this will bring them *pieng-an*, security, the absence of disturbances. Children, who are marginal to the rest of the ritual, are especially called out to 'cross the fire' (*guohuo*). I heard one man shout 'It can't burn!' (*buhui shao*) at his hesitant daughter, pushing her towards the flame. I also heard children say this to each other: 'It can't burn!', although people sometimes receive minor burns.

Instructing children to walk through fire may seem a strange form of *protection*, just as allowing children to play with firecrackers may seem a strange form of *anxiety*. But one boy explained to me that the *kng put* ritual was primarily a *bushen* activity, done to 'build-up the body-persons' of participants (many popular foods, tonics and folk remedies are also described as *bushen*). Many ways of dealing with children in Angang seem also to imply that strength is the best kind of protection. Children are sometimes portrayed as vulnerable, but the 'anxiety' surrounding this state of vulnerability (and the steps taken to remedy it) needs to be seen in context.

(3) Souls are unstable before birth; childbirth and children may 'pose a threat'

Some people in Angang recall childhood experiences related to the frights, but it could not really be said that *siu kia* rituals are performed in order to *teach* children something.[7] Quite often they are performed on infants and, in any case, the instability of souls is said to actually come before birth. In a discussion of ideas about women in northern Taiwan, Emily Ahern has noted that while a woman is pregnant, her child's soul is thought liable to move around the mother's bedroom (1975:196–7). More precisely, the Thai Sin (Placenta God), which at this stage is said to be the soul of the child, moves around. Rituals are performed to 'pacify the Thai Sin', and people are careful to avoid striking, breaking or cutting objects in the room, for fear of harming the foetus via its unfixed soul. The need for caution gradually diminishes: 'After birth the Thai Sin becomes attached to the child's body with increasing firmness, until, at about four months, there is no need to fear striking it inadvertently' (1975:197). The Placenta God, in addition to roaming around the mother's bedroom, is also present in birth fluids, which should be disposed of with great care in order not to harm the infant (1975:196–7). The overall impression is of a foetus, infant and child

2 A girl wearing a red incense-filled *xianghuo*, a 'fragrant fire'. This is taken from a spirit medium's altar, and is meant to protect the child from bad influences

at risk, and in need of protection from (perhaps unintentionally) careless and clumsy adults.

But menstrual blood and birth fluids are in turn believed to be dangerous to adults. Ahern suggests that this may, in part, be explained by the position of children and their mothers within Chinese kinship. Menstrual blood (as opposed to the father's semen) is said to actually become the flesh and blood of the child (1975:196). Newly born children, partly formed of menstrual blood, are also, in some ways, 'outsiders ... whose loyalties are unformed' (1975:210). They are thus, like their mothers, a potential (if necessary) 'threat' to the unity of patrilineal families. This combination of threat and necessity arguably makes the whole subject of outside women and their offspring especially fraught, and could help to explain why the process of birth is seen as unclean and dangerous.

These ideas might also be said to suggest that social relationships, the process of human life, and perhaps even childhood, begin before birth. The soul is very loosely attached to a foetus and to an infant up to four months, somewhat loosely attached to a child, and relatively firmly attached to an adult. Adulthood is a loss of vulnerability. But children are not simply at risk. A foetus is already influenced by the actions *of* others (it may be harmed), and it may have a powerful, and dangerous, influence *on* others. Children, in turn, are not simply passive objects (at the mercy of careless adults), but have their own powers as well (because of their 'unformed loyalties'). Children may pose a threat.

(4) The survival of children is celebrated

The excitement generated by marriage, pregnancy and childbirth in Angang, and the affection often showered on children, may render the suggestion that Chinese children 'pose a threat' rather implausible. But might not the (culturally magnified) 'dependence' of older generations on their descendants at least raise the anxiety-making possibility of descent gone wrong? Parents in Angang often express mild concerns, for example, about the health of their children or about their prospects in school. Could these relate to deeper concerns: that a child might die (leaving parents childless), that a child might turn out to be a bad person? The public celebrations which surround birth and childhood in Angang do not, however, have the character of explicit attempts to turn children into something else (e.g., into good descendants or full persons). By this I mean they are unlike initiations. Instead they primarily celebrate survival, and are as well attempts to safeguard the future.

In any particular family, events to mark the stages of childhood may vary.⁸ This variation relates to personal preference and family tradition, but also to the amount of money parents and grandparents are prepared to spend. People say that this, in turn, depends on two things: the extent to which a child was particularly *hoped for* (more effort is usually made for boys), and the extent to which a child is thought to have been *at risk* during its lifetime.

One month after a child is born, the parents will usually mark the occasion with a 'full month' (*manyue*) celebration, which includes both a brief private ritual, and an elaborate public banquet.⁹ This is one of many occasions for 'inviting guests' (*chia lang-kheq*), and it comes at the end of a period in which mother and child are secluded from public view. It is considered a matter of great pride to have produced a descendant. So much so that, in some families, similar celebrations are held at the fourth month. Then, when the child reaches its first birthday, parents may again 'invite guests' to a banquet and conduct rituals to celebrate *manyisui* or *manzhousui* ('full-one-year' or 'full-annual-cycle'). Similar events marking the passage of time since birth are common throughout China. They take place with reference to the individual date of birth, as opposed to the lunar new year (*guonian*, i.e., the Spring Festival) when everyone collectively becomes one year older.

As with all celebrations of happy events (*xishi*), the symbolic emphasis is on long life, fertility, prosperity and completeness. At the *manyisui* celebrations I attended in Angang, which were for boys, the infants were given new sets of clothes, gold rings, and hats with three gold medallions (all symbolising wealth and good fortune). A pig, a chicken and a goat were sacrificed and offered to Thi Kong ('Heaven'), along with a request for future protection. The infants were waved up and down in front of ancestral tablets and images of gods in an approximation of a bow. Special foods (such as steamed 'red turtle' buns (*honggui*), and red and white sweet rice-ball soup (*tangyuan*)) were first offered to the gods, and then consumed by the guests. Those attending the *chia lang-kheq* (they include relatives of the father and mother, as well as neighbours, friends and work associates) were expected to bring cash gifts in red envelopes (*hongbao*) for the child.

The 'full month' and 'full year' celebrations are linked to what happens much later, during the sixteenth year of a child's life. Then, offerings are made on the seventh day of the seventh month, specifically in thanks for the survival of the child. Some people describe this as the point at which a child is no longer a child, he or she has grown up (*zhang da*), and is no longer in need of protection.¹⁰ In some cases, a fairly simple ritual will be held at this time, e.g., offering the gods or the Seven Fairies¹¹ 'red turtle' buns to thank them for their protection. In other cases, a pig is sacrificed to fulfil a 'contractual' agreement with Thi Kong (payment is made upon survival of the child to an agreed date). If a child has been unhealthy while growing up, his or her parents may have specifically asked for divine help in this way. One woman told me that due to her son's recurring health problems, she had made an agreement with Thi Kong and sacrificed a pig in *advance* of his sixteenth year. (Similarly, many parents sacrifice a pig in thanks after a son completes military service without harm.)

These celebrations (after the passage of one month, one year and sixteen years) *mark* a completion and a transition. In them gods are thanked (retrospectively) for protecting the child from problems. As I mentioned, the events are *most* elaborate when there has been serious doubt about survival, or about existence in the first place. It is being publicly acknowledged that a child has survived a naturally risky period of the life-cycle. The public focus is arguably not so much on the child, as on the parents who have been clever enough to have one. Given the future dependence of the parents on the child (however 'unreal' this dependence may seem), they are felt to have good reason for celebration.

(5) Children become persons through learning

But this view of the *manyue* and *manyisui* (as events which do not transform) may be misleading. Rubie Watson (1986) has noted that children are also given their names during the 'full month' ceremony. After this (at least in some areas of China) a man, particularly one from the educated élite, may go on to accumulate many names during his lifetime. A woman does not, and in some ways loses the name she has, eventually being called by a category: 'old woman'. Watson argues that men become full persons in part through this process of naming and renaming, while women never 'attain full personhood'. This argument may seem to contradict my suggestion that children in Angang are thought of as already social, and therefore not in need of being made social. Bear in mind, however, that the naming practices Watson describes are, as she emphasises, directly linked to literacy and to scholarly attainment (for example, illiterate women are unable to participate in the clever name-related discussions of men). In other words, this model of becoming a person is part of the Chinese educational tradition. (It is 'Confucian' not only in the sense of being learned, but also in the sense that good names make classical allusions).

Although names are a matter of concern in Angang, both men and women do not in general have the level of education required to engage in scholarly speculation about them. But this does not at all mean that they are uninfluenced by Confucian ideals, and Watson's material does suggest the possibility of two interconnected models of Chinese personhood and childhood. In the one I have so far been describing, being a child is a natural process, marked by celebrations of survival (and not by attempts to turn children into persons). You do not *learn* to be a person, because you *are* one. In the other, life is a matter of cultural achievements, and especially of 'learning'. Both versions would have important implications for children because they would imply two different roads, two ways of being a child and of becoming something else.

But could a child not live with this difference? Evidence for both models, and of their interconnexion, is found in Taiwan, as shown by Thompson's discussion of Chinese ideas about the life-cycle (1990). On the one hand, he notes that many of the metaphors used to describe the ageing process (*both* in the theories of Neo-Confucianism and at the 'village level') are natural or organic (sprouts, trees, water, rice, etc.) He also mentions the notion that 'the growth process of humans, like that of rice, *should not be forced*' (1990:108, my emphasis). This seems consistent with the idea that life (and therefore childhood) is a natural process. But, on the other hand, Thompson notes (citing Munro) that 'a central strand of Neo-Confucian thought is concerned with the question of authentic human ageing, the *process of becoming human*' (1990:105, my emphasis). This view of 'becoming' is partly described through organic/natural metaphors, but is as well closely tied to Confucian notions of education:

Commitment to learning, and to self-cultivation, are essential to the process of authentic ageing, of properly becoming a person ... Education, nourishment of the mind, was thus rated very highly in Neo-Confucian thought ... the process of maturation is coterminous with the acquisition of culture (*wen*). The character *wen*, however, has as a constituent part of its meaning, an inextricable association with 'writing' on the one hand, and 'sinification' on the other. Thus, on this continuum of maturation, becoming 'older' (i.e. becoming more human, more a person) is associated with sinification, acculturation and literacy, all considered an ineluctable part of the process of humanization and self-cultivation. (1990:112)

The implication of this, as Thompson says, is that 'the illiterate, or the uncultured, are seen as incomplete human beings' (1990:112). Similarly, Watson notes that (illiterate and 'nameless') women are seen as less than full persons. However, as Thompson rightly points out, 'the extent to which such cultural representations actually inform and become reflected in practice is a complex issue' (1990:102). His own material illuminates part of this complexity: the way in which family-based ambitions for children may both contradict and overlap with Confucian ideals of what it means to be a good child and a proper person.

(6) Middle-aged children need protection; even the elderly may be childlike; the dead must be controlled

Obviously, the process of moving through and out of Chinese childhood might be conceptualised in different ways. But when is that process thought to end? I have already suggested that the starting-point is before birth. And, as noted, when a child is sixteen the 'end' of her childhood is celebrated, with offerings to repay the gods for protection. This is given as the age at which she could get married, but adulthood is arguably only reached when a young person *does* marry and produce children. This goal is so taken for granted, that it may be wrong to speak of it as an achievement. It might be said negatively: to not marry and to not have children is seen as a move towards achieving non-personhood. But in Taiwan many young people now go through an extended childhood while waiting to finish school or military service, and before they marry. During this time they often maintain economic relations with their parents which are those of childhood. Some are supported fully by their parents, while others who are out of school and working may send most or all of their income home (usually to be saved for marriage expenses). Does the boundary of childhood expand with delayed marriage?

There is also a sense in which people remain 'children', even *after* becoming adults by marrying and having children of their own. Just as 'social interactions' and some of the problems of childhood seem to start before birth, certain of the responsibilities and risks of childhood seem to push into mid-life and beyond. Women in Angang frequently make enquiries at spirit medium altars about the health and prospects of their adult sons and daughters (many of whom live in other locations in Taiwan). Often they specifically ask local gods for long-distance intervention on their behalf. These 'children' have many obligations towards their ageing parents, and it is in the interest of parents for them to receive spiritual protection well beyond childhood.

This is a matter for gods, spirit mediums and priests; it is 'religious'. But Confucian ideas about filial obedience (*xiao*) which are taught in the schools also imply that childhood is an ongoing process. Elementary school students in Angang read the following:

Xiao (filial obedience) applies to men and women, regardless of age; everyone must be utterly *xiao* to their parents. For example, Lao Laizi, over seventy years old, wishing his parents to be happy, often wore brightly coloured garments and practised children's singing and dancing, in order to amuse his parents.[12]

Filial obedience is in some ways a relationship of ongoing childhood, undertaken with reference to ongoing parenthood, and in denial of the passage of time. This is true in both the 'naturalistic' and the 'Confucian' views of childhood and the life-cycle.

In Angang, there are certain social contexts in which the elderly take the position of children *vis-à-vis* their own elders and ancestors. One of these contexts is the funeral ritual. But in funerals 'children' can be said to show both respect and disrespect towards their deceased parents. They are once again both vulnerable (open to bad influences) and powerful (able to manipulate the parental dead). For example, some of the food symbolism in Taiwanese funerals suggests that the dead are being told by their descendants to leave the living alone (Ahern 1973:197–8, Thompson 1988:80–91).

The bones of the deceased (not at all childlike and in some ways the symbolic opposite of children in their dryness) are also manipulated (almost literally 'kept in line') in order to direct good fortune toward their descendants, and to avoid bad luck. At the funerals I attended in Angang the descendants ('children') anxiously watched over the geomantic placement of the coffin by the Daoist priest. In later reburials, as James Watson describes, descendants take further steps with the increasingly ancestral bones of the dead to ensure that they are properly controlled:

> in order to be effective, the bones must be cleaned of every minute scrap of flesh. The people of San Tin and Ha Tsuen usually employ exhumation specialists to undertake this final chore. These men, who rank somewhat higher in status than corpse handlers, polish the bones and arrange them in ceramic pots ... for final reburial. Once the bones have been so treated they become, in the words of my informants, 'neutralised' or 'digested' (*hsiao hua*) and ready to transmit geomantic influences to the living. (J. Watson 1982a:181)

Would we say that dead people are thus made social, or sociable? Like children (before and after birth) they are both dangerous and vulnerable. And, like children, they are subjected to a process which is not so much one of being *made* social as one of being controlled within ongoing relationships.

Conclusion
There I will stop, with the neutralisation of ancestral bones, because it seems time to place this rather abstract discussion on a firmer grounding, i.e., in one place and time. In this chapter, I have tried to help situate that

ground by selectively outlining some Chinese ideas about childhood and the process of life. Among these are the following:

Souls are unstable before birth
Childbirth and children may 'pose a threat'
The souls of children may be frightened away
Children should 'cross the fire' for protection
The survival of children is celebrated
Middle-aged children need protection
Even the elderly may be childlike
The dead must be controlled

As I have said, these ideas, edited in this way, imply that people are always already 'social', by definition, even before birth, during childhood, and after death. Processes which we might describe as attempts to 'make social' are as likely to happen to dead people as they are to happen to children. There is nothing in Angang resembling an initiation, in which children are taught what they should be, or made into what they should be, *unless* this is how we would describe what happens in school. And, if that is how we would describe the school, then our description would be consistent with the overlapping and yet distinct ideas concerning the life-cycle which I have described as Confucian: 'children become persons through learning'.

In Taiwanese schools there is undoubtedly an emphasis on 'the proper way of being a person' (*zuoren de daoli*), and there is little question that schooling is seen as an important, and perhaps the most important, occupation of childhood in Taiwan. But, as I noted in the Introduction, what people in Angang emphasise about schooling is not morality (which is already known) but rather competitiveness. This competition (which, unlike the morality in schools, is unpredictable) seems to produce anxiety, both for parents and for children. Might this anxiety be related to the worry about and celebration of survival, or to the concern with soul-loss? From the perspective of the family, school is not where children are *made* Chinese, it is where, with effort and with luck (this is where the anxiety comes in), they *express* their Chinese values. They specifically show a willingness and a capacity to respectfully and obediently support their parents. In Angang, this responsibility is one which is learnt long before the arrival of children in school, and its veneration is part of community life. What that community life consists in, and how this veneration is expressed, are the themes of Part 2, which follows.

PART 2
ANGANG

2

Ghosts are not connexions

I recall having selected Angang as a good location for fieldwork partly on the basis of an illusion, namely the illusion of stillness. On summer days when the clouds break and the hot sun beats down on the village lanes, people mostly stay inside. Occasionally someone goes past, perhaps a woman slowly pushing a cart loaded with greenery for her goats and deer. An old Daoist, sweating and serious, bicycles along and ignores her. Children in blue uniforms silently read in their classrooms, the school-gates framed by the steep hills behind them. A puff of smoke rises from the Ma Co temple, the remnant of some private grandmotherly act of devotion, while a fishing boat makes its quiet progress out of the harbour and towards the Pacific, the 'ocean of great peace' (*taipingyang*). Then a blast of noise: a string of firecrackers is set off, celebrating who knows what, or a motorcyclist races at full speed through the middle of the village, sending chickens and dogs into a momentary frenzy, but apparently leaving everyone else unimpressed.

This shatters the illusion of stillness, and any adequate description of Angang would have to do the same, for *movement* (of people, spirits and forces) is a fundamental concern of the people there. I have said that schooling is seen not so much as a matter of learning as of competing. But it could also be seen as a matter of moving, because one of the most obvious effects of the educational system is that many students move (out of home, village, etc.) in order to study and to work. This is only one of the many ways in which the goings and comings of children (and adults, and spirits) are of significance to local people. In this chapter I will provide a partial description of life and movement in Angang, but I will do so in a rather unusual way, and one which requires some justification.

I suggested in the Introduction that children in Angang have their attention drawn to various 'identifications', and in chapter 1 I argued that children are (in some popular views) seen as already being persons, embedded in a set of relationships. Within this set, the 'local' level of identification is particularly salient. As many writers have shown, association and differentiation by locality are extremely important features of popular religious activity, and much else besides, in China.[1] But what does it mean to be identified with a particular local community in rural Taiwan? Again, this relates in part to moving around, into, and out of a certain place, as I will describe. The specificity of this place, Angang, rests partly on the local economy, and also on the way in which local people differentiate Angang from other communities (e.g., in a sentimental way).

Having given some general information about this, I will then turn to more directly child-related matters, and back to the subject of movement. It is, as I said, a matter of concern, and something which contributes to local identification. It is also one of the few subjects about which parents in Angang *explicitly* instruct their children, and is therefore relevant to the issue of moral transmission. For example, parents warn that to go away from Angang is to encounter bad influences, and they also advise their children that to run around in a 'chaotic' way is to risk bumping into ghosts. One form of protection against these spiritual and social dangers is to be a settled member of a local community; then one may avoid isolation and also receive the protection of communally produced gods. However, as I will describe, the beliefs and practices related to these gods (by contrast with ideas about children's movements) hardly seem to be explicitly transmitted at all. Religion is done, not taught, and this doing is an important part of growing up in Angang.

Having outlined some of the ways in which the community deals with supernatural matters, I will then turn to a more mundane and everyday concern, child discipline. This may seem a private matter, unrelated to the description of a community, but I hope to show otherwise. Certain situations provoke parents, and an examination of these might shed light on what parents hope, through discipline, to teach their children. (Or what they hope their children will come to understand.) I will describe both the 'toughening up' of children through games, and more serious disciplinary techniques. These practices are often a collective matter, and also thus contribute to local identity in Angang.

Houses to walk through

There are several villages in Angang *xiang*, one of which is Beicun. Although the houses there are mostly the same as in the other villages, the layout of Beicun is different, because it is built on a narrow (but long) strip of land between a steep hill and the ocean. The houses in Beicun are thus built quite close to each other in several long rows, often touching or with only narrow alley-ways in-between. These rows of houses face the ocean, and from the sea-wall in front of the village boats can be watched coming in and out of the harbour. The land in Angang is not particularly expensive, nor is it very productive, and agricultural activity is of secondary importance in what is, after all, a fishing community. Yet the village does not spread out onto the surrounding land. Instead, houses are placed close together, forming a series of cement blocks with cement courtyards, a pattern common in both rural and urban Taiwan.

Villagers sometimes mention the beauty of the surrounding countryside, which by the way is striking, but no one *lives* there, or even seems to want to spend much time there. Nor, within the village, do people want to stay alone. While at times complaining about the demands of living in a close-knit community, they seem to agree that only a strange (*qiguai*) person would choose to lead a lonely life. To be alone for even one night is thought dangerous, an open invitation for trouble from evil spirits, so, for instance, people prefer not to sleep in empty buildings. The cluttered and connected architecture of Beicun and, more importantly, the flow of human activity running through it, are seen as forms of protection against social and spiritual isolation and the trouble they may cause.

Even the noise of the village (which is often impressive) is sometimes said to be good because it frightens away ghosts. When people walk into empty buildings they often announce their presence by making noise. They apparently value a certain kind of noise and crowding, much as they value the 'hot and noisy' bustle (*lau-ziat*) of a religious festival. It is as if this good kind of happy disorder (*lau-ziat*) provides protection from a bad kind of unhappy disorder (*luan* or *o-peq*), the kind caused by ghosts or by social instability. Angang is not very 'hot and noisy' by Taiwanese standards, not even during a festival, but the human contact of everyday life is still close and valued. People are regularly told not to wander away from the protection which this provides. For example, my tendency to go alone for walks on the rocky ocean-front was a source of concern to my friends. Their advice about this became more pointed until finally I was specifically instructed not to 'wander aimlessly' (*luanpao*) along a section of road which was 'unclean' (*bu ganjing*), where angry spirits hovered at the scene of a violent death. If I was foolish enough to go to this isolated spot I would be taking a personal risk, but I would also, and this was worse, be dragging bad luck back to the village with me. Such concerns lead people to take a personal interest in the movements of their neighbours.

Because buildings are in rows, in some parts of Beicun it is easier to walk through someone's house than to walk on the street as a means of moving between two points. For the sake of efficiency, they say, villagers thus regularly walk through the homes of their neighbours, who may or may not be relatives in this multi-surname community. Many front and back doors are left open, and even houses which lead nowhere usually have open doors. This means that it is possible to walk in on any number of activities unannounced: people may be eating, drinking, sharing betel nut, playing cards, watching television, preparing fishing equipment, doing homework, arguing, gossiping, worshipping at their domestic altars, engaging in divination via spirit mediums, and so on. Generally, little needs to be said to the occupants in passing, and people seem not to mind having their homes used as semi-public pathways. This is not to say that they are unconcerned about privacy, but almost everyone in Beicun, and in Angang for that matter, is said to have some connexion with everyone else, to be a friend or a relative. People are free to walk into or through the *kheq-thia*, the main or 'guest' room, which is the public space of a private home (the bedrooms are off to the side). In the evenings, but also on days when the weather is bad or the lunar calendar is unpropitious for fishing, there is a steady movement, a circulation of villagers throughout the community.

All of this could be taken as evidence of a kind about human relationships on a day-to-day basis in Beicun: houses are virtually stuck together,

3 Homes in Angang, built close together

and people are accustomed to living surrounded by people with whom they are closely associated. Obviously, there are other kinds of evidence about relationships, but I wanted to present this view first, in order to emphasise that such connexions, at least in the case of Beicun, are lived with quite literally. Throughout Angang, there is a similar feeling of *closeness* to social life. In a moment, I will describe some things which follow on from this, but first I want to provide more detailed information about the community.

The economy of Angang

As I mentioned, Angang is a (*xiang*), a rural township which is part of a county (*xian*) in southeastern Taiwan. Many of Taiwan's Malayo-Polynesian aborigines,[2] commonly referred to as 'mountain people' (*shandiren*), live in the southeast, as do many retired soldiers (from various mainland provinces) who came to Taiwan with Chiang Kai-shek after Mao's victory on the mainland. But the residents of Angang township are, with only a handful of exceptions, Han Chinese descendants of migrants from Quanzhou prefecture (in Fujian province), and, in common with the majority of Taiwanese, their first language is the Fujianese dialect Hokkien.

Geographically, the southeast is relatively isolated from the rest of the Taiwanese island, divided from it by a long mountain range. The industrialisation and prosperity which have transformed Taiwan since the 1950s (miraculously, they say) have been slower to arrive in the southeast, and the effects have, at least superficially, been less miraculous. However, standards of living in the *xiang* have risen dramatically (from quite serious poverty) during the post-war era. Efficient public transportation also now links all parts of Taiwan, and migration in and out of Angang affects virtually every family. Young people often move to cities such as Taitung, Kaoshiung and Taipei to continue their studies beyond middle school (*zhongxue*), or to take up jobs in factories and offices. Angang, unusually, does not have local factories of the sort which have industrialised much of the Taiwanese countryside, and where local young people might be employed closer to home.[3]

According to a publication from the *xiang* government (*xianggongsuo*) the population of Angang in 1985 was about 4000 persons, divided between three main villages (*cun*). This same source indicated that 85 per cent of the population were supported by fishing. But the local fishing industry was, at the time of fieldwork, in decline, increasingly overtaken by heavy industrial concerns based at larger Taiwanese ports. The local industry primarily consists of line-fishing from relatively small boats (one to five-man crews), which usually make one-day outings in the vicinity. Crews may be recruited on the basis of kinship or friendship. Many families engage as well in small-scale farming (mostly growing peanuts, potatoes and other vegetables, medicinal plants, and animal fodder) and small-scale animal husbandry (primarily of pigs, chickens, goats and deer). Virtually all of the fishing is done by men, whereas women are often responsible for the agriculture. I was told that when fishing is bad (as it often seems to be), the men depend, or 'lean' (*kao*), on the women's farming. But very few families earn income from the latter, and most of the food for family meals is bought on credit from local stores.

Some local people are in government employment, for example in the schools, township (*xiang*) and village (*cun*) administrations, the post office, or the fishermen's association (some of these jobs go to 'outsiders' with appropriate qualifications). Others work at government installations which are within the *xiang*, but outside of the villages. These kinds of employment are considerably more stable than fishing, and the life is said to be less 'bitter' (*xinku*). Tourism also provides some employment, as do small shops.[4] Many families also have important economic ties with relatives in other locations in Taiwan, periodically going there to work, and the money which is sent back to Angang from children in the cities is also of considerable significance. Indeed, few parents now have the expectation that their children will settle in Angang; instead they are mostly expected to become workers in other Taiwanese towns and cities.

It is somewhat misleading to describe the economic situation of a single family, because what is most typical is diversity. But here, in order to at least give an impression of the economy, I will give an example of one household, consisting of a couple with four unmarried children (two of whom live outside of Angang). At the time of my fieldwork, the husband worked on a small fishing boat; this meant that his income was highly variable. For example, an extended expedition of over a week (unusual in itself) brought the crew a combined income of NT$70,000, but after expenses this meant that his share was under NT$10,000 (or about US$350 at the time). I was told that fishermen's monthly incomes were usually less than this (NT$10,000). In world terms, this may seem rather high, but it should be seen in light of the relatively high cost of living in Taiwan. It should also be compared with incomes from other occupations; for example, this man's brother was a construction worker in Taitung making NT$1000 per *day*. I was told that fishermen generally earn about the same as factory workers in Taiwan, but the income is unpredictable and the work considered more difficult and dangerous.[5]

In addition to the man's income from fishing, this family were also raising several deer, pigs, goats and chicken. They also grew peanuts and sweet potatoes on small plots outside of the village, on which wife, husband and children divided the work. The woman was also a spirit medium, and was sometimes paid for her services (although the money was said to be spent on the upkeep of her altar). This, in itself, is unusual, but it is not unusual for families to have income from secondary sources. They also sold religious items (including incense, spirit money and charms) and betel nuts, which they bought in bulk. From time to time, out of fishing season, the husband worked on public projects (jobs obtained through friends). For example, for several days he helped to install a new drainage system in the *xiang*, at NT$500 per day. The family also periodically received money from their son who was working in another part of Taiwan. At the time of fieldwork this was sporadic (usually several $1000 per month), and about to be halted temporarily by his military service, but their retirement plans clearly took this income into account.

As for expenses, they estimated that they spent about NT$10,000 per month, roughly the same as their income, primarily on food, utilities, school-related expenses for their children (e.g., the cost of uniforms and school lunches), and social expenses. The latter consist of obligations to give money and gifts to neighbours and relatives on important occasions ('one-month' celebrations, weddings, funerals, etc.), to support collective religious activities (temple construction, festivals, etc.), and to share food, drink, cigarettes and betel nuts with friends. In a place where everyone is known, these obligations can be quite heavy, as I will later discuss.

Of course, not every family in Angang is in a comparable economic situation, but the majority of families do rely to some extent on fishing income (especially in Beicun), most families do (or will) receive income from outside of the township, and *every* family has substantial social expenses. Although people in Angang tend to stress that they are not wealthy, and this is probably true by comparison with other Taiwanese, they also point out the change in standards of living over the past few decades. Interestingly, they often express this in their descriptions of the lunar New Year. They say that when they were children, new clothes for the festival would be pulled out of the box in which they were stored, and worn for only three days. Now, they point out, people have new things to wear all the time. Before, good food was eaten for three days and then, after the festival, everyone ate potatoes (no rice). Now they eat good food all the time.

Levels of identity
The villages in Angang are multi-surname communities. Each is numerically dominated by one or two surname groups, mostly made up of direct

descendants of early settlers. Some village districts house many people with the same surname, and there is a history of tension between certain of these groups, a history of friendship between others. But lineages, as such, seem unimportant. There are no lineage halls, and no collective ancestor worship. People are inclined to help their close relatives when possible, and are obviously concerned with the continuity of their immediate patriline. But larger agnatic groupings do not usually play a major role in community life.[6]

In previous generations, there was a high rate of marriage within and between the villages in Angang; now this is fairly uncommon. But the practice has had important implications both for the closeness of ties within the community (e.g., between villages and surname groups) and for the status of women. Most of the women who married locally continued (and continue) to have very important and everyday links with their natal homes, which are often only around the corner (cf. Judd 1989). This may have reduced the extent to which members of descent groups could think of themselves as belonging to self-contained units.

A person in Angang belongs, at least in theory, to various groups within the *xiang*, e.g. on the basis of immediate kinship (whether through birth or marriage), shared surname, common residence in a village or in a house, and so on. All of these groups are potentially exclusive, but their boundaries are often rather ill-defined. For instance, the boundary between close and distant kinship seems more a matter of practice than of definitions. Some of these vague boundaries relate, again, to inter-marriage. A woman who is born in one village, but then marries into and lives in another, is from both villages (if and when she wants to be). There is sometimes competition between villages, but in my experience this was usually good-natured, and while residents very often describe themselves as 'Angang people', it is less common to identify with a particular village.

There are some notions which go along with identification as an Angang person. These are partly a matter of sentiment, ideas about what the place feels like. They are also rather general, and could undoubtedly be said of most rural communities in Taiwan, but this does not keep people from invoking them to describe their own sense of attachment. First, Angang is seen as a place where everyone is known (*renshi*), in contrast to the anonymity of cities. Everyone is said to be either a relative or a friend (*qinqi, pengyou*); people in Angang 'watch out for' (*zhaogu*) each other and are always ready to 'assist' (*bangzhu*) when the need arises. But the sense of closeness in the community does have its drawbacks. Villagers are constantly called upon to help people out in different ways, including financially. They also say it is difficult to profit from each other, and one result of this is that most of the local trading business is done by 'outsiders'.[7]

Second, people express the idea that the residents of Angang are more or less on the same economic footing, and less well off than most Taiwanese. This notion of equality is rather misleading because there is considerable economic inequality within the township itself (e.g., families with access to government contracts make substantially more than the average, as do some families with useful connexions outside of Angang). Nevertheless, they say that one of the good things about Angang is that the people are 'all the same' (*dou yiyang*), and more or less 'equal' (*pingdeng*). They contrast this with other parts of Taiwan where some people are extremely wealthy, while others 'do not have rice to eat'. Villagers will at times go to some lengths to keep neighbours from learning of special income they receive (e.g., gifts or assistance), because this might generate bad feelings and jealousy.

Third, people describe Angang as *baoshou*, 'conservative', and as *chunpo*, 'pure and simple' or 'sincere'. This is related to the maintenance of local traditions, and to the perceived simplicity of country life. Again, such a description might be appropriate for much of rural Taiwan, or for the entire south of the island. But people in Angang feel it is especially appropriate to their community. One component of this is the sincerity they bring to religious activities. Unlike wealthier Taiwanese, they are unable to invest large sums of money in festivals and temples, but they (at least those who are religious devotees) do invest a great deal of effort, devotion and 'goodheartedness' in the worship of the gods.

Finally, they describe Angang as a place in which people 'love to laugh' (*ai chiou*) and to 'make jokes' (*kai wanxiao*). This is more important than it might seem, partly because humour is certainly a central part of daily life in Angang, but also because it is often an expression of closeness. Angang humour seems especially funny (to people from Angang, of course!) because it relates so closely to the situations and people they know. Someone who moves away misses this familiar, local sense of humour.

These, then, are some of the features which differentiate Angang (even if not very differentiating features) in the minds of the people who live there: familiarity, mutual assistance, modesty of means, equality, conservatism, simplicity, sincerity and humour. What makes these general features particular is the way in which they are familiarly enacted by people in Angang. But it is important to remember that the residents of this 'simple' community have had, almost without exception, experience of the outside. If nothing else, they are connected by television to much that is happening in Taipei and around the world. And this goes in both directions. People in the Taiwanese countryside are associated with the cities through relatives and friends who live and work there. Similarly, many Taiwanese who live and work in the cities regularly return to the countryside to visit families and friends, to participate in rituals, and so on. It is this movement to which I now turn. (And here I will again enumerate some 'widely distributed' sets of representations about childhood.)

(7) The outside is where children go bad
People in Angang sometimes express the view that when children are outside of the *xiang* (and not inside it) they are more likely to become bad (*phai*). This is one topic related to 'morality' which they seem willing to discuss with their own children in direct, if fairly abbreviated, terms. I knew of several instances in which parents prevented their children from moving away from Angang specifically for this reason, and more generally because other parts of Taiwan were simply felt to be too 'chaotic' (*luan*). Most of them will, as I have said, eventually go away, but preferably not while they are too impressionable, and the point at which they are no longer too impressionable is, of course, a matter for dispute. In one of these cases a middle-school student, a boy of about fifteen years, told his mother that he wished to move to Kaoshiung (a large city) and to work there for a few months. She advised him to be *xiaoxin* ('little hearted', i.e. cautious) in making such a move. She warned that people in the city say all manner of things, and they might say something that he would believe. Then he might go off with them and become a bad person. The boy's father gave similar advice. People would ask him to go out on the town and he'd want to go. The boy, for his part, agreed it was true, that he *would* want to go, but also stressed that even if he went out he wouldn't smoke or drink. He also pointed out that, in any case, he would be living with relatives (on his mother's side). In the end, he was allowed to go away and stay with these relatives, but only for a short time, and only after he and his mother had requested protection from the gods.

This problem of the outside is also commented on by the young. One young man, the very model of filial obedience, described for me what had happened when his *gege*, elder brother, had gone away from Angang for several years. He felt that his *gege* had, during that time, come under bad influences, especially while performing military service. Specifically, he had started to smoke, drink, gamble and chew betel nut, four activities which are common enough among adults in Angang, but which are widely seen as expensive, wasteful, and inappropriate for the young. On his return to

Angang the elder brother had subsequently moved out of his father's house, claiming that he wanted to be independent (*ziyou*). The younger brother described what had happened using a maxim about the influence of bad companions: 'Things near red ink become red, things near black ink become black.'[8]

I have discussed elsewhere another example of the 'outside' being seen as the place where children go bad (Stafford 1992). In that case a young man had moved away to the city to work in a factory (into which he had been introduced by his elder brother). Although he was a good son, he was also thought to be rather suggestible. In the city, he wasted both time and money running around with friends from the factory, and earlier had even fallen under the influence of Christians. His mother was a regular devotee of a spirit medium cult in Beicun, where she often asked about the health and activities of her sons (all of whom lived outside of Angang). During one divination session she was told that her son, for his own safety, should not go out on a particular day, information which she passed on to him at once. He nevertheless went out on the day in question, and was hit by a car. Following the accident, he returned to Angang to recuperate and joined with his mother in local religious activities. He became a special case for the local mediums and priests, but what was striking was the extent to which his treatment focused on his movements, just as his earlier refusal to listen to the god's advice about movement had seemingly led to the accident. He was advised not to pass by a number of locations in Angang, and his return to the city was also delayed for some time.

(8) Children should not make 'black-white' movements
Return for a moment to the image I gave of Beicun. Here the houses are linked together physically, but also in the sense that a noisy current of human activity flows through them. This human activity centres on family and friends, and I mentioned that being outside of this flow is seen as dangerous; even to step outside of the village puts one at risk from bad influences (such as ghosts). Going further afield puts one at risk not only of being isolated (because people in the cities are not all family and friends), but also of actually being transformed into a bad person (*phai-lang*).

This is partly a matter of moving out of line, or leaving the community. But it also might relate, more generally, to matters of thinking, acting and speaking. When children (and others) are told what they should not do, or are criticised for things they have already done, the Hokkien expression *o-peq* ('black-white', meaning 'mixed up'), and the Mandarin expression *luan* ('disorderly') are often used.[9] For example, if someone has said something foolish, it may provoke the ridiculing comment 'black-white talk!' (*o-peq kong*), or 'chaotic talk!' (*luanjiang*). Someone who expresses a strange idea may similarly be told not to have 'mixed-up thoughts!' (*luanxiang*). At other times 'black-white!' (*o-peq*) is used on its own, as an expression of mocking disbelief. It is wrong, in many different ways, to be 'black-white', but this kind of criticism often centres, as I have said, on movement. People are told not to 'run around' in a 'black-white' or chaotic fashion (*luanpao*), advice which is, at times, explicitly linked to the chaotic movements of ghosts.

As children know, the surrounding countryside is said to be peopled with unhappy spirits who may seek revenge for their grievances: premature deaths, the neglect of their graves, etc. This is particularly true during the seventh month 'ghost festival', when spirits are freed from hell and are themselves said to 'wander crazily' around (*luanpao*), even within the community.[10] But ghosts are an ever-present risk, especially near the water, scene of many untimely deaths. The spirits of drowning victims are said to be particularly unhappy because their bodies have not been recovered, as a result of which they have not been given a proper burial. These unproperly situated dead people are a risk to living people who unproperly wander outside the normal bounds of the community. For example, children told me of a ghost on the beach near Beicun who attacked the hearts of lone passers-by. Many children in Angang, their houses built next to the ocean, do not know how to swim because they've been told by the gods (via spirit mediums and via their parents) that they should *not* swim, that it will bring bad luck. More precisely, they would risk attack by an angry spirit. Children told me that even walking alone to the harbour at night was an open invitation for attack by a devil (*mogui*).

There are also many dangerous places away from the water. Children advised me not to go up into the hills behind the village, where I might encounter *heibai wuchang* (literally 'black-white never-constant'), the ghosts who announce a person's death.[11] Several children also said that it was dangerous to be near the schools alone or at night, and many people expressed surprise that I was willing to stay in the teacher's dormitory alone during one holiday. The school buildings, though strictly speaking within a village, are set off from the rest of the community, and unusually isolated. Children say that the elementary school (*xiaoxue*) was built on an old graveyard, and that the middle school (*zhongxue*) is located on an old execution ground, thus ensuring a steady stream of unhappy spirits.[12]

These are all reasons why children should not make 'black-white' movements. But, again, it is not simply a matter of movement.[13] One young man told me his mother had explained to him that if he hadn't done bad things (*huaishi*), then he needn't worry about 'ghosts knocking on the door in the middle of the night'.[14] It is also said that 'good people don't fear ghosts' (*haoren bu pa gui*). But this boy's mother had, just to be safe, advised him *not* to swim during the ghost festival. (He and his friends had secretly gone swimming during the festival in any case.)

(9) Communal religion protects children's movements

As I have suggested, protection against bad influences comes in different forms, including being a full member of a community, and being a 'good person'. This is somewhat redundant, however, because a good person, one who will not fear ghosts, is by definition a person who is fully part of a human community. But these overlapping forms of protection (community ties or goodness) are not seen as absolutely foolproof. As I mentioned in the last chapter, parents take a number of additional steps to protect their children. Certainly in Angang there is a great deal of ritual activity which is primarily protective (*hu*). But this, again, is *community*-based (i.e., local). People individually ask the gods for help, but, as I will later discuss, it is only because the community is properly 'connected' that these strong gods exist in the first place. This circular logic could be summarised as follows:

(1) people in the flow of human activity are less at risk from ghosts;
(2) people who obey the morality of human relationships will not be at risk in the first place;
(3) the product of proper human relationships (gods) can protect people from risk.

In a moment I will discuss the relevance of this for children. But first I want to give some examples of worshipping for protection, to show how this relates to community identity, and to movement. It should be noted however that protection, in the narrow sense, is far from the only benefit seen to arise from worship. Much of what happens in local religion is directed towards 'striking it rich' (*fa cai*), or being successful; there is as much of an emphasis on requests for productivity and fertility (in the broad sense) as on protection.[15]

But when people are asked why they worship, perhaps the most common answer is that they are requesting 'security', *pieng-an*. *Pieng-an* has a range of meanings ('peace', 'lack of disturbances', or, literally, 'flat and secure'), which overlap somewhat with the meanings of *an-cuan* ('security', 'defense'). Villagers define *pieng-an* as an absence of problems (*meiyou shi*, 'not having things happen'), as their examples show:[16] 'In [one part of

Taiwan], during a flood, an entire village of aborigines was wiped out, except for one house where the people worshipped [*paipai*, i.e. were not Christians].¹⁷ In another area, the one building left standing after a flood was a temple. After seeing this, many aborigines became Buddhists.' Another story similarly stressed the ability of the gods to provide security, *pieng-an*:

> During the war, when bombs were being dropped, Angang people had gone to hide in caves and up in the hills. They looked out and saw the following sight: [the goddess] Kuan-im catching bombs which were going to hit Angang. She caught them in her dress and dropped them into the ocean. She didn't let Angang people get hurt.

In a similar way, the gods are often asked to defend people who are making movements of various kinds. One exasperated 'outsider' (a woman who worked for the township government, *xianggongsuo*) said: 'Angang people ask the gods [*wenshen*] about everything. Even if they only want to go out to play [*quwan*], first they ask the god. If the god says don't go, they don't go!' There are many everyday examples of this. For instance, a fisherman was considering whether or not to go spear-fishing alone (a fairly dangerous activity) on a day which the lunar calendar listed as dangerous. He asked the goddess Ma Co (by dropping divination blocks) if it would be safe to go, and received an inconclusive response. At first, the goddess seemed to be saying not to go. As often happens with enquiries made through divination blocks, the question was then shifted (changing the time of departure), but he was still unable to get a clear response. In the end, lacking a firm answer, he decided not to go because it might not be safe.

When people are asked why they worship particular gods, as opposed to worshipping in general, they often say that a god protected them in the past, and often during travel or movement. A middle-aged woman told me that when she was young, and working in a Taipei-area factory, she had been in a bicycle accident in which she was run over by a car. She was wearing a charm (*xianghuo*) from the goddess Kuan-im and so was not hurt. Since then she had worshipped the goddess. A local man said that, when he was a child, he had fallen into a river. He did not know how to swim, and as he was being pulled under he said to himself that if he was saved he would become a 'foster son' (*yizi*) of Kuan-im. He somehow survived, and had since worshipped the goddess.

I was also told the story of a local fishing boat, which had gone out in bad weather and had been caught up in a typhoon. The family of the captain of this boat, back in Angang, had worshipped Ma Co, asking her to protect him, to give him a safe voyage. Ma Co agreed, telling the family (through a spirit medium) that in return they should help build a new temple dedicated to her honour. The boat returned safely. When a new Ma Co temple was constructed in the centre of Beicun, the captain's family made substantial contributions to it, and the captain himself became an important member of the temple committee.

Trips (for fishing, or to other parts of Taiwan) will often not be made on days listed in the lunar calendar as 'inauspicious', and even on auspicious days, gods will be asked to provide protection. As I've noted, much of the travel in and out of Angang is done by the young. On the morning of travel, it is very common to see mother and child on a motorcycle, driving up into the hills to worship at the local cave-temple to Kuan-im, asking for protection. Similarly, fishermen, who go back and forth, are thought to need extra help from the gods.

But this kind of help cannot be taken for granted, and 'outsiders' are sometimes criticised for presuming to tap into the local gods. More precisely, they are very welcome to worship, because this reflects on the power of the deities. But in general they are unable to fully benefit from this worship because, unlike locals (who learn of such things through spirit mediums), they do not know what the gods are thinking. For example, the local cave which houses an altar to Kuan-im has water which is said to have healing powers. People say that if you have a cut, and you put this water on the cut, it will heal very quickly. Stones from the cave are also powerful. But Kuan-im has said people must have her permission to use the water and stones (by dropping divination blocks), and this is something which many outsiders don't know: 'Some people took stones from the cave, they were going to take them home, but they didn't ask if it was alright. So their journey was stopped by bad weather, and when they finally got back home they became very sick.'

To conclude this section, communal religion is seen as a way of providing protection, e.g., for those who travel. This is not by any means restricted to children (and it is thought crucial for fishermen), but it is considered very important for children for two reasons. First, they are thought more vulnerable than adults to bad influences, and thus more in need of protection. Second, (like fishermen) the young tend to travel quite often, and thus are more likely to be exposed to various risks.

(10) Geomantic and other forces may also help or harm children
Here I should at least briefly mention some related notions of what may affect the fortunes of a child. First, geomancy. When I asked one woman to tell me something about *fengshui*, 'winds and waters' (i.e. geomancy), she

related the following incident. One day, when she was a girl, she began to have severe stomach pains. When her father learnt of this, he remembered that earlier in the day he had hastily repaired the roof of the family home with a plank of wood. Because of his concern about his daughter's illness, he removed the plank and properly fixed the roof with cement, in case his carelessness had been the cause of her distress. She quickly recovered, and her parents accepted that the placement of the board had literally directed the problem towards her stomach.[18] Although this kind of layman's *fengshui* is not uncommon, and the geomancy of graves is an important matter, there are no local *fengshui* experts, and it is not generally a matter of everyday concern.

Nevertheless, the kinds of forces invoked in discussions of 'winds and waters', along with astrologically inspired notions of fate and destiny, are, in a rather unsystematic way, held to influence, or even determine, the lives of children. For example, one man told me that when his elder brother was a child, his parents had gone to a fortune-teller (*suanmingren*) in the city to ask about his prospects. The fortune-teller advised them that the total number of strokes in the characters of his name was unlucky, so they changed it. (Parents might also select a new, more auspicious, character to include in the name, e.g. one which had the radical for 'gold' in it, indicating future prosperity.)

Even the *statements* of adults are a potential risk to the fortunes of children; I was told by a local woman that I should not, in front of a child, say that she was 'fat' (*pang*) or 'good' (*guai*). She said that the spirit (*shen*) inside of the child might change upon hearing such a thing, and the child might then become sickly (i.e., not fat) or bad. To praise a child is thought, potentially, to attract the attention of malicious spirits. Children are thus sometimes given ugly names or nicknames, as a way of making them seem less worthy of attention from ghosts.

(11) Children are not taught religion, instead it is done for them

I have described Angang as a closely knit community in which communal gods give protection. But aside from simply living there, how do children in Angang learn about religious matters? As I mentioned in the Introduction, Schipper has described the transmission of Daoism as 'l'enseignement sans parole' (1982:237–75). In Angang, there is indeed no formal instruction in religious matters (the only seats in temples are for the gods), and only rarely do people set out to teach *themselves* by reading religious texts. Such texts do exist, and are usually freely available in local temples, but are rarely read.[19]

One result of this lack of instruction or study is that both children and adults often have only very sketchy ideas about the gods whom they worship. They would know that Ma Co, for instance, protects fishermen, that she was a young woman from Fujian province, etc., but beyond this the details are scant. They do sometimes watch operas at temples which relate the stories of the gods. But at spirit medium altars many people must even be told the name of the god from whom they are about to make a request. Rare are the discussions of doctrine or religious philosophy (i.e. philosophical Buddhism or Daoism), as such. But there are, by contrast, especially among serious devotees, a great many conversations about arrangements for ritual activities, the details of spirit medium sessions (including what is revealed in them), and the activities and movements of locally worshipped gods and other spirits. Children certainly hear and sometimes participate in many of these discussions, but they are never, to my knowledge, arranged for children's benefit. If a child was listening, she would undoubtedly learn something. What she overheard would, as likely as not, be about how to do something (but there is a moral in that, as well).

Although children do not seem to be taught about religion, they are certainly *made to participate*, sometimes literally put through the motions of rituals. When I asked one group of children how they had learnt about religion, they said that they had watched their mother and other adults *paipai* (worship). However, children quite often do not even manage this much. For example, one boy I knew did not go to watch an opera (a rare event in Angang) which was performed at the Ma Co temple, a few steps away from his home.[20] This meant that he also missed seeing the rituals associated with that particular occasion. At first, he told me that the opera was 'not good to watch' (*buhaokan*), i.e., not entertaining enough, and that in any case he would be 'watching without understanding' (*kanbudong*). Many other children did watch the opera, although everyone stresses that such performances are intended for the gods, not for people. The boy later told me that in fact he hadn't gone because his mother had forbidden it. She said the opera was intended for Ma Co, and that adults might watch as well, but that children should not. (Sometimes these performances can be rather 'adult', and include strippers, but this was not true on this occasion.) He said his mother told him that children (she specified children still in school) shouldn't watch, because they might 'go crazy' (*feng*). At other times children are similarly excluded from religious activities, ostensibly for their own protection. For example, some rituals, or parts of rituals, are seen as dangerous, and children may be told to leave a house in which such an activity is taking place. They may also be sent away from a spirit medium session in which sensitive or private matters are being discussed.

Another, very important, reason children sometimes do not watch religious activity is that they are too busy. This usually means that they are at school, or they are doing homework. The school follows the national calendar (*guoli*), i.e. the Gregorian/solar calendar, while religious activities follow the lunar calendar (*yueli*, or *nongli*, agricultural calendar). Because rituals are held on auspicious (*jili*) days, as indicated by reference to the lunar calendar and/or divination, rather than on convenient days, the best day for a ritual may very well be a day in which all children are in school.

Here it is worth stressing that whereas I was never told that the point of religious activity was to *teach* children, I was often told that the point of religious activity was to *protect* them. The fact of children being kept away from rituals or festivities, or being in school when they happen, is secondary. What is important is that children receive the benefits of religious activity. This is consistent with what I was told by one (unmarried) young woman about her own participation in religion. She said that she only worshipped when her mother took her to the temple. Otherwise, when she was away from Angang she didn't worship, because she 'didn't know how to do it'. She said that most women will consider starting to worship only when they have their own children and start to worry about them, or perhaps when they worry about their husband's health. Then they might learn what to do.

However, as noted, even the knowledge which parents have about religion at times seems insubstantial, as shown by a discussion I once held with a spirit medium (*tang ki*). Mediums, as a matter of routine, go out of their way to claim ignorance about what they do; only when possessed do they have expertise. But this man said, with reference to religion in the community in general (as opposed to his own practice): 'We really don't know very much, just a little bit. The god says do something, and then we do it. We don't understand very well [*bu tai liaojie*].' I asked how the local Daoist priests (who are 'unofficial' in the sense that they have no specialised training, little special equipment, and a limited range of techniques) know what *they* know, and he said: 'They study some, but not much. Mostly the gods tell them, especially in dreams.'

Alongside this rather passive stance towards transmitting and acquiring religious knowledge, there is evidence of a positive dislike of direct religious transmission. In Angang, at the time of my fieldwork, there was a small group of missionaries from the Yi Guan Dao sect (which combines ideas from Buddhism, Daoism, Confucianism, Christianity and Islam). The young missionaries, most of whom had been factory workers in Taipei before joining Yi Guan Dao, and being sent down to suffer for their faith in Angang, tried to convince local residents to participate in their unorthodox rites. They rely very much on daily study, and on (earnest) discussion. But local people were very suspicious of Yi Guan Dao. Once I was walking down the street with a local boy, and we passed some of the missionaries. I started to speak to them, and the boy nervously dragged me away, saying it was unlucky to do so. There are a number of reasons for this mistrust (including the sect's strange reputation, and a dislike of the 'mixed up' nature of their doctrines). But I was also told that people in Angang dislike Yi Guan Dao specifically because the missionaries *talk* too much (*jiang tai duo*); nobody can stand to listen (*women shoubuliao*).

(12) Children should learn to 'take punishment'
Having described some of the ways in which the community deals with supernatural matters, I now want to turn to something more mundane. I have noted that religious protection at times centres on movement, i.e. something seemingly 'physical'. But now I will discuss ways in which something seemingly 'physical', punishment, is closely related to the moral and spiritual. As I said in the Introduction, although there is an anxious discourse about children, in practice they do not seem to be over-protected (e.g., in rituals they are told to walk through fire). I suggested they were sometimes toughened up. In order to better explain this, I will describe some of the everyday ways in which adults and children interact, but it should be stressed that this is a community matter.

In Angang there is a great deal of openly expressed affection between parents and children. There is also, among friends and relatives in the community, a kind of affectionate physicality, which sometimes leads into rough-and-tumble teasing. Against this background, adults also often slap and pinch infants and children. This is done (rather hard) on the face, arm or leg, as if it were a kind of game, although they may act serious at the moment of hitting. Parents do this to their own children, but also to the children of friends and relatives, and children also sometimes do it amongst themselves. The correct response is no response, a blank stare, and very young infants learn not to react to being hit. When adults playfully (and yet firmly) slap a child, and the child does not respond, the adults often smile and laugh with delight. (And it can be quite funny to watch.) This may seem a very minor thing, but it is part of everyday life in Angang, something that routinely happens alongside displays of affection between adults and children.

Sometimes the scenario is more complicated, if predictable, and involves encouraging children to hit older people. For example, I once saw a young man teasing an infant, until the baby started crying. At that point, the man began to gently slap the baby on the face, telling it not to cry. The baby's grandmother, who had been watching in amusement, then laughingly intervened, hitting the young man in mock anger. She also took the baby's hand, and tried to get it to slap out at the young man as well. Somewhat older children may be teased by adults who instruct them to hit other adults, for example those who have fallen asleep in chairs. I once saw a married couple tease their son's daughter (not yet old enough for school) about some small matter until she started crying. Showing no sympathy, they then instructed her to go up and hit a man (also a relative, her father's father's sister's husband) who was sitting, unawares, nearby. The rather brave child went up and hit him, hard, crying all the while. The man looked surprised, but had no further reaction. Then she was left alone. I should emphasise that in most cases this teasing and hitting (which in an out-of-context description undoubtedly sounds somewhat cruel) takes place in a relaxed atmosphere of joking among friends. Children sometimes get upset, but usually it is a game.

When I asked why it was done, I was most often told that it was *haowan*, 'fun', or 'fun to play'. One young woman also explained that parents were made happy by any evidence that their children were strong, able to withstand hardship (*shouku*, 'take bitterness'). But the teasing is often done by people other than the parents, although usually by their close friends and relatives. One day some young friends of mine (a group of sisters, along with some cousins) were hitting each other, quite hard, trying not to react amidst the laughter. They told me they were 'taking punishment' (*rong-xing*). At a local shop I came upon a group of adults standing around a small baby who did not respond to being pinched and teased. One neighbour-woman praised the child, laughing with great merriment: 'He won't cry! You can't make him cry!' On another occasion, a grandmother bragged about her two-year-old grandson, who took a very hard fall and managed to constrain his tears: 'It doesn't matter how much he's hurt, he doesn't cry!' Again, this relates to local identity. A fifteen-year-old girl once laughed as she told me about an 'outside' child who had visited Angang. The child had lightly skinned her knee and then had cried about it as her mother made a big fuss. The local girl said that children from Angang would not be that way. A child who cries in public is as likely as not to be ignored, or simply to be told that 'people are laughing at you'.

(13) When they do wrong, children should be punished; but they are expected to do wrong

Playful hitting is perhaps a kind of game, which should bring no response. Nor should a skinned knee bring a tearful response. But serious discipline is another matter altogether (or is it?) I will relate one (fairly complicated) example of this. A group of children were playing on a village street, when a young girl did something which momentarily put a young boy (to whom she was not related) at risk of physical injury.[21] This was witnessed by the boy's mother, who was obviously frightened, but who said nothing. It was also seen by the girl's paternal grandmother, who flew into a rage. She picked up a stick and started beating the girl for putting the boy at risk, but the boy's mother intervened, grabbing away the stick and telling the older woman to stop.

Instead, the grandmother picked up another stick, and chased her granddaughter into a house, followed by the boy's mother. She then told the girl to hold out her hands to be beaten, which the girl refused to do. Every time she refused, her grandmother thrashed her legs and back with the stick. The mother of the boy was now obviously concerned that things had gone too far and tried to intervene, pinching the grandmother and telling her to stop. Finally, the little girl held out her hands, and her grandmother whacked them with the stick. Then the girl was made to sit on the floor for fifteen minutes, holding a tray of betel nuts on her head, quietly crying.

There seemed to be two problems. The first was that the girl had threatened the good health of another child, and this is what she was punished for. But, secondly, (as a typical Angang child, trained to 'take punishment'?) she was fairly strong-willed herself, and her refusal to give in to her grandmother (and hold out her hands for hitting) provoked extra wrath. About a week later, I saw the grandmother testing the granddaughter, calling her over and telling her to hold out her hands to be beaten. The girl again refused to give in (apparently preferring to take the extra beating she would receive), and the grandmother got a stick. But as she was about to start hitting the girl, she was called away to deal with some other matter. The girl's mother (i.e. the daughter-in-law of the woman who had been doing the beating) had been watching from the side and called her daughter over. She told the girl to hold out her hands, which this time the girl did, and then the mother picked up a stick and hit her, as promised.

The grandmother later told me about her own childhood. She had once fallen out of a tree in the mountains where she was gathering fruit. She bled quite badly from the back of her head. This was in the days when no doctors were to be found in Angang, so she went up to her mother, in tears. Her mother only pinched her for being so stupid as to hurt herself. Another time her father had become uncharacteristically angry at her for being *tiaopi* (naughty or mischievous), and had struck her over the head with a stick, causing an injury to her forehead. Now the back and front of her head often hurt.

In these practices there is something of a paradox. Children are playfully hit in order to teach them how to 'take punishment'. And they are also seriously hit in order to be punished. On the one hand, parents seem to want to control their children, while on the other hand, they seem glad to have evidence that their children are uncontrollable. Indeed, I was often told that parents are happy if their children (both boys and girls) are 'naughty' or 'mischievous' (*tiaopi*) because it is felt that this translates, in later life, into cleverness (*congming*). Being somewhat bad is seen as a good thing, and as something which one eventually outgrows.

Children are often called 'little ghosts' (*xiaogui*) by teachers and parents (just as people who drink too much, or drink *alone*, are called 'wine ghosts', *jiugui*). People also sometimes say that petty theft is carried out by children, whereas (in a community as closely-knit as Angang) adults would supposedly never do such a thing. For example, when it was discovered that some cash offerings had been taken from a local temple, it was assumed that only children could have done it. During one festival for Ma Co's birthday, her temple was filled with offerings, including red envelopes with cash (*hongbao*). During the festival, someone was assigned to stay in the temple every night, specifically to protect the valuables from children.

Conclusion

From the beginning I have suggested that family-based morality in Angang is not transmitted in an explicit way. But in this chapter I have given many examples of ways in which this morality could be said to be transmitted to children. For example, parents tell children to take steps to avoid ghosts (which is, as I hope to have shown, another way of saying that they should stay in and with the community). By extension, instructing children to avoid ghosts, or telling them that by being good they will not have to worry about them, is perhaps a way of instructing children in the morality of properly ordered human relationships (although it is never said in such a way).

Children are also explicitly advised by their parents not to leave Angang in certain cases, and forbidden to do things which might lead them to become bad. They are reprimanded for putting the physical integrity of themselves at risk, and even for putting the well-being of other children at risk. When this happens, might they not learn something about the *shen*, the 'body-person' of a child? And when they are playfully hit, they might learn something about family-based notions which value strength and resilience. Just as they learn that to go outside is to become bad, they know that, in other ways, they are already assumed to be naturally mischievous. Their identification with Angang is also inextricably tied up with these notions, including the way in which Angang both protects them from harm, and strengthens them to resist it. This is arguably quite a bit of learning, and later I will return to a closer examination of the ways in which this takes place.

In chapter 3 I will begin to describe learning inside of the schools. There, it seems clear that morality (*daode*) is directly transmitted, for example in texts which make distinctively moral propositions, which teachers then explain. By contrast, when children in Angang are told by their parents what they should or should not do, the emphasis is on commands rather than explanations. The seriousness of the moral tone of school life is something which is opposed to the informal tone of daily life in Angang. (This may seem a vague manner in which to describe a difference, but the difference itself is clear and striking.) In public life in Angang, people laugh at those who are seen to take themselves too seriously.[22] Also, and again within the Confucian tradition, the morality of the school is thought to be transmitted through the 'exemplary' behaviour of teachers. But parents in Angang are in some ways (both by their own estimation and by the standards of the school) *bad* examples for their children. In many cases they lack the education they would need to live up to the example of textbook parents. Nor can they live the austere lifestyle promoted by the schools, not if they are to meet the intense social demands of their collective life in Angang.

3

The proper way of being a person

In chapter 2, I described some movements in and through Angang, leaving aside one of the most obvious and important: that of children going back and forth between their homes and the schools. Within the *xiang* there are three 'national elementary schools' (*guomin xiaoxue*), and one 'national middle school' (*guomin zhongxue*). Students obviously leave home to go to these buildings, and in many cases they must leave their villages to do so, coming back in the evenings. Once they have graduated from middle school, if they are to continue in education, they leave Angang altogether, only to periodically return. This moving back and forth, as I have suggested, also entails a shifting in and out of different ways of learning. In this chapter I want to discuss several of these ways: reading texts, watching television, becoming acquainted with certain role-models from popular culture, becoming consumers, imitating the pattern of teachers, and being bribed and punished by them. This may seem a strange way of describing what happens in schooling, but my argument is that children see the pattern of teachers, and interpret the proper way of the school, against the background of a much broader set of representations.

(14) Studying and being a person are inseparable
The following text (read in the fifth year of elementary school) conveys the tone of much school-based rhetoric. Interestingly, it also asserts the value of practical non-school learning. The text is entitled 'Studying and being a person', *Qiuxue yu zuoren*. A more accurate, if clumsy, translation would be 'Seeking learning and conducting oneself as a person'. *Qiuxue* can simply mean to attend school, or to study. But *qiu* implies supplication (e.g. to *qiu pingan* is to 'request security' from the gods), and *xue*, 'learning', also has rather grand associations (e.g., one of the Chinese classics is 'The Great

Learning', *Da Xue*). The expression *zuoren* means 'to be a person', but more precisely 'to conduct oneself as a person'; to *zuo* something is to do it (e.g. to *zuofan* is to cook a meal, 'do the rice').

Studying [*qiuxue*] and being a person [*zuoren*] are inseparable. The goal of our studies is to learn the proper way of being a person [*zuoren de daoli*]; we must be clear about the proper way of being a person, otherwise study is impossible [*you fei qiuxue bu ke*]. From this we see that studying and being a person are inseparable, they are two sides of the same matter, the relationship is extremely close. We know that coming to school to study is not only about learning what is in books, what is more important is the use of this knowledge in our daily lives. Only then will it be meaningful to study, only then will we not be reading dead books [*sishu*].

Having suggested that what is learnt in school must be put into practice, and that what is learnt in practice must be brought to the school, the text then goes on to argue that schools have no monopoly on learning:

Most people take the scope of study to be narrow, assuming that the information studied in schools counts as learning [*xuewen*]. But this is a serious misunderstanding. We must appreciate that the scope of learning is very great. The information in books and the reason [*daoli*, 'the proper way'] of teachers is only one small part of learning. In our lives there are many new matters we should study, and many other kinds of reason [*daoli*] await our understanding. These are the most important kinds of learning. We can say: all of life is a great book; the society we are born into is a great school. Only if we use our intelligence, seek knowledge, search our minds for answers, only then can we achieve truly rich insights [*fengfu de xueshi*].

The text then attacks those who *only* possess book-learning:

Some people assume that studying and being a person are two separate things. In spite of reading books, in spite of learned talk [*toutou shi dao*], when it comes to being a person and handling matters, what comes from the mouth is evil-hearted [*wangwang kou shi xin fei*], the talk is not trustworthy, the attitude towards others is dishonest, and matters are handled perfunctorily [*fu yan se ze*], not even coming up to the level of the uneducated. This kind of person has not understood that studying and being a person are one matter. We can say: they do not have true learning. In sum, we see that the truly learned know the proper way of being persons. And when it comes to learning, those who know the proper way of being persons will inevitably show great skill [*gongfu*].[1]

The argument of the text, set out in somewhat repetitive detail, is that the opposition between studenthood and personhood is false. To put this another way, the school *should* be embedded in communal life. In chapter 4, I will suggest that many of the texts read by students do provide evidence of a continuity between school and community. Texts about filial obedience, in particular, appear to share many of the concerns and values of family life. But before examining these, it is useful to think, at least in an impressionistic way, about the context in which they are read. This context includes not only home and school, but also two interrelated sources of many representations of childhood and personhood in Taiwan: television and popular culture.

(15) Schooling is a process of going out of the house

A girl from Beicun will spend the first few years of her life in the village (usually rarely leaving it, except perhaps to go to the next village), surrounded mostly by close relatives and family friends. She will become part of the ongoing movement through the houses there, watching and participating in conversations, rituals, meals, games and so on. The older children around her, perhaps brothers and sisters, will meanwhile go to school. Every morning they assemble, in uniforms, along the sea-wall, and together walk away from Beicun towards the next village. She will also certainly know young people who have gone to, and come back from, more distant places in Taiwan. In this manner she has contact with the world outside of Beicun, including, it could be said, the knowledge which is transmitted through the schools. Many older siblings, friends, and perhaps even her parents, will have gone through at least part of the educational system.

There are other important ways in which her village life is not clearly delimited. Television, for instance, brings to her attention many ideas 'from outside'. Almost every home has a set, and they seem to almost always be on, (even if, much of the time, they are only half-watched). Occasionally, the programming touches directly on beliefs which are part of her everyday life. For example, I spent one rainy afternoon watching television with a family (parents and children) who were devotees of a spirit medium cult in Beicun. The programme was a docu-drama of sorts, which went as follows:

A jealous wife, convinced that her husband is having an affair, has a nightmare in which she kills him. Made anxious by her ominous dream, she goes to a fortune teller. He explains that the dream relates to a problem from one of her previous lives. The fortune teller also gives her charms to put on the door of her house and under her husband's pillow. She does so, but her husband finds the charms, and, in a fury, he rips them to shreds. Husband and wife then fight, partly because she remains convinced that he is having an affair. In the heat of the moment, she grabs a knife and stabs him with it.

The moral of the story (explicitly stated, and given by an announcer directly to the camera) was that dreams are created by people, and not by gods or something else. But if they are given too much emphasis, they influence behaviour, becoming self-fulfilling, sometimes tragic, prophecies.[2]

This programme, along with much of the prime-time programming in Taiwan, was in the 'national language' (*guoyu*), and in some ways it shared the values of the school. Its anti-superstition[3] message seemed directed against things which are commonplace in Angang (spiritual consultations, interpretation of dreams). Both schools and television are centrally controlled in Taiwan, and many television programmes anticipate, in important ways, the moral transmission of the schools. As a girl grows up in Beicun, television helps to make the boundary between her village and the outside world less distinct.

Then, when she is old enough, the girl's parents buy her a uniform, and she is sent to elementary school. In the mornings she joins other children on the sea-wall, for the sleepy walk to the next village.[4] This new way of spending time has, of course, a number of important implications. First, it is her point of entry to a system which will occupy her attention for many years, and in which she will be expected to work (quite hard) towards success. Second, as I have said, it is a shift to a different way of learning, one which is much more direct than that embedded in village life, one in which reading and writing is of central importance, and one which comes to her in the 'national' rather than the local language. Third, it is the point at which teachers become an important part of her life (and their influence is felt to be particularly significant). Finally, it is her most concrete introduction to identification with a community outside of her home. This is true, for example, in terms of classroom composition (which is increasingly diverse), but also in texts which identify her, as the reader, with the nation. Somewhere along the line, for the first time, she learns that she is a citizen (*gongmin*).

But this wider community, even if evoked from the very beginning, is slowly arrived at.[5] The first stage, which after all lasts for six years, is elementary school (*xiaoxue*), in which most of the girl's classmates will be from Beicun or the next village. Her 'national education' thus begins in a classroom in which she is surrounded by many relatives. Most of the men and women who teach her are also from Angang, not from the outside. Only after six years does the girl transfer to the middle school (*zhongxue*), which is attended by all of the children in Angang, regardless of village, regardless of surname. There she is taught sometimes by local teachers but, more often, by teachers who are from the outside. Then after three years, and depending on her examination results and the resources of her parents, she might either remain in education or begin to work. For example, she might attend a *zhuanke* (a sort of 'junior college'), or *gaozhong* (high school). But this would mean leaving Angang, and probably going to the capital of the county, where the schools draw their students from different places.

Along with many other students, she would probably stay with relatives there. But in general, the higher she moves up the educational ladder, the further she moves away from her immediate family and natal community. This migration is, at the same time, something her family would be proud of and encourage (although they would still be concerned about her physical and spiritual well-being). In any case, the movement through educational sites coincides with an important expansion of the idea of community. All along the way, the content of courses in the various schools she attends would emphasise her identification with the nation (i.e., a non-kinship, non-local level of identity). Here there would arguably be a tension which related back to her original commitment to a family. (I will later discuss several texts which deal with the relationship between families and the state.)

(16) The student road has divergent ends
Although not every student manages to arrive there, and very few from Angang ever do, Taipei is at the far end of this movement through educational sites in Taiwan.[6] It is the centre of commercial, political and intellectual power, and even those who have never been there are influenced by it. In Angang, for instance, many of the middle school teachers are recent graduates of universities in Taipei. There are many things which might be said about this capital city and its influence, but in the context of this discussion of schooling and movement, I will mention a road, which arguably symbolises some tensions arising from Taiwanese education.

Taipei is cross-cut by a long east–west avenue called *Zhong-xiao Lu*, i.e., Patriotism-and-Filial-Obedience Road. The name is, of course, interesting in itself, reflecting the Confucian notion (as interpreted by the schools) that filial obedience (*xiao*) and loyalty/patriotism (*zhong*) are twinned virtues. More precisely, filial obedience is seen as the path to patriotism and all other admirable forms of conduct, just as membership in a family is seen as the first in a series of commitments which leads to citizenship. Most of the major avenues in Taipei have similarly virtuous names derived from Confucian or Nationalist doctrine.

Patriotism-and-Filial-Obedience Road also arguably symbolises a tension which arises from educational migration in Taiwan. The western end passes in front of Taipei's main railway station, the focal point of internal Taiwanese migration (much of it school-orientated). In the neighbourhood around the station are found dozens of revision schools (*buxiban*), which are attended by thousands of (often very tired-looking) students. After school, at times still wearing their uniforms, these students descend on the *buxiban* in order to improve their chances of success in the highly competitive university entrance examinations. At times, this district of Taipei seems to be filled with hard-working students and virtually no one else.

The opposite, eastern, end of Patriotism-and-Filial-Obedience Road has a different atmosphere altogether: it is a shopping district, a monument to consumption and prosperity. Here thousands of smartly dressed young people stroll between high-rise department stores, fast-food restaurants, karaoke bars and cafés. While the western end of the avenue, with its railway station and *buxiban*, could be said to represent the migration and dedication which are explicitly linked to the process of education in Taiwan, the eastern end could be said to represent the reward for this work: success, prosperity and consumption. It may also represent, in its consumerism, a notion of individuality which is arguably promoted by the schools, and which is a potential threat to family loyalties. As Thompson notes, although parents in Taiwan usually see education as an investment, the actual process of schooling is partly a process of 'individuation', which may free children from parental authority (1990:117). In any case, Taiwanese youth culture oscillates between a work-ethic and a consumer-ethos, both of which are well-known to students as they leave their homes in order to study.

(17) Teachers are what students should become

Just as students from rural Taiwan could be said to be on the way to Patriotism-and-Filial-Obedience Road (if never actually arriving), teachers in Angang could be said to be coming back from there, and representing its mixed message in the countryside. If Chinese education is expected to be moral, then Chinese teachers are equally expected to be both transmitters and living examples of this morality. The notion of teachers as 'patterns' is consistent with traditional Chinese images of learning as a process of direct, personalised transmission. Students of calligraphy, for example, trace and imitate the calligraphy of a master, down to every stroke and nuance, in order to achieve mastery. Students of *taijiquan* should also imitate the movement of someone who already understands the pattern and the significance of *taijiquan* movement. School-children are similarly expected to live up to the upright example of their teachers, in some ways to become them.

It is easy, in modern Taiwan, to be cynical about such a proposition, but I was told by many country people that teachers are still the most respected members of society. This aura of respect is often explicitly traced back to Confucius. One young man explained to me that teachers should be, for their students, an example or 'pattern' (*bangyang*) of virtue or morality (*daode*). Furthermore, they should be *qinggao*, 'morally lofty and upright'. When asked what this meant in practice, he explained, laughing: 'They don't make much money, but they have a lot of virtue!' He specifically said that teachers should be the kind of people who refuse 'red envelopes' (*hongbao*), i.e., bribes.[7] Then everyone would *zun shi zhong dao*, 'respect the teacher and respect his way' (i.e., respect his teachings).

Teachers are often cited as a direct source of moral guidance; for example, several times children told me they had learnt what was a bad thing to do (*huaishi*) because their teachers, as opposed to their parents, had explained it to them. Teachers themselves stress that their aim 'isn't simply to teach the knowledge in books, but also to teach the proper way of being a person'.[8] When I asked them where they obtained the material for classes in morality, and how they knew what to say, they pointed out that they (being relatively young) had recently gone through the whole system. They needn't rely on manuals, they knew what was meant to be said.

This 'saying', however, happens in different contexts, and is not restricted to courses on morality. For example, among the many activities in the school, there is a more or less constant cleaning up of classrooms and the school grounds. This purification often seemingly happens whether or not it is strictly necessary, and it takes up a substantial proportion of student time. Teachers explained to me, and more importantly to the students, that it was intended to 'foster the labouring spirit' (*peiyang laodong de jingshen*). Teachers also place a considerable emphasis on proper posture. One teacher in particular became very angry when students failed to sit up straight. She said that when they sit properly they are able to concentrate (*zhuanxin*). If they do not sit properly then their minds will wander and they will think of other things. But also, as she often told her students, it was a sign of disrespect towards her, as the teacher, if they did not have a proper bearing in the classroom. Her own posture was impeccable at all times, for their edification.

The outside teachers in the Angang middle school mediate in a complex way between the township and the world beyond. On the one hand they are enforcers of school-based discipline (correcting student posture, 'fostering the labouring spirit', etc.), pushing children in a particular direction. But on the other hand they are patterns of what students should become, and they are expected to *attractively* represent the ideals of school and nation. In Angang this mediating role is perhaps heightened by the fact that they are almost the only local representatives of their age-group. Because young people from Angang emigrate for school and work, there are not many villagers aged between about sixteen and thirty years. But these outside teachers, having been sent to a rural area as a first assignment, are relatively young, mostly between the ages of parents and children. This heightens the sense in which they represent everything new and modern in Taiwan, in contrast with the old and traditional pattern embodied by parents and grandparents in the village.

(18) Children might follow *phai* or *ke'ai* role models
The pattern exemplified by teachers should be seen against the background of other potential role-models in Taiwan. Here it is worth mentioning an interesting tension between two opposed role-models in Taiwanese popular culture, both of which are viewed with some ambivalence. I will call these the 'loveable' (*ke'ai*) and the 'rotten' (*phai*). The *phai* or 'rotten' role-model is perhaps best exemplified by what are known as *liumang*. These are (here I am discussing an image) the hard-living young hoodlums and gangsters who are part of the Taiwanese underworld. When parents worry about their children being led astray (as I discussed in the last chapter), it is often the influence of these underworld types they have in mind. Given the concern that children not 'wander aimlessly', and that they receive communal protection, it is worth stressing that the term *liumang* literally means 'drifting rascal' (*liushui* is 'flowing water'). *Liumang* are, rather like ghosts, disengaged from normal society.[9] In the popular image, they are thought very likely to fail miserably in their traditional social responsibilities. They waste money by gambling, smoking and drinking, and they are felt to be destined for a tragic end, a conclusion spelt out more or less constantly in popular fiction and televised drama.

But this so-called negative role model unquestionably has its attractions for many Taiwanese; for example, many youths, even quite 'good' ones, superficially take on the style of the *liumang*. (Part of this involves acting sullen instead of cheerful.) Parents also value, as I have said, a certain kind of toughness (lawlessness?) in their children, and sometimes themselves behave in a rather tough manner. Parents in Angang would undoubtedly be quite offended to be described as 'rotten', and they are openly critical of *liumang*. They also (as I have pointed out) think of 'badness' as something learnt on the outside. Still, they are themselves quite likely to smoke, drink, chew betel nut, etc., and to indulge in various forms of 'wastefulness' which are criticised by the school and the media. These activities, in certain contexts, are seen as unavoidable parts of rural Taiwanese social life. So parents are not necessarily (in the terms of the school) good examples for their children, even if they see themselves as exceptionally good-hearted persons. And while they would obviously despair if their children became gangsters, a little bit of *phai* can be a good thing.

The contrasting *ke'ai* or 'loveable' role-model is perhaps best exemplified by many of the young pop stars and celebrities who perform on Taiwanese television. These performers are an important part of the youth culture industry based around the concept of 'loveableness'. (This may seem trivial, and the very name evokes triviality, but the industry has an important influence on young Taiwanese, and a closely related concept and industry of 'loveableness' are found in Japan.) The archetypal *ke'ai* person is 'cute', bursting with energy, humour and happiness, and surrounded by large numbers of friends. This is, of course, meant to be positive, but being too *ke'ai* may be seen as a bad thing. Some of this ambivalence is expressed in uses of a different term, *guai*. When doubled (*guaiguai*), it is a term of endearment for children, and a way of saying that they are good, 'well-behaved'. But it can also be used sarcastically, to mean 'goody-goody'.[10] It should be noted that the *ke'ai* image is more often associated with girls, whereas the gangsterish *phai* image is more often associated with boys.

In different contexts, both *phai* and *ke'ai* role-models have a considerable appeal, not only to young people but also to adults. The opposition, somewhat overdrawn here for the sake of clarity, is an important one for an understanding of the imitation aspect of learning and growing up in Taiwan. I say this in order to say what may seem obvious: that the young teachers in Angang are, in certain ways, living examples of the loveable role-model as opposed to the rotten role-model. More generally, the schools and the media promote energetic loveableness as a good thing, something which children should aspire to.

Loveableness is perhaps not what would be expected of a traditional Chinese teacher. In Angang, these young men and women who teach must deliver the austere moral message of the school, and they take quite seriously the disciplining of pupils (see below). And yet, as persons, they represent something attractive, 'loveable', and good (and also, perhaps, 'goody-goody'). They are meant to be non-smoking, non-drinking, non-gambling, and almost hyperactively energetic. This is, in modern Taiwan, part of being 'morally lofty and upright', and part of what students are meant to become.

This struck me most clearly during the visit to Angang of a group of university student-teachers from Taipei (again, the importance of movement to and from that place). They were training to be teachers of biology, and came to the countryside to organise and lead a two-day 'Biology Activity' in which a limited number of students from the elementary and middle schools (selected on the basis of academic achievement, and on being 'good') gathered plants and animals, participated in games and contests, attended special classes, etc. But above all, the children had privileged access to the guests from Taipei. The visiting student-teachers, in terms of clothes, attitude, way of talking, way of moving, etc., were clearly representatives of modern 'loveable' Taiwanese youth culture; they enthusiastically went about their task.

They were also literally pulled into Angang life by the school-children. On one of the nights of their brief visit, children came to the teachers' dormitory to take the guests for a walk in the moonlight. They (children and student-teachers) later sat for some time near the beach, telling ghost stories, stopping on the way back to the school at the nearby Earth God temple. Amidst laughter, everyone bowed to the assembled gods and read out divination slips from the wall. (This was not irreverent, as such; local people often laugh and joke in temples, and in many contexts it is not thought necessary, or even desirable, to be sombre around religious buildings and images.) In other words, the student-teachers, although 'modern', were not somehow separate from the world of ghost stories and temples, i.e., from life in Angang. Instead, they presented a model of a new way of moving through that life. By the end of their stay, these soon-to-be teachers were treated as celebrities; the students swarmed around them, asking for autographs.

(19) Teachers were our children; students should be disciplined
Student-teachers, as loveable visitors, may be pulled through Angang, but they are outsiders who already know (on many levels) what to expect from such a 'conservative' place. They, after all, end up in universities in Taipei having gone out of homes somewhere (often in the countryside). They already know many ghost stories, and are familiar with divination slips. They also know traditional Chinese ideas about learning, which means that, no matter how loveable they are, they will have to be prepared to discipline their pupils. When loveableness fails, it is time for punishment.

I mentioned that children in Angang are apparently taught to not react to physical punishment. But some parents also think that children learn better if hit from time to time. For example, I was asked to teach English to the children of one family, but eventually I had to tell the father that I had been unsuccessful. His children did not seem interested and, after all, I was not a very good teacher. He said 'you should hit them!' (*ni yao da tamen*). When I said that I couldn't possibly do such a thing, he said 'I'll teach you!'

Teachers also often told me that punishment is an important part of learning; it encourages students and helps to maintain discipline in the school. But they were surprised at how little children in Angang responded to punishment. They also seemed to resent very much the policy on these matters (corporal punishment is technically forbidden), seeing it as the result of a Western view of education, imported by Taiwanese alumni of American graduate schools. This approach holds that students should be loved and not hit ('But they're not loveable!' lamented one teacher). They characterised this anti-disciplinarian approach as something distinctly un-Chinese, and as a failed policy in Angang. At the middle school there is a rather high turnover of teachers (who come on short-term contracts before being posted to other locations in Taiwan). The group who were there during my fieldwork were highly critical of the preceding group for being lax on discipline. They said that the earlier teachers had been *chong'ai*, 'over-indulgent', with the children. In response, they had collectively adopted a policy of being 'severe', *yange*.

This new policy made it somewhat easier to enforce discipline, but the teachers were still very frustrated by the lack of interest their students seemed to have in learning, especially beyond the boundaries set by examinations. One very conscientious teacher complained to me that the emphasis placed on examinations made it difficult for him to discuss anything which was not clearly exam-based. Students would simply not listen. They and their parents expected him to rely heavily on set texts, because these are known to be the source of exam questions. All of the teachers were frustrated, he said, because they would develop new ways of teaching, new ways of making learning fun, but these were rarely put into practice because if the exam results were bad then it would be traced back directly to the teacher. The principal would ask, 'What are you doing with these children?'

If both loveableness and discipline had failed, how would the students be encouraged to learn? One teacher had developed a more productive method for increasing student interest, one that was certainly very familiar to children from Angang, even if they had never seen it in school. This was to award cash prizes to students for performance. He compiled their results and gave money in 'red envelopes' (*hongbao*) to the highest achievers. The students were so motivated by this that he realised to his surprise at one point that he had committed himself to handing out several thousands of dollars worth of prizes. So, in this case, a morally upright teacher, one who would refuse 'red envelopes', was instead distributing them to his students, as a quirkily traditional way of holding their interest.

(20) Children often have more schooling than their parents
As I noted before, it is parents who shout at their children to *thak cheq!*, 'read books!' Ironically, parents also often complain about the pressure generated by schooling. Everyone agrees that this pressure is bad for the health and spirits of children, but it seems inevitable. Children must work hard in order to compete in the extremely competitive system. But the relentlessness of this is seen as counterproductive. One woman complained to me that her children were always staring at books and never had time to learn from life, whereas: 'When we were small, we spent half of every day on our parents' backs, up in the hills'. And yet, her own daughters were routinely sent to supplementary schools in order to help them succeed academically. She also told me, with some anxiety, that her son (only a preschooler) showed little academic promise. 'Now,' she added, 'if you haven't graduated from high school, no matter what you want to do, it's difficult.'

Parents also often express regret about their own lack of education, which they ascribe to their relatively impoverished background. One fisherman explained that he had completed elementary school with good marks, but that his parents decided it was better for him to make money than to take the entrance examination for middle school. He noted that a friend of his, who was not especially clever, had taken the examination, and as a result had eventually settled into a comfortable government job. He, by contrast, had begun to fish as a youngster, and still was dependent on that dangerous profession.

I have noted that parents (who are too involved in community social life to be austere) are not necessarily good 'patterns' for their children. Another related problem is that they themselves, in many cases, have not become full persons by the standards of the Confucian model of personhood. They have limited education, and it is difficult for them to exemplify for their children the so-called 'proper way of being a person'. Changes in schooling expectations have come to Angang in one generation. This can be seen by examining the possibilities open to the members of one household, consisting of a husband (in his forties), wife (in her thirties), daughter (in elementary school), and two sons (one in elementary, one in middle school). While telling me about his own lack of education, the man carefully wrote out the expression: 'Rarely do the sons of farmers study' (*nongjia zidi dushu nan*). In fact, as a fisherman's son, he had completed elementary school, and was able to read and write, and to speak Mandarin with relative ease. His wife, along with a number of women of her generation, had not attended school. She was unable to recognise even quite basic characters, and spoke unusually halting Mandarin. But they were both keen followers of the academic progress of their children. For example, although the father praised his eldest son's physical strength (*tili*), and was sure that he would be a good worker, he was very concerned by his apparent inability to make progress in school, indeed to even recognise characters (*renzi*). He felt that it was a 'new world', and that even someone destined for physical labour should be able to at least read and write.

The conversation in which these comments were made was held when the man and his wife had received the listings, sent to all parents, of the standing of all students in their various subjects. That is, they (and everyone else in the community) had just seen precisely how badly their son was doing. By contrast, their younger son was faring much better. But the best student in this family was the daughter, who had been sent away to attend a supplementary school.[11]

But beyond saying that parents show an interest in the academic careers of their children, it could not be said that they become directly involved in the process of schooling. They almost never participate in school-based rituals (e.g., graduation ceremonies), they express little interest in the content of courses, and they have limited contact with teachers. I was told that parents in the cities express a greater interest, and it should be said again that educational opportunities for those from Angang are seen to be very limited. People in Taiwan migrate specifically in order to live in good school districts, and Angang is certainly near the bottom of the hierarchy of these districts in Taiwan. Local children are, in fact, automatically given a boost to their examination scores in order to help them enter schools beyond the ninth grade, but parents who have the resources are inclined to move their children out of Angang altogether at some point. They are aware that living in Angang puts their children at a disadvantage in the competitive examination system. As one woman told me: 'In Angang you can be number one (*diyiming*), and then, when you go off to the city, you're the last.'

4

Textbook mothers and frugal children

This account of learning in Angang began with textbooks burnt in the home of the Stove God. Now I return to these books which are read and reread, and which prompt local people to say 'the more you read, the more it makes you crazy!' Here I will thus move away from descriptions of learning contexts, towards the *content* of what children are taught in schools, and specifically to the moral content of the textbooks they read. But why examine this morality which, in any case, is viewed as commonsensical? In part because it is not as obvious as it first appears to be. However the point is not so much the moral issues themselves, as their relation to crucial questions of identity. Why, then, look for this morality in textbooks, and not somewhere else? There are several reasons for doing so.

First, because textbooks are a reasonable guide to the explicit content of schooling. Due to the competitive nature of education in Taiwan, examinations are of fundamental concern. Examination questions are, in turn, based directly on textbooks, and teachers are expected, above all, to prepare students for their exams. Textbooks thus present a reliable (if incomplete) outline of what is taught in the classroom. Beyond this, it is observably true that children in Taiwan read and study the texts intensively over a period of many years.[1] I make no assumptions about what they learn during that process, but there is no denying that students in Angang, even the least accomplished, are repeatedly exposed to whatever is represented in textbooks.

The second reason is that texts are central to a Chinese conceptualisation of learning. Reading and writing, as opposed to other occupations, are seen as the defining activities of studenthood. The attainment of literacy, and the on-going attainment of advanced literacy (which is seen to be particularly difficult because of the nature of the Chinese language), are at the core of the very notion of what it means to learn, and to be a student. The folk version of this, as expressed in Angang, is that a student is fundamentally one who 'reads books' (*thak cheq*), and one who 'writes characters' (*sia zi*).[2]

The third justification for studying the texts is that they are, themselves, cultural products, both created and consumed in Chinese settings. They are artifacts of a kind: objects written, taught and read. As written traces, they touch on subjects which seem close to, without being quite the same as, many of the concerns found in communal life in Angang. In this way they arguably provide an official (or 'officialistic') account of the unofficial ways in which people live. In particular they seem useful for thinking about Chinese kinship, a subject they deal with at length.

Finally, the texts merit examination because they arguably draw the attention of children to certain forms of identification. Among other things, they provide an insight into the relationship between the family and the state. This relationship, which is seen as problematic, and is without question of central concern in the Chinese cultural tradition, is at times directly addressed by textbooks. If through schooling children have their attention drawn to the nation, then these texts may illuminate some of the tensions inherent in that wider sense of community.

The choice of particular texts for analysis still remains to be justified. It should be re-emphasised that students are taught many things other than morality in school. Mathematics, biology, geography, social studies, Chinese language and literature, and history are each arguably given as much emphasis as morality, in the narrow sense. However, in both elementary and middle schools, a special course is set aside for moral issues. In elementary school this is *Shenghuo yu Lunli*, roughly 'Life and Ethics', and in middle school it is *Gongmin yu Daode*, 'Citizenship and Morals'. Additionally, many other courses often touch directly or indirectly on ethics; this is true of *Lishi* ('History'), and *Shehui* ('Social Studies'). And it is especially true of elementary school *Guoyu* ('National Language') and middle school *Guowen* ('National Literature'), where many, if not most, of the stories read and studied deal with moral issues in some way. Together, these courses form a significant proportion of mandatory schooling in Taiwan. Beyond these courses and their texts, as I have already noted, a moral tone is an everyday part of school life and a defining feature of the relationship between teachers and their pupils.

Because of my own interests, I have, within the larger set of moral texts, focused on a highly selective group. In the first instance, I have been interested in stories which relate directly to questions of kinship (these form a substantial subset of the overall moral curriculum). They could be said to highlight certain patterns of relations between kin. Children in Angang, the readers of these texts, live out similar relationships. But in considering the texts side-by-side, one thing is rather striking. Although it seems almost natural to think of Chinese kinship as fundamentally a set of relationships between men (through patrilineal descent), and especially between fathers and sons (as expressed through filial obedience), the elaboration of the texts seems to be in other directions. Perhaps not surprisingly, virtually nothing is said about descent groups, as such. More is said about fathers, but what is said about them tends to be rather mundane, and usually does not convey a strong sense of what the father-child relationship should be. What is striking is the series of very emotional texts which relate to mothers and their children; often these are specifically about widows and their sons. And, as will become clear, many of the texts which address the affinity of family and state do so through representations of mothers.[3]

My intention here is primarily to provide translations of the texts, and in later chapters to explore some of the issues they raise. But several recurrent themes will be obvious to readers from the outset. One is the notion of a complicated form of reciprocity between parents and their children. As I will discuss in the next chapter, in Angang this is enacted through, among other things, perpetual transfers of food and wealth. Descriptions of this reciprocity in the texts are found alongside another theme, the expression of an apparently 'physical' connexion, or contiguity, between parents and children. Parental anxiety about the physical and spiritual well-being of their descendants is prominent. The final point to make is that my selected texts, which are read by girls and boys, are primarily about women as mothers, and men as sons. These are far from the only 'roles' assigned to men and women in texts, but they seem of particular importance, as I will later discuss.

(21) A child cannot repay a mother's care

The Hymn to Mothers (*Muqin Song*), which verges on mother-worship, conveys the mood of many of the texts.[4] The first section describes what a 'loving mother' does for her children (the accompanying pictures show a girl and a boy), including the provision of food, clothing and concern. Particular stress is given to the anxiety surrounding parenthood, which may lead mothers to forget their own needs. Note that this anxiety arises when the 'physical' health of the child is in question.

Under the winter sun, warmth;
Beside a loving [*ci'ai de*] mother, endless happiness.
When I am hungry, she prepares food and rice,

When the weather is cold, she asks if I am warmly dressed.
She worries when the wind blows, when it rains, bringing clothes and umbrella,
I encounter difficulties, fall ill, she is anxious, for my sake forgetting to sleep and eat [*wei wo fei qin wang can*].
From morning to evening, she bids me work bravely,
From childhood to adulthood, wishing me happiness and peace.
Under the winter sun, warmth;
Beside a loving mother, endless happiness.
A mother's loving care
Is the fountainhead of life [*shengming de quanyuan*];
A mother's consideration [*shensi*]
Is that which one could never finish repaying [*yongyuan baoda bu wan*].

Having noted the sacrifices which a 'loving mother' makes, the second section of the hymn sets out the difficulty for children of making an adequate return for what has been given, including instruction. In the end, this return is specifically linked to the pursuit of knowledge and to the practice of good citizenship. (Recall here the neo-Confucian idea that learning is the path to full personhood).

How difficult to repay [*baoda*] a mother's kindness!
The kindness [*enqing*] of my mother is as deep as the ocean.
Supporting me from childhood to maturity,
Suffering greatly, with all her heart.
I shall be obedient [*xiaoshun*] and serve her [*shifeng*],
To make her greatly pleased [*huanxin*] ...
Her earnest instructions bear future rewards.
Diligently shall I pursue knowledge [*dunpin qiu xuewen*], and become a good citizen [*hao gongmin*].

Later I will return to the question of why good citizenship should be seen as a way of repaying one's mother. But this text also outlines two important, and related, themes. The first is the notion that mothers contribute to the health, well-being and education of their children. They do so by providing food and clothing, but also by engaging in an emotional relationship, involving anxiety, suffering, consideration, encouragement and instruction. The second, related, theme in the text is the sense of (unrepayable) obligation which a mother's contribution instills in her child.

(22) Virtuous mothers produce great sons

Some stories provide examples of mothers making sacrifices specifically for the education of their sons, who subsequently become great figures in Chinese history. A short series of these is given in 'Virtuous Mothers of Ancient Times' (*Gudai de Xianmu*).[5] For example:

When Mengzi [Mencius] was young, his father died, and he thereafter lived with his mother. She felt he should receive a superior education [*lianghao de jiaoyu*] and thus paid careful attention to his surroundings. At first, they lived near a graveyard, and Mengzi watched as the bereaved buried their dead. When he was at play, he would imitate burials. Mother Meng felt this was inappropriate, and soon they left for another place. They then lived next to a slaughterhouse. There Mengzi watched as the pigs were killed, and when he played he imitated butchery. Mother Meng felt this was also inappropriate, and they quickly moved again. Finally, they moved near to a school. Here Mengzi saw the people reading books, and he soon learnt to read. His mother felt this place would be good for her child, and they settled, no longer moving.

Note the idea of the child's susceptibility to his environment. The story concludes by asserting that Mengzi's greatness was 'entirely due to the education (*jiaoyu*) provided by his virtuous and intelligent (*xianhui*) mother'.

A similar conclusion is reached in the story of another 'virtuous mother' and her son:

Ou-yang Xiu, the Song Dynasty writer, grew up in poverty, lacking even the money to buy paper and writing brush. His mother, in order to teach him to write, gathered reeds to serve as brushes, and taught Ou-yang Xiu to write on the ground. Later, when he had become an official, his mother repeatedly urged him to govern with caution [*yongxin zhengshi*], and to care for the people [*aihu renmin*]. It can be said that Ou-yang Xiu's ability to write and his success in governing were entirely due to his mother's instruction.

Again, the text emphasises the mother's direct responsibility for the child's learning, a theme which is taken up in many other texts. It is worth repeating here that most parents in Angang (and especially women) have limited schooling, and are therefore sometimes unable to help their children directly with school-related work. They do obviously support their children during schooling, that is seen as the important thing, but they cannot teach them.

As mentioned, several of these stories detail the relationship between widows and their sons, and the way in which sons are able to make their mothers contented and proud. For example, one middle school text recounts 'The Childhood of Wang Mian' (*Wang Mian de Shaonian Shidai*).[6] According to the story, after the death of Wang Mian's father, he was supported by his mother. But eventually, due to financial hardship, he was forced to give up his studies and to begin working as a shepherd. When given food by his employers he would take it home and 'respectfully present' (*xiaojing*) it to his mother. He also saved enough from his modest income to buy books, which he studied in the countryside. One advantage of his work was that it placed him in beautiful surroundings, which he also diligently studied. He was inspired to begin painting, gradually developing a name for himself as an artist. With the money from his first sale, he bought gifts to, again, 'respectfully present' to his mother. Finally his success was great enough that he was able to give up his work as a shepherd and devote himself to study and painting. The story ends by noting the happiness his success brought to his mother: 'Gradually he no longer need worry over food and clothing, and his mother's heart was joyous (*huanxi*).'

(23) Textbook mothers instruct children privately

A rather more complicated tale of the debt which a famous son owed to his widowed mother is found in 'Mother's Instruction' (*Muqin de Jiaohui*), an autobiographical sketch written by the modern scholar Hu Shi.[7] According to the notes accompanying the text, when Hu Shi was five years old, and his mother twenty-three, his father died. She then 'supported him to adulthood' (*fuyang zhangda chengren*). Hu Shi's mother is described, in the notes, as a woman who 'possessed our nation's traditional womanly virtues' (*you wo guo chuantong meide de nuxing*). The story begins by recounting the morning routine of mother and son, relating this directly to the son's eagerness to be a good student:

Each morning at dawn, mother would call me awake, saying to dress and sit up. I never knew how long she had been by my side. She would look at me, just awake, and tell me what I had done wrong yesterday, what I had said wrong, wanting me to recognise my mistakes, hoping that I would be a conscientious student. Sometimes, she would tell me of my father's virtues. She would say: 'You always want to follow your father's footsteps. In my entire life I've only known that one truly complete person [*wanquan de ren*], you want to study him, and not fail to live up to his example.' When she spoke of her sorrows, the tears would fall.

When the sun was up, she would make certain I was well-dressed, and then rush me off to school early. The keys to the school were at the teacher's home, so, having glanced at the school entrance, I first went to knock on his door. Someone would hand out the key, and I would then run back to open the school, sitting down to read a new passage. Eight or nine out of ten days, I would be the first to open the doors. Waiting for the teacher to arrive, I would memorise the text, then return home to eat breakfast.

The story then turns to the way in which Hu Shi's widowed mother fulfilled her dual parental role, that is, also acting in the manner expected of a father. The texts translated above stressed the 'loving kindness' (*ci'ai*) of mothers. In fact, the word *ci* ('kind') has, as one of its definitions, 'maternal'. It is very often used in the combination *cimu*, 'loving mother', which could arguably be taken to mean a 'motherly mother', i.e. one who acts in the expected way.[8] Men, by contrast, are stereotypically referred to as *yanfu*, 'strict father', and one of the definitions of the term *yan* ('stern, strict') is 'father'. In short, to be loving is to be motherly, and to be stern is to be fatherly. And so it is in Hu Shi's tale:

My mother's control of me was extremely strict [*wo muqin guanshu wo zui yan*]. She was a loving mother acting as a stern father [*ta shi cimu jianren yanfu*]. But she never cursed or hit me in front of others. When I did something wrong, she would simply look at me. Seeing her stern and far-seeing eyes, I was truly frightened. If what I had done was a small thing, she would wait until the next morning to reprimand [*jiaoxun*] me. If it was more important, she would wait until the quiet hours of the evening, close the door, first scold me, then punish me, or make me kneel, or pinch me. No matter how severe the punishment, I would never cry or make a sound. When she reprimanded her son, it was never for others to hear.

Obviously, this account of direct moral instruction differs from my account of parent–child interactions in Angang, and I cannot fully discount the possibility that such private instruction might have taken place in Angang. I know that parents and children do at times have private conversations. However, there are several reasons I find it unlikely that this is an important way in which children receive instruction. First, as noted, in Angang there is in general little scope for privacy. As I described in chapter 2, there is a constant flow of people through many of the houses in the community, and much private or domestic life is thus relatively public. Because people are closely related (through kinship or friendship) they also tend to know each other's affairs.[9]

Following on from this, things which in other places might be 'private' are often handled here in public. By this I mean, for example, that family fights will often be held in full view of neighbours. If people want to say something to their children (e.g., to scold them harshly) they seem perfectly happy for others to hear it. The incidents of child discipline I mentioned above were noisy affairs held in full public view. Also, when I spoke with children and young people about 'morality' (e.g., ideas related to filial obedience or to religion) private parent–child instruction was never mentioned. Finally, as I have been stressing, the morality of the community is thought of as something which school-aged children would already know ('ordinary knowledge'), even if their mischievousness kept them from living up to it.

To return to Hu Shi's story, he then recounts an occasion on which a careless sarcasm provoked his mother's wrath. The situation which gives rise to the sarcasm should be noted: Hu Shi places his health at risk by refusing to dress properly.

One evening in the early fall, after dinner, I played in the doorway, wearing only a light vest. At that time, my mother's younger sister, Aunt Yu Ying, lived with us.

She was afraid I would be cold, and handed out a garment for me to wear. I wouldn't put it on. She said, 'Wear it! It's chilly [*liang*].' I replied sarcastically: 'What's this talk of mothers [*niang*]? Even Father can't control me!'[10] As I said these words I raised my head to see my mother walking out of the house; I hurriedly put on the jacket. But she had heard my sarcasm. In the quiet of the evening, she made me kneel, and punished me severely. She said: 'Such a happy thing for you to not have a father! You brag about it!' She was shaking with anger, and would not let me go to bed.

But this punishment, brought on by the son's sarcastic rejection of 'mothering', itself actually leads to a health problem, and then to a literally physical connexion between mother and son:

I cried, kneeling, using my hand to wipe away the tears; I don't know what germ I rubbed into my eyes, but afterwards I had over a year of trouble, which was treated to no avail. My mother felt regretful and anxious. She heard that eye disease could be licked away with the tongue; one night she woke me up and actually used her tongue on my diseased eye. This was my strict teacher (*yanshi*), my loving mother.

The story ends with a comment on the extent to which the author relied upon his mother's instruction:

I lived under her guidance for nine years, and was profoundly influenced. When I was 14 ... I moved away [to attend school]. In the midst of this sea of humanity, I wandered for over twenty years, with no one to control me. If I have learnt a shred of good behaviour, if I have learnt anything about human relations, if I am able to forgive and to be sympathetic, I must thank my loving mother.

(24) A frugal child is able to make a return

One of the texts students read in the fourth year of elementary school addresses not only the sacrifices mothers make for their children, but also the way in which a return can be made for their kindness. This is entitled 'Frugality and Savings: a Model Child' (*Jieyue Chuxu de Mofan Ertong*).[11] It is hardly a fascinating piece of writing, but I will quote it at length because, in its mundane way, it does address points of central concern. In it, a clear moral value attaches to the ability to save money, and economic austerity is explicitly tied to the ability to repay one's parents for their care. Once again, the parent is a widowed mother who provides food, clothing and money for her son. And, once again, her maternal contribution is directly linked to his education:

Zhang Xiao-hua is a fifth-grader. When he was five years old his father died, and his mother took in cleaning to support him. The income was small, but because his mother loved him, she not only carefully attended to his clothing and food, he also never lacked materials for school, and she even gave him spending money. He lived a carefree life. So that he could study even more, and live in greater comfort, his mother took in cleaning night and day.

But eventually he recognises the sacrifice his mother is making for his benefit, and the toll it takes on her own health:

One cold and stormy night, when he was in the third grade, Xiao-hua was doing his homework and preparing for bed. Then he saw his mother with her unkempt hair, bent at the waist, still in a corner of the kitchen washing clothes, the unceasing round of back-breaking labour [*xinlao jianku*], and it made his heart ache. He could not stop a tear from falling. In his heart and mind [*xin*] he thought: if we owned a washing machine, mother wouldn't have to work so hard.

Then, when trying to think what *should* be done in such a situation, the textbook child turns to what he has learnt at school from his teacher:

He remembered that in the second year his teacher had recounted the story of Wu Xun, who collected alms and eventually opened a school. Why can't I save? He was determined to buy a washing machine for his mother, to decrease her hardship. From that day, Zhang Xiao-hua saved his money. He never ate snacks, never went to the cinema, never spent without thinking. He cherished every kind of material; even a pencil stub, a small piece of paper, he wouldn't waste. He found a box, taped up the lid, opened a small hole in the top, and started saving money. Every day all the money his mother gave him went into the box. His income from the New Year and other festivals also went in.[12] Gradually his savings grew, over two years and seven months.

When he thought he had enough money to buy a washing machine, he took his savings box to an electrical goods store. Because his mother washed many clothes for other people, the best thing would be to buy a large model. So he pointed out a large machine and asked how much it cost. A saleswoman told him it was 6000 yuan. He opened his box, poured out the money and counted it, and found he only had around 4700 yuan, still short by over a thousand. He stood for a moment, heart aching and hope lost, then put the money back in the box, bowed his head, and said with embarrassment to the saleswoman, 'I'm sorry, I'll come back next year to buy it'.

But this moment of defeat is soon overcome by a rather miraculous intervention:

At that point, a gentleman [*shenshi*] happened to be standing behind him, and seeing what transpired, he went up to enquire into the details. He wrote down the boy's name, age, school and address, then kindly told him to take his money home. In the afternoon, the gentleman personally delivered a washing machine to the boy's home. He had been terribly moved to see the filial heart of someone so young, a boy who could economise and save. So he especially delivered the machine in order to fulfil Xiao-hua's wish.

This private praise for a filial child is then turned into a wider statement of public approval:

At the same time [the gentleman] notified the boy's school of the incident. At a school assembly, the principal gave Xiao-hua an award for exemplary frugality and savings. When he received the award, all the teachers and students cheered him wildly, and burst into thunderous applause. Everyone felt that he was not only a filial son, but also a model of frugality.

If this seems an over-stated ending to a story with a somewhat mundane moral, it should be stressed that in Taiwanese schools frugality is presented as a matter of national (not only familial) concern. The story, which seems to be about a boy saving to buy something for his mother, is accompanied by the motto: 'Frugality is the basis of national construction' (*jieyue shi jianguo zhi ben*). One of the questions following the story is: 'What is the relationship between frugality and national economic construction?' And one of the rhetorical questions in the 'Self-examination and putting-into-practice' section (*fanxing han shijian*) is: 'Would I gladly use my savings to honour the hard-working armed forces (*jing jun lao jun*)?' Here, frugality is tied not only to filial obedience (*xiao*) but also to patriotism (*zhong*). In a later chapter I will return to this theme, and to the apparently ambivalent relationship between families and the state.

But first I want to consider the reciprocity between parents and children which is outlined in these texts. The schools seem to support enthusiastically the moral basis of this reciprocity (and even apply it to the wider goal of national construction). But by the time children in Angang arrive at school the notion of parent-child reciprocity has long since been learnt; it is 'ordinary knowledge'. This learning happens in part through a whole series of complex transactions in food and money, and this is the theme of chapter 5.

5
Red envelopes and the cycle of *yang*

The school textbooks read by children in Angang outline certain features of Chinese kinship, including the notion of a reciprocal tie between mother and child. Such representations might or might not find reflections in the community. (But where is the boundary between a story and the child who reads it?) Textbooks draw attention to certain parent–child scenarios, creating possibilities: the recognition of, or enactment of, similar scenarios in non-school life. In the texts, the obligation between mother and child is composed around a series of transactions. In particular, economic interdependence is highlighted (a mother washes clothes to send her son to school, while the son saves money to reduce her hardship). And a form of 'physical' interdependence is also implied. (A son fails to protect his health, and his mother subjects him to corporal punishment. Later, made anxious by his illness, she uses her tongue on his diseased eye.)

Here, descriptions will be given of the community-based version of parent–child reciprocity, in particular its evocation through transfers of food and money. Looking at these phenomena, three things become apparent. First, some of the transfers seem obviously symbolic or ritualised (the giving of 'red envelopes' at the lunar new year), whilst others seem more substantive (the provision of financial support). But here it is difficult, and also perhaps misleading, to draw a firm contrast between the substantive and the symbolic.[1] Second, these transfers, which might be said to underline certain relationships and thus to influence identification, could equally be said to *produce* the relationships in the first place. It is the giving back and forth of sustenance which actually defines the association of Chinese parent and child. More than recognition is at stake. Third, transfers of food and money between parents and children in Angang only make sense in the context of much wider circulations of support (including the offerings collectively made to the gods). These wider circulations, I will argue, make apparent a child's identification with a community beyond the family.

(25) Children must respond to parental support
In Angang, children learn both in the community and at school that they are obliged to *yang*, or *fengyang* their parents. *Fengyang* means 'to respectfully support'. But *yang* has a range of meanings, including 'to give birth to', 'to cultivate', 'to educate', and 'to nourish' (a 'food' radical is in the character). When used in the context of filial obligation it generally means 'to support and provide nourishment' to one's elderly parents.[2] The same term (less the 'respectful' *feng*) is used to describe what parents do for their offspring: to *yang haizi* is to 'raise children'. *Yang* also describes the nurturing or development of many things, e.g. 'raising pigs' (*yang zhu*), or 'growing flowers' (*yang hua*). Chinese parent–child reciprocity, in all its complexity, develops from this rather simplistic formula: first, parents *yang* children, and then children *yang* parents. The process unfolds differently for daughters than for sons, and is in practice more complex for everyone than the formula would suggest. But whatever its complexity in practice, the principle is clear, and of fundamental importance.

The obligations of *yang* are often described as if they were not optional, and duties performed by parents and children are clearly seen to have a reciprocal efficacy. Parents raise their children, but children thus acquire obligations towards their parents. These include producing grandchildren to continue the family line, providing life-long financial support, and performing rituals to ensure that support is maintained in the next life. The cycle of *yang* is repeated with each new generation, and one's own willingness to care for the elderly is seen to guarantee one's own future care.

While the affective nature of filial obedience is stressed, certainly in the school but also in the community, the directly economic content of much filial action is clear. As I said at the outset, educational achievement is seen as a way for children to set about making a return to their parents, to repay *yang*. If they succeed even moderately in school they are thought more likely to find secure jobs. This should help ensure that their parents, as they grow older, will have fewer worries about money. In practice, the support given to parents by children (successful or not) comes in many forms, and sometimes not at all. The elderly may or may not live with their children. They may receive regular and substantial payments which are their principal income, or they may receive relatively insignificant amounts, or gifts, which are intended to show affection. But support in some form is clearly anticipated, even if not always given.

(26) Children must be scrupulously reverent
What a child learnt about this process in the school and in the community, regardless of differences in the way of learning, would be somewhat similar. For example, each of the texts in chapter 4 highlighted the contribution of a mother to her child's upbringing, including the provision of food, clothing and concern. Many of the stories also described how a child might repay or respond (*baoda*) to this contribution. They were mostly tales of extraordinary people, but the relationship of *yang* outlined in them, no matter how exceptionally moving, is in certain ways quite ordinary. School texts about filial obedience do clearly reflect concerns which are found in Angang.

If textbooks were the guide, we might say that the essence of Chinese childhood is *xiao*. This term has usually been translated as 'filial piety', but now is often translated as 'filial obedience'. This has the advantage of evoking the hierarchical sense of the Chinese term (recall that the character *xiao* is 'elder' over 'son'), but also of shifting away from the moralistic connotations of the English word 'piety'. *Xiao* is undoubtedly a moral relationship, at times piously invoked, but it is equally practical, and it would be misleading to separate the two facets. However, this separation does sometimes happen in China.

The textbooks children read in Angang turn, not surprisingly, to Confucius (Kongzi) in order to explain *xiao*. According to the texts, Confucius did not so much define it, as describe its working through a series of examples. This was part of his policy of 'teaching according to the ability of the students' (*yin cai shi jiao*). His teachings thus proliferate in answer to the same question, 'what is truly *xiao*?' (*zenyang cai suan shi xiao ne*). His explanations (that is, the textbook accounts of them) stress that *xiao* is not simply a matter of 'support' (*yanghuo*):

> What is today called *xiao*, is really only supporting [*yanghuo*] one's parents. But people also support dogs and horses! If sons and daughters merely support their parents, and are not scrupulously reverent [*jinshen gongjing*], what distinguishes that from the support of dogs and horses?
>
> ... What is truly *xiao*? ...
>
> The most rare is this: to submit to one's parents cheerfully [*duidai fumu heyan yuese*]. For example, when some matter arises, deal with it for them. When it is time to eat and drink, ask them to eat first. Otherwise, how could this be called *xiao*?

82   Angang

... What is truly *xiao*?

When your parents are on earth, in caring for them you should observe protocol [*hehu lijie*]. When they die, in burying them you should observe protocol. When they are dead, in commemorating them you should observe protocol.³

(27) Supporting and obeying parents is what 'should be done'
The observance of filial obedience, according to this text, should be less a matter of practical support (*yanghuo*), and more a matter of form ('observing protocol') and spirit ('cheerful submission'). However, in Angang, although form and spirit are sometimes important, practical support (*yang*) seems at the forefront of notions of *xiao*. Support and obedience also seem, at times, to be given automatically, without question. I soon learned that people found it strange for me to ask about their feelings or thoughts concerning matters related to filial obedience. Time and again the answer was that actions which were *xiao*, or which related to *yang*, were things which simply 'should be done' (*yinggai zuode*). For example, I spoke with a young woman whose paternal grandmother lived with her parents one out of every three months as part of their obligation to support her. I asked the young woman whether her parents liked or disliked this arrangement. She said it was not something they either liked or disliked, simply something they did and should do. Support of elderly parents is seen to be obligatory, even if not always given.

Following the decisions of parents (out of the sense of filial obedience) is also, in theory, obligatory, something to be done rather than something to express opinions about. For example, one young man's romance with a local woman ended when the woman's mother decided he would be an unsuitable marriage partner (she disapproved of his career plans). I asked the young man what his girlfriend had wanted to do about this. He replied that what his girlfriend wanted to do was beside the point (*wusuowei*), it was her mother's opinion that mattered. Another young man moved back to Angang from the city because his elderly father needed help with his work. I asked the young man what he felt about having to return. He replied (eloquently, I thought) that his father, who was seventy years old, had told him to come back and he had, of course, come back.

This is not at all to suggest that children and young people somehow feel nothing about the obligations of *xiao* and *yang*, and only obey. At times, on the contrary, feelings run high. For instance, the same woman who told me that her parents cared for her grandmother simply because it should be done, on another occasion expressed resentment about her own lack of independence (*duli*). All decisions, she said, were left to her mother and

Red envelopes and the cycle of yang 83

father. However, the reality of this perceived lack of independence was quite complex. She and her fiancé had decided to remain in Angang, after marriage, so that her parents 'would not be lonely' (this was her formulation). But her boyfriend's elder sister (*jiejie*) had disapproved of this plan, and insisted that they move to the city instead. In the end, the woman's parents approved of these new arrangements, but not before interventions by all concerned, including the woman and her fiancé. The key point is that, at the level of rhetoric, she continued to describe her parents as the arbiters of the important decisions in her life. In what contexts is this spirit of obedience (if not necessarily the reality of it) taught or learned? Why is it natural to say that repaying obligations to parents is simply that which 'should be done'?

(28) Children are pressed to take red envelopes

Chinese celebrations emphasise transition or process. People do not so much 'spend' a holiday, or 'celebrate' it, as 'pass through' or 'cross' it. One 'passes through a birthday', *guo shengri*, just as one 'crosses the street', *guojie*.[4] The most elaborate and extended celebration in the calendar is the lunar new year, or Spring Festival (*Chun Jie*). This is usually referred to as *guonian*, literally 'cross-year', a verbal construction which again emphasises the *passage* into a new cycle. People collectively become one year older at this transitional moment. Ideas about what should and should not happen during the festival also highlight the interdependence, over the passage of time, of ancestors, parents and children, and the related themes of family wealth and longevity.

At the family meal on the last evening of the old year (*chuxi*), fish is often eaten because the (Mandarin) word for fish (*yu*) rhymes with a word for 'extra'. This 'abundant' food, collectively consumed by the family, is said to bring 'year after year of abundance' (*nian nian you yu*). Meanwhile, the scraps of paper which accumulate around the house (e.g., in the courtyard because of the detonation of fireworks) are not to be swept away, for they represent money. Children are meant to stay awake overnight, to ensure that their parents have long life (*shou*).

Many children told me the best thing about the festival is that they are given *hongbao*, red envelopes containing money, by their parents, relatives and other adults. (Recall that they are given money during the life-cycle celebrations as well.) The most important of these transfers, that between parent and child, happens as part of the ceremony in which they honour the ancestors and their elders by bowing in front of them on the last evening of the old year. In Hokkien this is usually simply referred to as the giving of a 'red envelope'. But in Mandarin the money is called *yasuiqian*, which has sometimes been translated as 'anchor the year money'. *Ya* literally means 'to press' (and even 'to extort'), and one young woman suggested to me that parents use *yasuiqian* to press down (*ya*) on their children, to ensure that in the future the children will care for them.

One 'outsider', a former mainlander living in Angang, gave a different explanation for the name. He said that ('long ago') Chinese children would refuse to accept this money from their parents, and so it was placed under their pillows, where it was 'pressed down' (*ya*) by their heads. To the best of my knowledge this does not happen in Angang, although I do know of children declining to accept *hongbao* (and other gifts) from adults *other* than their parents. But this explanation does give an interesting perspective on the transaction, and one which arguably underlines the ambivalence with which generosity is viewed within Chinese culture. To oversimplify for the moment, acceptance of generosity, between persons who are unrelated, is seen as acceptance of obligation. However, refusal of generosity is seen as over-politeness, as displaying 'the air of a guest' (*kheq-khi*). When people decline hospitality they are told it is not necessary to behave like a guest (*m kheq-khi*), and told that they will not be obligated if they accept. But being guest-like is also precisely a way of remaining a guest (*lang-kheq*), instead of establishing a relationship, with all the obligations this might imply.

In theory, this talk of politeness is irrelevant within families (and in the case of the new year *hongbao*) because children are already, by definition, under a heavy obligation. However, children do sometimes refuse to accept support from their parents, and in some contexts this is described as an honourable thing. Not because it is polite, but because it is a sign of respect. For example, one woman boasted to me about the behaviour of her youngest son. He was performing his military service, and his income was not enough to cover his own expenses. This meant that he was unable to send money home to *yang* his mother. But she noted with pride his refusal to accept assistance from her. Similarly, a young married woman proudly told me that she had declined financial help from her parents, even though she and her husband could certainly have used it.

Return to the symbolic transaction for a moment. Declining to accept a new year 'red envelope' from one's parents could be seen in two very different ways. On the one hand, it might be seen as a sign of respect or politeness, a refusal to take advantage of parental generosity. On the other hand, it might be seen as a way of not accepting the obligation it implies (that of providing support to parents later on). Placing the envelope under the pillow, where it will be pressed (*ya*) by children's heads, would then imply a *forcing* of generosity, and of obligation, upon them. Given the delight with which children in Angang accept *hongbao*, this reading may seem farfetched. But even if not placed under pillows, and not called *yasuiqian*, red envelopes are very clearly linked in China to a kind of pressure. They are the standard way of transferring money in a symbolically loaded way, and the expression 'to give a *hongbao*' is a common euphemism for 'making a bribe'. Inducements to the powerful are made in *hongbao*, as are payments to powerful gods (packets of spirit money offered to them will usually be covered with a slip of red paper). In these cases, the transfer of a red envelope suggests a power relationship and, obviously, it is not the giver who has the power. *Xiao*, filial obedience, is conventionally portrayed as a hierarchical relationship in which the child is controlled by the parents. But at the centre of the lunar new year, representative in many ways of this hierarchy, we find a transfer of money which arguably evokes the opposite: the power children have over their parents.

(29) Children should think of the future
The money which parents give to their children (e.g. at 'one-month' celebrations and at the lunar new year) is a symbolic manifestation of a very

4   A woman preparing steamed-rice buns (*baozi*) to be offered to the gods during a festival and then eaten by devotees for *pieng-an*, the 'absence of problems'

complex and long-term economic relationship which continues well beyond the boundaries of childhood. From one perspective, this seems a dyadic exchange. Parents *yang* children when they are young, and children respectfully *yang* parents when they are old. But this process is not a simple settling of accounts; rather it is immersion in a system of total support (economic, social and spiritual). It is as if the filial child were situated in an eternal chain of filial children. Property, substances and 'forces' coming from the ancestors (including land, blood, bones, food, good fortune and merit) are returned to the ancestors in the form of spirit money, food, descendants, assistance in negotiating the after-life and so on. Nurturance coming from parents is returned by their children in the form of this-worldly and other-worldly nurturance. This is seen not only as a proper response to a past obligation (what children owe their parents), but also as the best guarantee of a future return (what children can expect from their own descendants.)

One woman complained bitterly to me about a son who moved away from Angang to raise his own children. It is, of course, not unusual for people to move away and set up their own households, but he did so without consideration, and provided his family with no financial support. Her other sons were not always able to send money home, but when circumstances allowed they would do so, and this made life easier. The criticism of her 'bad son', however, came in a way which stressed more than her own hardship. What she specifically emphasised was that he was not thinking (in fact was 'unable to think', *ta bu hui xiang*). What would become of him when *his* children had grown up? They would see what he had done to his own parents, and then refuse to care for him. In this sense, parent–child transactions are clearly seen as having a connexion with the past and with the future.

(30) A child's obligation comes partly from 'yang'

When asked why parents are supported in old age, people often first mention child-rearing expenses. Specifically they refer to the costs associated with providing food, clothing, shelter and education, as well as marriage-related expenses (which are often very high). They find the failure of westerners to make a return for these expenses hard to understand (cf. Thompson 1990:102). One group of children, when asked about filial obedience, cheerfully brought to my attention a passage in an elementary school text which deals with American nursing homes. It is sometimes said that America is 'a young person's heaven and an old person's hell', precisely because Americans are lacking in the Chinese virtue of *xiao*. With *xiao*, the elderly are guaranteed support because they have formerly given it.

But is the support children give their parents entirely due to what they have formerly received? The connexion between the obligation to give *yang*, and the experience of having received *yang*, can in part be clarified by considering cases where children are fostered.[5] That is, where support (*yang*) is given, but children are not the 'blood and bone' of their foster parents. For example, one man in Angang had, as a child, been 'given by his father' to a man of another surname to raise. This man thus became the boy's *yangfu*, 'foster father'. Note that the term is *yang*-father, i.e. 'supporting father', as opposed to a father who is *qin*, related by blood.[6] In this case, the child took his *yangfu*'s surname, and was expected to support him in old age (as repayment for received *yang*). No support was given to his *qin* father. However, because he was not the biological son of his *yangfu*, he was later allowed to marry someone of his own (adopted) surname, which in other circumstances would have been highly inappropriate.[7] In other words, the care he received did put him under a kinship-related obligation, but did not entirely determine his own kinship status.

Another local man had been cared for by a *yangfu* and *yangmu* (foster mother) after the death of his own parents. He explained to me that, in return, he now gave them money on special occasions, such as festivals and birthdays. But he did not provide regular support, as would have been expected from a biological son, and in some cases from a foster son. He said it was unnecessary 'because they have lots of money and sons'. Instead he preferred to do favours for them (taking bags of fruit, etc.), leaving the issue of substantial support to their biological sons. His attitude was rather similar to that of many women in Angang towards support for their parents. It is seen to be mostly voluntary, done out of affection, by contrast with the support given by their brothers. Indeed, this man's wife specifically told me that his way of supporting his *yangfu* and *yangmu* was more like that of a daughter than of a son. She pointed out that she herself similarly gave money to her own parents on special occasions as an expression of affection, but not as full support. This suggests that giving *yang* to parents is not simply a matter of having received it.

However, as I mentioned, received *yang* is often given as *the* primary reason for supporting parents in old age. This view is closely related to ideas about why certain ancestors should be worshipped, while others are not.[8] I discussed this with one young man who told me that what was most important about ancestor worship was that offerings should be made to those who had taken care of (*yang*) you. This is a very short-term view of ancestor worship, but his own situation in this regard was very complicated. His father had come to Angang from the mainland, and it was therefore impossible for father or son to tend the ancestral graves. If he stressed immediate *yang* as that which generates an obligation (as opposed to ancestral substance) it may have been related to the difficulty, for him, of acting on filial obligations stretching back into the past. But his circumstances were also interesting, and equally complex, when seen projected onto the future. The young man was the only biological son of his father, but he did have foster brothers. Specifically because of his blood-relationship with his father, he was to be given a larger inheritance than the others. However, one of the foster brothers (along with his wife and children) had continued to live at the family home, and gave almost all of his income to his *yangfu*. Because of this economic contribution, and because he had provided substantive *yang* (his wife, for example, often prepared the family meals), this foster son was to be given a larger share of inheritance as well.

I cite this example to show that the connexion between received *yang* and given *yang* is a very complex one. When people say why children should support parents, the issue of *yang* is at the forefront. But there is considerable variation in the terms in which people discuss this return, and parents often deny that they are self-interested in the matter. For example, one woman who was very ambitious for her only child, a daughter, went out of her way to stress that she was only concerned for her daughter's happiness. She was making sacrifices and working hard for the girl, but she expected nothing in return.[9] Others are happy to state things in more pragmatic terms. A fisherman told me that it was very important to have children while young. He said that if you marry early and have children, then they will support you when you are old. If you wait too long, you may be dead before the children can do anything for you.

(31) Children contribute to wedding expenses and to the family wealth

It is important to stress, however, the contrast between different kinds of uses for the money children give to their parents over the years. In many cases the money is *not* used for living expenses, especially if it is given before parents stop working. Instead the transfer resembles, as people point out, a banking transaction. They specifically say that the money given to parents is put in the post office (i.e. in an account) and not used. In many cases, it is saved for the marriage-related expenses of the same child, what for a son is often described as 'buying a wife' (*mai taitai*). Money is needed to cover the expense of wedding ceremonies and banquets, to buy a house for the new couple, to provide it with furnishings, and so on. Children thus contribute to the cost of a process which will establish them as adults. They still rely on parental help, however, because the costs of marriage are high.

But even after these marriage expenses have been met, the sending of money to parents is still seen as something of a banking activity. This is because the family wealth (*caichan*), to which all sons *should* make a contribution, is later divided between those who *have* made a contribution. (Inheritance is usually not given to daughters, who in theory do not contribute to the estate.) As one man told me, if you don't give money to your parents, how can you expect to have a share of the inheritance? Again, it is interesting to consider the position of fostered children. In one case I knew of, a man had died, leaving an estate, and the division of the family property among the sons was then overseen by his brother. This man decided to give a full share of the estate to a foster son, on the basis that he had lived at home and provided support to his parents. Another (biological) son, who had moved away and not contributed to the family wealth, was excluded from a share. In other words, the money given to parents by sons is not simply for parental support, in many cases it is a guarantee of their own future security.

Clear benefits are thus seen to accrue to children (but especially to sons) who give money to their parents, whether this is seen as 'support' or as a banking activity. First, it helps ensure that they will receive *yang* from the next generation (i.e. from their own children). Second, it means they will have continued support from the family for expenses beyond childhood, primarily those of marriage and establishing a household. Third, it earns sons a right to a share in the family estate when it is divided.

(32) Daughters are 'also children'
The way in which I have formulated this discussion will undoubtedly seem strange to those familiar with Chinese kinship, because I have tended to minimise the difference between sons and daughters in the cycle of *yang*. It is often assumed, and people in Angang also say, that the support of parents falls more heavily on sons than on daughters. Quite often, people say daughters have no obligation whatever to support their parents, and anything they do is optional. Generally, it is sons who contribute to the family wealth, and who divide it amongst themselves as brothers. Listening to this talk, it would be easy to assume that *yang* (and even *xiao*) is a matter for men and not women. But the reality is rather variable, and I would argue that traditional perceptions are now being transformed. Daughters are increasingly seen by their parents as potential sources of wealth and

support. This is partly because of declining family size, but also partly because in Taiwan the career prospects of women are now thought to be quite good. In fact, in many cases their short-term prospects are better than those of sons. Young men in Taiwan spend up to three years in military service, during which time they are unable to work or study, and may need financial assistance from their parents. Daughters, by contrast, are able to earn money immediately upon leaving school, money which they usually give to their parents until marriage. Because the average age of marriage in Taiwan is now quite high (the preferred age is in the middle to late twenties), daughters may work for many years and send home a substantial amount of support in the meantime. In many cases this is simply saved for marriage expenses, but in other cases it is an important part of family income.

Even after marriage, many women in Taiwan now continue to work, and many use their income to provide some form of support to their parents. One woman (a widow with sons) told me that originally she had disapproved of her only daughter studying beyond elementary school, because a girl 'marries out' (*chujia*), and her future is a matter for someone else. But the woman said people had explained to her that 'a daughter is also a child' (*nu'er ye shi haizi*). They advised her to pay attention to her daughter's future, and to support her. She had done so, and, to her delight, the daughter turned out to be very supportive in return (financially and emotionally). After marriage, her daughter's new husband had encouraged her to stop working, saying she should care for the home and the children instead. But later, when their children were in school all day, she took part-time employment. Her husband began to tease her, asking why she didn't send money home to her mother. She then began to send money on two 'national' holidays: Women's Day and Mother's Day. Another young working woman in Angang, as yet unmarried, told me that she planned to continue sending money to her parents indefinitely. She saw this as an important reason for remaining employed after marriage, so that she would have 'her own' money to send to them.

These are examples of 'optional' *yang* being given, but it is also interesting to consider examples of families who *only* have daughters. In the absence of sons how do they deal with parental support? I spoke about this with a woman who had three young girls. Her husband's parents, with whom she and her husband lived, felt very strongly that they should continue trying to have a son. But the woman said that three children were enough, and that boys and girls were the same (*dou yiyang*), it made no difference to her. In particular she seemed unconcerned with the economic consequences, saying that would take care of itself, and that she expected nothing from her daughters. Note, however, that it is fairly common for parents to say they do not expect support from their children.

And what do the children say? Another local woman had four daughters and no sons (she was separated from her husband). The daughters said that they would unquestionably support their mother when she was old, and arrange for her to be worshipped after death. They would do so specifically because they had no brothers, whereas if they had a brother, he would be responsible for their mother's support. Traditionally, such a situation might have been resolved through uxorilocal marriage, i.e. by 'inviting in' a son-in-law. But this has rather negative connotations, and one of the daughters said that most women (herself included) would not want to marry the kind of man who would *need* to marry uxorilocally. The solution, for this family, was for the daughters to take over the role of sons, and to provide their mother with economic support.

So far, my inclusion of daughters in the cycle of *yang* has either been related to changing opportunities (the seemingly improved prospects of daughters) or to 'exceptional' circumstances (the absence of sons). I have also given examples of women who simply wanted to show affection to their parents, and gave some limited form of *yang*; but this, by contrast with the support provided by sons, was not seen as obligatory. But what about the position of women in more 'traditional' arrangements? Financial support which is given to a woman's parents after her marriage, if it *is* obligatory, is commonly thought of as coming from the son-in-law, rather than from the daughter. This is usually the result of a marriage agreement in which the son-in-law undertakes to send regular payments to his parents-in-law. But this kind of agreement could arguably be seen as the repayment of the *yang* which parents have invested in their daughter; the difference is that it is less direct than the repayment from sons.[10] In other words, a woman's husband repays her obligation to her parents.

There is another, more obvious, way in which women are involved in the cycle of *yang* even after marriage: they take on the obligation to support and nurture their husband's parents. Daughters-in-law, especially in the traditional view, are responsible for the everyday feeding and care of their parents-in-law. Focusing on the financial aspect of *yang*, as opposed to feeding and nurturing, might lead us to underestimate the role of women in repaying the debt of *yang* which their husbands owe to their parents. Having been nurtured by her own mother and father, at marriage a woman's primary obligation shifts to her husband's parents. Indeed, in practice, husband and wife have important obligations to *both* sets of parents. In this way, sons and daughters are fully implicated in the cycle of *yang*.

(33) Children must learn that waste is wrong

I have been stressing the economic aspect of reciprocal *yang*, but it is important to remember that economic relations are here seen in simultaneously practical and moral terms. Recall the text cited in chapter 4, in which a son saved money in order to reduce his mother's hardship. His ability to be frugal was explicitly linked to his determination to be *xiao*. Frugality was a moral issue because of its connexion to filial obligation and, beyond that, to national construction.

So they say in the schools, but frugality is also a moral issue in the community. People in Angang become quite upset when confronted with examples of waste (*langfei*, literally 'a wave of expenditure'), whether these involve money, property or food. For instance, I have seen a mother hit her daughter for dropping a small piece of food on the ground, and it is said to be wrong to leave even a single grain of rice in a bowl at the end of a meal. This everyday condemnation of waste is in contrast to the recurrent need to be wasteful on certain occasions. Villagers support, for instance, the extravagant consumption which is part of local festivals and celebrations. This kind of waste is seen to be inevitable and necessary, in spite of official (and some local) criticisms of it. Feuchtwang paraphrases a temple notice sent out by the mayor of Taipei in 1967 as follows:

> To have feasts and to worship Heaven as the ancestors' equal is to act against original principles ... The Ch'ing Manchus and the Japanese were guilty of perpetrating the fallacy of feasts, which are like nausea and madness and seriously affect health, strength, domestic economy, and social order ... feasts are against the spirit of the New Life Movement and are especially wasteful at a time when the country is at war. (1974: 288–9).

However, as Ahern (1981b) notes, this 'waste' is seen to be crucial for ensuring prosperity and, when it comes to public celebrations, illiberality is seen to be wrong.

But outside of necessary extravagances, people are generally severe in condemning waste. This is closely related to mutual economic support, and thus especially relevant to the cycle of *yang* and to children, in three ways. First, people say that it is wrong to waste something which comes from someone else's labour, and this especially applies to what children receive from their parents. Second, more generally, because children and parents are economically interdependent, anything that a child wastes is seen as a loss to the parent and the family estate. Third, the condemnation of waste often applies to food, which as I will discuss, is a crucial element of *yang*. Although I know of many cases of children being scolded for wastefulness, frugality is a generalised moral which applies to everyone, as the examples I give will show.

One of the stories I was told most often in Angang (and which all the children knew) was of a ship which ran aground during the Japanese occupation of Taiwan. The ship, bearing Westerners (*xifangren*) and filled with their 'high quality' goods, landed near one of the villages. The details of what then happened are disputed, but the emphasis in different accounts is fairly consistent. Villagers stress that during the occupation people in Angang were very poor, and they enumerate the luxury goods on the ship (meat, alcohol, cigarettes, etc.). The Westerners (presumably surprised to suddenly find themselves in a Chinese fishing village) are said to have given some of these items to local people, but the Japanese occupiers were unwilling for the locals to have them. (A different version is that some goods were stolen.) The Japanese then seized the goods from villagers, placed them in a pile on the beach, and set them ablaze. When old people tell and re-tell the story (with some emotion) it is the intentional destruction of food and luxury items which they seem to find particularly offensive.

But even unintentional waste provokes strong reactions. One of the couples I knew best in Angang had a very good relationship; they rarely argued, except in a joking way. When they did have a dispute, the woman, who had the more forceful personality, was very vocal in her own defence. One day I went to their house to watch them remove antlers from their deer, to be used in an expensive medicinal wine. The blood from this operation is very carefully gathered up; it also is for medicinal use, and quite valuable. The wife took the antlers from the courtyard into the house, and somewhat carelessly placed them in a sack on the floor. A few moments later the husband walked in and saw blood from the horns seeping through the cloth, being wasted. He flew into a rage, and shouted at his wife: 'That's $300!' She became very flustered, looked up guiltily, and uncharacteristically said nothing at all in response. She set about trying to gather up the blood, and he remained angry for the rest of the afternoon.

In order to show that criticisms of waste are very pervasive, I will here relate some personal experiences. These are of interest because people normally went out of their way to be polite to me, and to be forgiving of my mistakes. On one occasion, I helped a fisherman to place a net along the coastline. While we were carrying out this complicated manoeuvre, swimming some distance from the shore in fairly choppy water, I lost sight of the large rice bag in which we had been carrying the net, and it drifted out to sea. When the fisherman discovered the loss of this easily replaceable item he lashed out angrily (and untypically) at me.

On another occasion, I borrowed a camera from a schoolteacher and inadvertently wasted part of a roll of film. He reacted angrily to this loss, and I was left in no doubt that what I had done might have been accidental, but it was nevertheless wrong. The teacher was normally very friendly and consistently generous with me, always insisting that I should use his things rather than waste money on my own (*buyao langfei*, 'don't be wasteful!'). Indeed, during the months when I lived with the teachers I felt rather constrained by their moralistic attitude towards money. (Did this come from what they had learnt from their families? It was certainly consistent with what they taught their students about waste and citizenship.) They were, for example, unhappy if I went to the local shop to 'waste money' on food or supplies. (The teachers may also have felt that my need to *buy* things would have placed their own generosity towards me, as a guest, in question.) I soon found myself making purchases rather furtively.

One of the things I hoped to buy, for health reasons, was bottled water, which in Angang is sold primarily to tourists. Local people drink boiled water, and consider bottled water to be a fraud, tap water for which one must pay. As time went on, I became friends with the owners of the shop nearest the school where I made most of my purchases. Soon this family of shop-keepers themselves began to tell me that I was wasting money buying bottled water, even if it was from them. In the end this criticism became fairly pointed, it was foolish and wrong to waste money unnecessarily, and eventually I gave up on the bottled water.

These examples, of course, are not remotely of the same kind: the wilful burning of luxury goods, carelessness with a valuable medicine, the accidental loss of an everyday item, the making of unnecessary purchases. But what ties them together, and makes them all morally wrong, is that they involve the waste or destruction of wealth in some form. Again, the examples given do not specifically relate to filial obedience, and my own experiences seemingly had nothing to do with kinship at all. However, as I said, the concern with frugality is by definition related to the cycle of *yang*, because any wealth which passes through individual hands is by extension family wealth, and it is wrong to waste it. But in certain contexts being lavish, and even wasteful, is seen as appropriate and necessary. This should become clearer in the section below, where I turn to other aspects of the cycle of *yang*, and especially to food.

(34) Children must feed their parents
As noted, the character for *yang* contains a 'food' radical, and the parent–child relationship is often described with explicit reference to food. At times, the obligation to provide food seems even more fundamental than the obligation to provide financial support, and the meanings of food and money often appear to be virtually conflated. Food and food-related symbolism are obviously very important in China, and have received considerable attention from anthropologists.[11]

In Angang one quickly learns that various foods have meanings (*i-su*), because people often point out that food means this or that. For example, long-life noodles, *shoumian*, represent long life. They are said to resemble long white hair, or a long white beard, and eating them 'means' one will (hopefully) live for 100 years. For this reason, they should be swallowed whole rather than broken with the teeth. If broken, a long-life noodle means something else. To give another example, when people marry and establish a new household, the first meal at the new house includes chicken, because the word for chicken is similar to the word for family; their meanings converge. Villagers also often worship with, and consume meaningful foods such as 'eternal-life peaches' (*shoutao*), a kind of pastry which derives its significance from the Banquet of the Daoist Immortals. Red pastries in the shape of turtles (*honggui*) are also given to the gods, and then divided amongst devotees. Drinks may be meaningful as well. At times villagers consume 'absence-of-problems (*pieng-an*) tea', made from water gathered in the local temple-cave to Kuan-im. A complete list of these foods and drinks would be very long indeed.

Ways of eating or not eating together also represent something. For example, if a person resists accepting food from someone else in a particular way, then that person is displaying 'the air of a guest' (*kheq-khi*), whereas sharing food may be seen as a public acknowledgement of a connexion. Providing food for others also represents something. For example, if I offer a particular food to my father's spirit, it means not only that I respect him, but also that I have not forgotten what he enjoys eating. Some of these notions will be explained in greater detail below, but for the moment I wanted only to stress that food-related symbolism is very prevalent, and of importance in many different kinds of social interaction in Angang: everyday meals, public banquets, offerings to gods and ancestors, and so on.

It is in the context of this prevalent food-related symbolism that obligations between parent and child are expressed through the idiom of food. Recall that the texts cited in the last chapter included the provision of food as a key element in motherhood. And in Angang, when children and young people talk about their mothers, they often spontaneously raise the issue of food. The apparently *inevitable* and on-going nature of a mother's duty to feed her child is evoked in the following ghost story which I was told by a young girl:

Once, in Taiwan, there was a young woman who became pregnant, but then died before giving birth. She was buried. Afterwards, inside the coffin, she gave birth to a child. Then every night she would leave the coffin and walk along the streets. She would go up to shops and buy noodles to take back for her child to eat.

Children, for their part, also seem almost *inevitably* obliged to provide food for their parents. The support they give to parents later in life (by contrast with earlier 'banking' transactions) is especially seen as 'care' or 'nurturance' (*yang*), and, more practically, as ensuring that parents are fed. Indeed, people sometimes minimise the extent to which providing this support is a burden, by pointing out that 'it's only one extra bowl of rice' or 'one extra pair of chopsticks'. The ability to provide this support for one's elders, to make a return, is, as I have been saying, tied to educational achievement. One woman with four children (three girls and a young boy) bragged to me about the talents of her son. She told him to write out numbers for me, something he had been taught by one of his elder sisters. The daughter of a relative was watching this performance, and the boy's mother teased her: 'You're older than him and you can't write! *Png-thang, png-thang!*' The expression *png-thang* literally means 'rice pot', and is used to mock a useless person, i.e. someone who is only good at eating rice, not producing it. A son who was destined for success would surely not be a 'rice pot', he would be able to feed his parents.

One of the most common systems for giving *yang* to the elderly is actually called 'meal rotation' (cf. Hsieh 1985). In most versions of this, parents live for a month with one child (almost always a son) before moving on to the next. The support given is not restricted to food, but nor should the provision of food be seen as a mere side-effect of the overall system. One elderly woman in Angang, on 'meal rotation' between her three sons, evaluated the experience largely in terms of the quality of food at each of their homes. More specifically, she said that one of her sons was the most filial (*xiaoshun*), commenting (in this order) that the food at his house was the best, that he gave her more money than the others, and that his home was the most 'relaxed' (*qingsong*). For her, *xiao* was not simply a matter of meals, but they were obviously a key issue.

Even after death, the parent–child connexion is partly enacted through food. The support provided for the recently dead takes different forms, and many things are transmitted to the other world during funeral rites: spirit money, paper houses, clothes, etc. But special efforts are made to keep the dead comfortable and well-fed, because it is under-fed spirits who most often become hungry ghosts (*e gui*). In short, the relationship between parents and children is mediated, on different levels, and even after death, by transactions in food. In the following sections I will focus on three seemingly disconnected parts of this overall process: the consumption of medicinal foods, the sharing of food in public contexts, and the foods used in religious offerings. Each of these usages draws attention to certain relationships, and also reveals ways of thinking about children.

(35) Medicinal foods protect children
In Angang many kinds of foods and drinks are seen to have medicinal properties, of help to those who are ill, or to those susceptible to illness. These qualities are ascribed to common foods eaten in everyday life, to luxurious foods eaten on special occasions, to traditional Chinese medicines (*zhongyao*), to commercially produced invigorating tonics (*buyao*), to alcoholic beverages and teas, and so on. Here I use the term 'medicinal food' to gloss these very different usages, meaning substances people eat or drink in order to improve or protect their health.

The emphasis given to these foods, and the prices many of them command, underline the fact that health and longevity are seen as highly desirable goals. Good health, reflective of one's moral state, is a basic filial obligation and something worthy of investment. Because health is a family (rather than an individual) preoccupation, medicinal or health-bringing foods and tonics are a matter for families. Recall that children are taught in school the Confucian admonition to protect their health for the sake of their parents, and that religious activities also often focus on 'protecting the body-persons' (*hushen*) of children. Similarly, many kinds of food and drink are regularly used either specifically as medicines (*yao*), or as tonics and remedies (*buyao*) to 'strengthen or supplement the body-persons' (*bushen*) of children. Of course, the consumption of medicinal foods is not restricted to the young. However, remember that they are thought more vulnerable than adults to certain kinds of harm, and more in need of assistance. Also, as I have been stressing, the future of the family relies in part on them surviving and flourishing, thus making the provision of medicinal foods a worthwhile investment.

One Taiwanese television advertisement succinctly portrayed the use of medicinal foods and drinks which I have in mind. In it, a young man is seated at his desk, alone in a large room, framed by the light of his desk-top lamp. He conscientiously works his way through a stack of books, but seems very tired, if not exhausted. His mother and father, smiling with satisfaction at his dedication, come into the room. Seeing his tiredness, they hand him a bottle of a commercial 'invigorating tonic' (*buyao*). He drinks some and is immediately, and obviously, invigorated. He then proceeds to pick up another book, with an energetic smile on his face, and resume his studies.

People in Angang do often drink such tonics, but they also produce a more traditional kind of medicine. Almost every household keeps one or more head of 'plum-blossom deer' (*meihualu*), from which the antlers are periodically removed. This is done while the antlers are still relatively new, and filled with blood. A rope is thrown around the hind legs of the animal, and it is then tackled and restrained while the antlers are removed with a saw. The blood from the operation is caught in a pan, and small caps are put on the bleeding stubs. The antlers are later sliced into small pieces and aged in rice wine and herbs. This deer-antler wine (*lurongjiu*) is said to make the body hot (*re*), and people drink it during the winter against the effects of the weather, saying it is good for the joints, and keeps one from 'fearing the cold', *pa leng*. Men (but not unmarried ones) drink the blood which comes from the antler-removal operation for sexual potency, while everyone may drink small amounts of the wine throughout the winter, particularly when they feel weak.

Deer penis (*lubian*), is also held to be particularly powerful as a *bushen* and 'hot' food (a single one can sell for around NT$8,000). The penis should be removed while the animal is still alive, and it is then chopped into small pieces, dried in the sun, roasted, and eaten by women (especially young women) and children.[12] I was told by women in Angang that this food makes them strong (*qiang*) and fat, and is a particularly good thing to eat during pregnancy and while breast-feeding. One woman told me that she had almost died while bearing her last child (and only son), but that she had eventually recovered and become strong, something she largely attributed to eating *lubian*. She continued to prepare it for her children from time to time, although she no longer needed it herself. Some people also claim that eating *lubian* makes one very agitated (*jilie*) during sexual intercourse (this is a very common claim made for various 'hot' foods). One man told me he would not dare (*bu gan*) to eat deer penis, because it was too powerful, although elderly men might safely do so. I was also told that if a young man ate it he would have to run to the beach and jump into the water to cool off.

Even outsiders sometimes still make special trips to Angang to buy *lurongjiu* and *lubian*. Belief in their efficacy is such that prices have, at times, been very high; and, until recently, the production of deer-based medicines was an important source of income for people in Angang. The recent flooding of the Taiwanese market with fake deer products has reduced profits, but people continue to produce for themselves, and to use other kinds of foods for protection and strengthening. What I want to stress is that deer products are very expensive. People in Angang rarely have to pay for them, but their production requires a considerable effort. Almost every day, throughout the year, someone from the household (usually the mother or a child) must go out into the fields to gather and bring back a large amount of 'deer-grass' (*lucao*) for each animal. The amount of medicine which is produced from this everyday effort is quite small, and *lubian* and *lurongjiu* are clearly marked out as luxury items.

Such medicines may seem strange examples with which to illustrate a discussion of food in the parent–child relationship. They seem to have as much or more to do with the strength of mothers, or the sexual prowess of married men, as with children. Indeed, certain kinds of medicinal foods, including the blood from antler removal, are specifically *not* given to children. But to explain why medicinal foods are family foods, and relevant to the parent–child cycle of *yang*, they must be seen in view of the moral aspect of health. Sickness, weakness, infertility, susceptibility to accidents or even death may arise from or reflect moral failures; they are all resisted. Conversely, strong and fertile body-persons (*shen*) are goals of every family. It may seem obvious, but much of what families aspire to (including the production of descendants, economic security and ritual continuity) is premised on the health and reasonable longevity of each generation. Investing in medicinal foods is one way of trying to achieve these goals, of making sure that the family is 'complete'. Both children and adults are part of this process, and it should be remembered that the women and men whose fertility is enhanced by expensive means are *also* the children of their parents.

A child in Angang would almost certainly know a number of things about deer and deer products. She might, for example, be sent out to the fields to collect 'deer grass', and would certainly know of this everyday task. She could not help but hear the cry they make when their horns are removed, and might watch the operation. If so, she would see men drink the fresh blood, and perhaps overhear a joke about sexual potency. At some point in her childhood, she would probably drink *lurongjiu* (and perhaps eat *lubian*). She would also know of the expense of the products, and know of outsiders coming to Angang to buy them. Within these various observations lies a potential for learning. She might learn something of the value attributed to her own physical health (her *shen*, body-person); or of the value attributed, in different ways, to the fertility of men and of women.

(36) Food reflects the child's family to the outside

Medicinal foods are used to protect and strengthen families, and this is a relatively private matter. But food is also, of course, an important medium for social relations, a reflection of the family to the outside world. I spoke with one woman several days before her son was to return to Angang from the city for a visit; she said he planned to bring a friend. She was already preparing food for the visit, and said this was important on account of her son's 'face' (*mianzi*). According to her, sons should always let their mothers know about guests in advance so that food can be prepared. The more notice they give, the better. If they arrive without warning, there is nothing to be done about it. She said that even if an elaborate meal was out of the question, the important thing was to do enough to show your 'kindly feelings' (*xinyi*). She related this immediately to a more general consideration of wealth and appearances. She said that when she visited her son, it was important to dress as nicely as possible so that his friends would ask 'whose mother is wearing such nice clothes?' If she wore something old and shabby, they might say 'who would let their mother wear such bad clothes?' In other words, the son's ability to care for (*yang*) her was reflected in her clothes, and their ability to care for (*yang*) each other was reflected in the food they, as a family, could serve to someone from the outside.

Her comments were not exceptional, for in Angang the concern with appearances of various kinds often relates to food. Perhaps the clearest, or in any case most extreme, example of this is found in public meals or banquets, which are a regular setting for the conduct of business and politics, and are explicitly viewed as a way of making and holding onto connexions outside of one's family. Even in Angang, where social interaction is usually quite informal and relaxed, formal meals are sometimes very important, and during them people occasionally conform to the standards of high etiquette.

For example, on one occasion the highest official in the rural township (the *xiangzhang*) hosted a dinner at his home. He wore pyjamas as a way of indicating to the guests his own sense of lowliness, and of expressing to them the honour they paid his family by eating in his humble home. On the next night, when he was invited to a meal in the home of the local doctor, he appeared wearing a suit and tie, an exceptionally rare sight in Angang, to show how honoured he was to be invited. The humility of the official and the doctor did not stop them from serving expensive and elaborately prepared meals. On both occasions, and in most *chia lang-kheq* ('inviting guests') situations, it is standard for the host to apologise for the fact that there 'is no food' (*bou chai*), even as more and more plates are piled onto the table.[13]

It is perhaps misleading to reduce these activities to their food-related elements. But in China the sharing of food often seems to constitute the fundamental transaction of social relations. When I unsuccessfully asked people to explain to me the details of various traditions, I would often be told simply that people in Angang emphasise the *chia lang-kheq* aspect of events more than anything else, including the formal rituals. For example, when I tried to learn about weddings, people would launch into a discussion of *chia lang-kheq*. One couple told me about their daughter's marriage to a man from outside of the *xiang*. When the groom and his family came to Angang for a banquet, the tables were filled with food, and the guests could eat all they wanted. But when the couple from Angang went with their daughter, the bride, to be guests of the groom's family, it was a different matter. It was true that there were plenty of people, that it was 'hot and noisy' (*lau-ziat*), but there wasn't any food to speak of (*bou chai*). Everyone remained hungry.

This grown-up world of banquets and appearances often *seems* to explicitly exclude children and women, because adult men usually represent the family to the outside. Even in relatively informal Angang, in *chia lang-kheq* situations women and children will often eat afterwards, or not at all. Sometimes they will loiter only on the edges of a meal, filling a bowl and walking around the room, or they may take over the table when the men have finished. But this apparent exclusion is misleading because they certainly know what is going on, and know that it reflects upon them. I was fascinated by the extent to which children in Angang, in spite of their absence from most banquets, create in their own affairs a similarly food-centred social world. When they organise parties and expeditions for themselves they often seem most interested in establishing the catering priorities: what food will be bought, who is responsible for it, at what stage in the proceedings it can be eaten, who gets to eat how much of it, etc. On these occasions, children often say to each other the same polite words used by adults.

For example, I was once invited to attend a child's birthday party. (Although everyone is said to become one year older at the lunar new year, individual birthdays are often celebrated in some way as well.) This party was for a middle school girl, and was attended by her classmates, but also by a seven-year-old boy from her village, next to whom I was seated. On this banquet occasion, the young boy was amazingly adept at using polite adult speech. He told me (in Mandarin) to *ganbei* ('bottoms up') my drink, told me to 'not be polite' (*buyao keqi*), told me I was eating 'without obligation' (*meiyou guanxi*), and that I should therefore eat a bit more of everything (*dou chi yidian*). All of these are very common meal-time comments directed at guests. Throughout the party, he filled my plate and glass, and pressed me to eat and drink. In short, word for word, gesture for gesture, he replicated adult *chia lang-kheq* behaviour. Some days later the same boy saw me eating in a street-side noodle shop and asked, again in adult tones: 'Why are you eating here? If you want to eat, come to our house! There you won't have to spend any money!' Children in Angang grow up surrounded by talk of food and of food symbolism. Clearly, they know from an early age how to behave politely when food is shared. Even when excluded from this sharing, they know that the presentation and apportioning of food is a reflection of their family to the outside world, a matter of appearances.

(37) Children should politely decline food from others
In this respect, it is important to know that children usually politely decline offers of food from non-kin. They usually say that they have already eaten (whether or not this is true), or that they are not hungry, or that they will eat at home. This rejection is so ordinary as to be automatic, but it may relate to notions of what it means to accept and share food. In banquets, sharing food seems to be a way of either highlighting relationships, or producing them. However, it should also be pointed out that providing food can equally be seen as a way of trying to control or to avoid relationships, or simply as a way of paying people off.

For example, in Angang, the helpers at funerals, who are not highly thought of, and who have inevitably accumulated spiritual pollution in carrying out their tasks, are always given a meal by the family of the deceased. This is hardly an attempt to establish close relationships, rather it is a form of compensation. Similar compensatory offerings are made to ghosts, sometimes called 'good brothers' (*hao xiongdi*). They are periodically given food and wine, which is left on tables in front of homes, and in these cases the hope is that, having eaten enough, they will go away, leave everyone alone, and not cause trouble. Remember that the existence of ghosts in the first place is often thought due to the failure of their descendants to care for their needs. People thus try to resolve the problem of ghosts by making a kind of false connexion with them, offering hospitality, and calling them brothers.

This concern with whether or not the ghosts have eaten might be related to the food hospitality which enters into everyday matters of etiquette, including the refusal of food by children. Two of the most common greetings in Angang are *ciaq-png be*?, 'have you eaten (rice) yet?' or *ciaq-pa be*?, 'are you full yet?' These phrases are shouted out and usually answered affirmatively, regardless of meal-times, in the absence of food, and often by people passing each other on the street. They are set phrases, but are still clearly associated with their literal meanings. For instance, people may communicate the 'have you eaten?' question to someone out of earshot by pantomiming the gestures of holding a rice bowl and using chopsticks to scoop out food. The proper response is to shake the head, yes.

If a person in Angang walks past or through a house where food is in fact being eaten, they will also usually be invited to join in with shouts of *ciaq-png*, 'eat (rice)!', or simply *ciaq*, 'eat!'. Usually it is sufficient to say *hou*, 'alright', and then to simply walk away. Children are usually not pressed further, but in some adult situations where the offer is genuine it is considered rude to decline, a rejection not only of food but also of friendship. What counts as a genuine offer is sometimes hard to determine, but it depends in part on whether or not food is close at hand, and whether or not the person making the invitation backs down.

If and when people are made to sit and eat (and this is true at banquets as well) the tension between offer and acceptance carries on. The host should ensure that the guest will not refrain from eating out of politeness. She will shout out *m kheq-khi*, 'don't have the air of a guest!' She may put food (*chai*, i.e. 'dishes') directly into the guest's bowl, after which it would be extremely rude to not eat. Meanwhile the guest, who may not be remotely hungry, will try to achieve a fine balance in terms of the amount eaten. To consume too little is to reject hospitality or even to suggest that what is on offer is not good to eat, *hou-ciaq*. But because people have often in fact already eaten, being asked to eat more is sometimes unpleasant. At the same time, to eat *too* much would be to take advantage of someone's generosity, perhaps to be seen as a *png-thang* ('rice pot'). But worst of all, to overeat might suggest that the guest was actually hungry. Underfed people on the streets, like underfed ancestors who become hungry ghosts, may need the generosity of those outside their own families. Children, in declining offers of food, are partly being polite, but also indicating that they eat enough at home.

Food symbolism arguably begins in the family, where obligations are most unavoidable. Every attempt to extend this outwards is also a serious business. In theory, one reason for restraint when someone outside of your family offers food is to reduce these obligations. But since most people say, and seem to genuinely feel, that they offer food on most occasions only to be friendly and generous, they become exasperated with guests who seemingly hold back. They sometimes use the expression *meiyou guanxi*. This is often translated as 'you're welcome' or 'never mind', but it literally means 'there is no connexion (or relatedness)'. It is a way of saying to guests that accepting hospitality is unimportant, and perhaps that food is not being used as a way of establishing obligation. To say 'there is no connexion' is a way of claiming, in the face of all the counter-evidence, that sharing food in this case means nothing. But everyone agrees that sharing food does mean something, and in fact when guests feel that they truly can eat or drink no more they often say *i-su*, *i-su*, which literally means 'meaning'. People say 'meaning' as a way of asking to consume enough to show the 'feelings of their heart' (*xinyi*) without having to eat or drink so much as to be made ill.

Children are expected to politely decline the 'meaning' of shared food as they walk through the community. But in other ways, the communal sharing of food, and its offering to the gods, is seen to produce a kind of protection for them.

(38) Food and money help produce the gods who protect children
In Angang the connexion between close friends (those with whom it is truly unnecessary to be polite) is often enacted through the sharing of food and drink. When people say that they can depend on each other during difficult times, this is also often expressed with specific reference to food. During a period of very bad fishing, one man told me, while pointing to an altar, that soon people in Angang would be reduced to eating the food offered to the gods. This observation was interesting, in part, because it suggested that such offerings would carry on through even the most difficult times. But it was also interesting because food offerings are explicitly seen as a collective effort for communal benefit, i.e. as an example of mutual support. For example, people regularly join together in groups (of relatives or friends) to raise pigs which will then be offered to a deity. The people themselves are seen to have had an important part in producing the offering in the first place, and they are closely identified with it (cf. Ahern 1981b). Once the god has 'consumed' the meat (or its fragrance, *xiang*) it is then carefully re-distributed to the members of the group which produced it, who then re-consume it, for their own protection.

In local religion there are many examples of this kind; devotees are often told that they should eat (*ciaq*) the offerings, because this will be good for their health (*dui shenti hao*). Furthermore, in common with most acts of worship, it will bring them *pieng-an* ('the absence of problems'). Indeed, people are sometimes specifically told by bystanders at religious occasions to 'eat security' (*ciaq pieng-an*), as they are handed various offerings. Through spirit mediums (*tang ki*), the gods often advise devotees to eat or drink particular kinds and quantities of various pastries, noodles, fruits, wines, etc., which are found on altars. For example, at one shrine the god regularly complained that children were not eating enough of the candy found in front of his image. These sweets, left by devotees, could protect them, but children were failing to take advantage of this divine help. Adults were told to eat the candy as well. One woman told me she had been injured during a religious ritual but that as soon as she had eaten the candy her pain disappeared. Gods regularly instruct devotees to drink water in which charms have been burnt. These charms are usually 'imperial decrees' against evil spirits, written on slips of paper by mediums or priests. In drinking the charm-water, believers are felt to be consuming the words of the gods, and acquiring their preventative power. Mediums complained that the charm-paper and ink had become quite expensive, but they continued to buy the highest quality supplies specifically because children could eat the charms without risk. (In cases of ill-health, these charms are used in conjunction with expensive medicinal and strengthening foods.)

Food offerings are obviously important, as is the consumption of various items, but other kinds of offerings are made as well. Supplicants also burn incense, and deities are regularly given large quantities of paper spirit money. During a festival, a local temple will thus usually be filled with incense, food and money offerings. The exact quantity and type of money is often a matter of detailed negotiation between mediums, priests, gods and their bureaucrats. In addition to burning spirit money, the underwriting of festival expenses (with 'real' money) is also seen as an important way of showing dedication. Temple walls are covered permanently with the names of those who have contributed to their construction (and the amounts they have given). Similarly, at festivals the names of all donors are prominently posted. In various ways, people in Angang give money and food to the gods, in the hope of a return.

But why are these religious acts said to be effective? Partly because the attention of the gods has been attracted to certain things. Groups of people make offerings as part of the overall effort to entice gods to pay attention to particular localities, families or individuals. Not only are the gods paid and fed, but the soldiers of the gods are often paid and fed as well. Sometimes even the horses of the soldiers of the gods are given grass and water and spirit money. This may seem an over-sensitivity to the culinary and financial needs of spirits and their hangers-on, but gods come and go with alacrity. It is necessary to try to hold their attention. At some divination sessions a kind of 'tea' incense is held under the nose of the medium, like a magnet being used in order to attract the spirit into his body. And when people spend money staging festivals for the gods they say the point is to entertain them, usually with operas or puppet shows, to feed them well, and to make them feel welcome. And, although this is less rarely said, the point is also to make them feel obligated to the community.

Such offerings are not only a way of enticing, obligating or paying off the gods, they are also a way of making gods strong and effective in the first place (cf. Sangren 1991). Consider the example of incense.[14] People offer incense out of respect, but this accumulated incense is itself of great power, and is often the thing which really 'represents' the god. It is also perhaps the most important symbolic manifestation of the fact that a collective effort produces gods and that such gods are infinitely redivisible. One consequence of this is that people prefer charms (*xianghuo*, 'fragrant fires') made with incense from altars where *many* people have worshipped, because they are thought especially effective. The charm is effective precisely because many people have offered incense at the altar of this god. The logic is, of course, circular. The god's power attracts worshippers, but accumulated acts of worship give the god power.

Local rituals in Angang also imply that strong gods come from communal worship and communal offerings. Eating food which has been given to these spirits is, perhaps, a way of consuming this collective effort. And it is this collective effort which ensures the divine protection of families and their children. But here things become rather complicated, for in the midst of this communal effort, we find an undercurrent of family self-reliance. Offerings are often cooperatively made by groups of friends and devotees, and festivals also usually include large public banquets. But every family usually brings its *own*, individual, offerings. These are accumulated, displayed together, and this is what makes the overall effect impressive, 'good to look at' (*hou-khua*), and of interest to the god. But after collective rituals, people usually consume the offerings of their own families. This balance between community-based and family-based action is repeated on many levels. People work together to make the gods and the community strong; but the basic requirement for a strong community is strong families, and this takes us back to food and politeness.

(39) A child's family should care for its own needs

If families fail to feed their ancestors properly, these spirits may become ghosts, wandering about to cause trouble for other families. Such ghosts must then be appeased by everyone else. But the best thing is if families take care of themselves, one might say *yang* themselves, without external assistance. Most people would prefer not to give the impression, when eating someone else's food, that they actually need help with having enough to eat. Children, in general, politely decline offers of food, and guests at banquets often try to eat modestly.

But recall here the question of politeness when food is being offered. When a host says 'there is no connexion', is this to be believed? People are told not to be like a guest (*m kheq-khi*), which may imply that one should eat like a relative. Shared food is sometimes described as if it does transform guests into friends or even relatives. When men eat together, e.g., they will often say that they are all brothers (*dou xiongdi*) or that they are from one family (*yijiaren*), especially when they are not. They seem to be very interested in making and using family-style connexions on this basis. But it is perhaps too easy to conclude that they use food as a way of producing and maintaining relationships, and to assume that when people say 'there is no connexion' as they offer food to guests that they are in fact proving the opposite.[15]

In Angang there is an ambivalence about the power of food, and an elaboration of the etiquette surrounding the giving and receiving of it. But the etiquette is so well-known, and the connexion between food and relationships so explicit, that people perhaps manage the manipulative potential of hospitality in ways that would be unthinkable if they had the idea that hospitality was meant to be disinterested. In Angang food *is* interested when it is shared between people, but everyone knows it to be so.[16]

Indeed, what people in Angang complain about is not the non-family obligations which arise from food, which may be seen and denied and which are in some senses optional, but the etiquette surrounding food which is obligatory, and often rather oppressive. They seem more concerned about being forced to eat than about accumulating obligations in this way. Consumption itself is often the heaviest obligation, and people complain about the unhealthy practice of public over-eating and over-drinking. Family meals, by contrast, are usually healthy, unwasteful and low-key affairs. This, it could even be argued, suggests that giving in to the demands of hosts means failing in the duty to protect one's health for the sake of the family. From this perspective, food, or too much of it, could be seen as a way of actually damaging families from the outside. But this is balanced by the protection and by the opportunities which outside connexions (established through extravagant sharing) may provide.

In thinking of the connexions which in theory are established by sharing food outside of the family, we have to be clear about what is being attempted. In Stuart Thompson's article on food in Taiwanese funerals, he notes that rice is primarily agnatic substance, 'coassociated' with semen, bones, offspring and ancestors (1988:92–5); also, 'rice is ideally not shared between families' (1988:93). In Angang, although people who are unrelated may informally share rice, as when someone sits in on a 'regular family meal' (*jiachang bianfan*), rice is usually not eaten as part of an elaborate meal or banquet.[17] This may suggest that hospitality is not, in the strict sense, an attempt to turn outsiders into relatives, because, as Thompson notes 'the eating of rice together in a real sense demarcates the family unit and reinforces kinship bonds' (1988:92). Leaving rice out of hospitality situations, and focusing on the *chai*, the dishes which accompany the rice, is justified as a way of focusing on the expensive and special, but perhaps it also signals that the very serious business of establishing a family-type connexion is not truly contemplated.

I have suggested that in Angang one reason for declining a gift of food is not so much that it implies an obligation but rather that it implies an inability to take care of one's own needs. Conversely, one of the reasons for wishing to share food with others is not so much to obligate them as to publicly express how well one is taking care of one's own needs. This means that eating together may indeed be a way of showing that there is no connexion between families: it is a way of asserting the ability of a family to take care of itself in style, and to have enough left over to impress the outside world.

(40) Schooling is for future 'yang'
Some families in Angang, through schooling and economic migration, have succeeded in remaining strong and have even managed to prosper. Successful children are good sources of food and money, and in this sense the 'connexions' of a local community such as Angang are less necessary. Plenty of food is there without the bother of wider obligations. In some senses this 'individualism' is exactly what is promoted by the schools. For while education focuses on filial obedience and encourages children to love and support their parents, it discourages the wastefulness of public festivals

and banqueting cycles in which large sums of money are spent, and large amounts of food and alcohol are consumed. And, as Feuchtwang notes, 'the philosophy underlying this education rejects mass participation and the exaltation of local community' (1974:288). I would argue that in some ways people find this government intervention a relief, because it gives them a moral basis on which to reject the obligation to over-indulge, and to reject as well the communal obligations which are sometimes felt to be problematic for smaller family units.

Among the teachers at the middle school were a young married couple, in many senses the embodiment of the moral philosophy in Taiwanese education. They were, in their own terms, hard-working (*yonggong*) and 'striving' (*zhengqi*), but also quite generous, kind-hearted and friendly. They once proudly showed me pictures from their wedding banquet, detailing the number of tables and the number of dishes at each table (which is a very common way of discussing such affairs). The husband told me that sometimes these banquets get out of hand because people want 'face'. If they see someone else has six tables, then they want seven at their wedding. Giving a wedding banquet is sometimes, as he reminded me, a money-making (*zhuanqian*) operation, because every guest brings a cash gift (*hongbao*, yet again) which more than covers the cost of his or her meal. But he said that at their wedding banquet he and his wife had declined to accept (*bushou*) money from their friends, and instead had paid for the banquet themselves. This was for them a matter of pride, because they had chosen not to play the old game of invitation and obligation; they positively did not want to put pressure on their friends. And yet, in other ways, these teachers were strikingly traditional in their thinking. Before marriage they had consulted a fortune teller (*suanmingren*) about the compatibility of their horoscopes, and about the most auspicious date and time for their wedding. They were also planning, after a few years in Angang, to move back to western Taiwan in order to care for (*yang*) the man's father in his retirement, out of their sense of filial duty.

These teachers face many of the issues which people from Angang face, feelings of being both protected and oppressed by cycles of generosity, reciprocity, obligations and connexions. The generosity of the community, sometimes enacted through sharing food, is some degree of protection against supernatural threat and hard times, but this enactment is itself oppressive. People say they prefer to live in close-knit communities and within strong families, partly to avoid ghosts and disorder in the broadest sense. But in practice they also find this solution claustrophobic. In a sense, education and the economic success of Taiwan provide one answer to this problem. Families seem to increasingly obtain their own food independently, without relying on local communities. In fact, this is an oversimplification. The older generation remains in the countryside, receiving money from the city, and this money is spent in the villages, for example for local religious activities and in the form of food and drink shared out with friends and relatives. The younger generations in the cities also have friends and business associates with whom they create new relationships. But people in Angang say that in urban areas it is much easier for people to end up without connexions.

'There is no connexion' (*meiyou guanxi*) is a way in which people say that they offer hospitality with no expectation of return. I have suggested that this could be genuine, partly because everybody knows what food means, and partly because the heaviest obligations connected to food symbolism are restricted to the family. But what follows on from the increased reliance on education and work migration as a way of ensuring the strength and independence of individual families? One result is a transformation of local communities in which food is widely shared. In Angang, even if they tend to over-state the reality, people claim that they help each other because everybody is the same (*dou yiyang*), and this conceptualisation goes beyond the family. In the city there is no pretence of this. People from Angang, in their attempts to discourage my occasional trips to the city, would point out to me that in the city people don't know who lives above them and below them and next door to them, and there are many ghosts. This is very different from Angang, where one can walk into a connexion at every turn.

Summary

In this chapter I have examined parent–child transactions in money and food, but this focus has taken me in many directions. Readers could be forgiven for wondering where exactly I thought I was going, but there is a logic to the presentation. I began by describing the economic aspect of the reciprocal obligation of *yang*: parents support children, and children must in turn support parents. Symbolic financial transactions (e.g., the New Year's 'red envelope') are found alongside practical financial transactions (e.g., the 'banking' activity of parents for their unmarried children, and the 'respectful support' of the elderly).

But *yang* is clearly not a purely monetary relationship. Parents are obliged to feed their children, and children to feed their parents (and eventually the ancestors). Parents also give their children (and themselves) expensive medicinal foods, as a form of private protection, and as a way of enhancing family fertility. Food may also reflect the family (and its ability

Red envelopes and the cycle of yang   111

to take care of itself) to the outside. It is an important medium for producing and emphasising relationships between families. In particular, the communal offering of food and money to the gods is seen as a way of producing communal protection and security. Much of this seems very far removed from the simple mother–child reciprocity of the last chapter. But it is the context in which a child in Angang would read a text which dealt with relationships of *xiao* and of *yang*.

6

Going forward bravely

Textbook renderings of filial obedience (*xiao*), and of parent-child reciprocity (*yang*), are said to be 'ordinary knowledge'. This is partly because the parent-child cycle of *yang*, enacted through transfers of food and money, is an on-going feature of communal life, something which children could not possibly overlook. And yet, as one reads the texts, and thinks about life in Angang, important differences emerge. I have mentioned, for instance, that parents seem disinclined to instruct their children in morality (as the texts imply they should). Parents may also, due to their own lack of education, or their participation in seemingly wasteful social transactions, be unsuitable patterns for their children to emulate. And while textbooks stress the form and spirit of support for one's parents, interest in the community seems more narrowly focused on the provision of money and food.

The texts in this chapter suggest another important difference. Parents in Angang take many steps to protect their children from different kinds of harm. They perhaps resemble the textbook 'anxious mother' who does whatever is possible for her child (although the texts scarcely mention religion, and certainly not spirit mediums). Parents, of course, want their children to survive, and any number of reasons might be given for this: love, attachment, the cultural valorisation of longevity, the commitment to patrilineal ideals, and so on. We might also say: parents want children to survive because they are linked with them in a perpetual cycle of *yang*, which should not be disturbed. Supplication for the 'absence of disturbances' (*pieng-an*) is often directly focused on children, who must endure for the sake of the family. But school textbooks, as I will now show, stress dying for the nation. This form of sacrifice is, perhaps disingenuously, directly linked in the texts to the issue of filial obedience. Now the key issue here is perhaps not death, as such, but rather the use of death as an idiom in discussions relating to identity and commitment. What is at stake is the tension between identification of children with a family (and obligations this implies), and identification with a nation (cf. Stafford 1992).

At the end of chapter 4, in which were translated a series of texts dealing with the relationship between mothers and sons, I related the story of a child who was a 'model of frugality'. Recall the motto accompanying the text: 'Frugality is the basis of national construction.' This implies that frugality is tied not only to filial obedience (*xiao*) but also to patriotism (*zhong*).[1] But the notion of a moral continuity (from *xiao* to *zhong*) goes well beyond the concept of frugality, and in this chapter I will consider some texts which deal with these broader implications.

(41) Children eat foods to commemorate a patriotic death
In the second year of elementary school, children read a story entitled 'Everyone eats *zongzi*.'[2] *Zongzi* are steamed rice balls (usually with a meat or vegetable filling) wrapped in bamboo leaves. In Angang, these are sometimes used as offerings, but are most closely associated with *Duanwu Jie*, the Dragon Boat Festival, held on the fifth day of the fifth lunar month. Here a child relates the story:

Mother has been busy these last few days, because it's time for *Duanwu Jie*. We all enjoy *Duanwu Jie*; there are delicious *zongzi* to eat, and interesting dragon boat races to watch. It is a very 'hot and noisy' festival! Mother bought some green bamboo leaves, in order to wrap the *zongzi*, both sweet and salty. She skilfully wrapped them and hung them up. Little brother was very excited, running back and forth in the room, first asking when we could eat them, then asking who invented *zongzi*.

Mother laughed and said: 'We Chinese people have been eating *zongzi* for over 2000 years. This is to remember a patriotic poet [*aiguo shiren*] from our country's ancient times; he was named Qu Yuan. Qu Yuan, on the fifth day of the fifth month, threw himself into the river and died. Everyone had great respect for him. They put rice in bamboo tubes, and threw these into the river for the fish, so that they would not eat Qu Yuan's body.' I listened along with my brother, and only then did we know why everyone eats *zongzi* on *Duanwu Jie*.

This brief version of the Qu Yuan story omits some important but well-known details (which are dealt with in subsequent texts).[3] Qu Yuan is said to have committed suicide because of despair over government policy, and the refusal of the emperor to heed his advice. He was a 'patriotic poet' (his verses often dealt with these matters), and his was a 'patriotic suicide'. Obviously, his lasting veneration (as a critic of corruption and incompetence), and his commemoration in a major public festival, is a popular tradition anyone in power in China must deal with.

But what is perhaps most interesting about this simple telling (intended for very young children) of a remarkable story is the way in which it is framed. The context is a mother's preparation of a traditional food for her own children. But the food she prepares, and which her children will eat, is of a special kind. On the one hand it commemorates a *patriotic death*. But, on the other hand, it is the food used to protect the integrity of Qu Yuan's body in the river. Remember that death by drowning is thought particularly horrible, and note that the dragon boat races are re-enactments of attempts to recover Qu Yuan's body so that it could be properly buried. This concern with bodily integrity is a central part of the family-based morality I have been describing, and a suicide, in normal circumstances, would be a grossly unfilial act. But the mother in the story acknowledges Qu Yuan as a great man ('everyone had great respect for him'), and she instructs her children in the meaning of the food (her child says 'only then did we know'). The implication is that a patriotic death is a good death, and it is a mother who draws her children's attention to this fact.[4]

(42) A child should repay the nation
In theory, a patriotic suicide, or indeed any other kind of violent, premature or accidental death, is problematic for a kinship ideology based on unbroken descent and long life. The flow of *yang* should not be made discontinuous by such disturbances. Several texts deal with this problem more or less directly. They argue, explicitly, that putting oneself at risk for the nation is not only something consistent with family morality, but is actually the highest fulfilment of Confucian ethics. One such text is found in the series on 'Virtuous Mothers of Ancient Times':[5]

Yue Fei was a famous hero of the people [*minzu de yingxiong*] who grew up in extreme poverty. His mother used branches and wrote on the sand in order to teach him, and also encouraged him to carefully develop his strength, hoping that in future he would become a master of the pen and the sword [*wenwu shuangquan de rencai*].

Yue Fei's scholarly and military talents were exceptional, but his mother further encouraged him to dedicate himself [*baoxiao*] to the nation, etching the characters 'repay the nation with utter loyalty' [*jinzhong baoguo*] on his back. Yue Fei dared not to forget his mother's instructions, and later had many great victories in battle, recovering lost territories, redressing the nation's humiliation, and earning the greatest admiration of the people [*renmen de zongjing*].

This version of the Yue Fei story does not mention his well-known hesitation over a military career, because of his mother's dependence on him for support. Again it is precisely the mother who praises patriotic action, indeed inscribes this praise on her son's flesh, seemingly unconcerned with the risk to the family, and to her support, it implies. I have rendered the term *baoguo* as 'repay the nation', although it is perhaps more accurately translated as 'dedicate oneself to the nation', or 'enlist in the national cause'. Note, however, that this *bao* is the same as that used to describe the 'paying back' (*baoda*) of parents for their care.

The same issues are discussed at greater length in a text entitled 'Filial Obedience: *xiao* to one's kin and committed to the nation,'[6] which tells the story of Chiang Kai-shek's childhood with his widowed mother:

From a very young age, First President Chiang was an obedient [*xiaoshun*] child. When he was nine years old, his father died, and he lived a difficult [*jianku*] life at his mother's side. He was extremely obedient towards her, and very hard-working in school. He rose early every day, swept the floor, and dusted the furniture; after school he also helped his mother start the fire, cook the food, and wash the dishes. Sometimes he went to the garden and helped her with planting and watering. He earned his mother's great affection.

Every evening, she would knit as he read by her side. In their small sitting room, the sounds of reading and the sounds of knitting mingled, harmonious and happy. At the same time she told him of the great heros in Chinese history, encouraging him to do important things. He took her teachings to heart. As he grew older, he became even more obedient.

One day, she said to him, 'You'll soon be an adult [*chengnian*]. You are extremely obedient, helping with the chores and studying diligently; obviously you're a good child. But you should know the true meaning of *xiao*. So-called *xiao* is not simply about being polite, labouring to support your relatives, carrying out the formalities. It really starts with loving-kindness [*titie qinxin, buwei qinyi*]. And you should also know that *xiao* and patriotism [*zhong*] are inseparable. When small, one should be utterly *xiao* towards one's parents, when grown [*zhangdahou*] one should be utterly loyal [*zhong*] towards the nation. If in the future you are able to sacrifice yourself to the nation [*xianshen baoguo*], to substitute *xiao* with patriotism, for the nation and the people to do great things, that would truly be the Great Filial Obedience [*daxiao*], and it would be my greatest hope for you.'

Chiang heard and was extremely moved, and set his heart on joining the army. Later he was a student in Japan, and followed Sun Yat-sen, participating in the Revolution. After the Father of the Country [Sun] had died, Chiang carried out his goals [*jicheng yizhi*] ... Chiang was for his entire life *xiao* to his kin and committed to the nation [*yisheng xiaoqin baoguo*]. He was not only the saviour of the Chinese people [*zhonghua minzu de jiuxing*], he was also a prophet of anti-communism, and one of the world's great men.

Again we find a mother encouraging dedication to the nation, specifically tying it to the principles of filial obedience. Chiang's mother says that '*xiao* and patriotism are inseparable'. She also challenges her son to 'substitute *xiao* with patriotism' (*yixiao zuozhong*), i.e. to be loyal to the nation in place of being loyal to his kin. Note, however, her argument that patriotism is an *extension* of filial obedience (rather than a replacement). She also uses the

116   *Angang*

5   Military service cadets at Angang Middle School

expression *xianshen baoguo*, 'sacrifice oneself to the nation'. This could perhaps be translated 'dedicate oneself to the nation', but *xianshen* literally means 'to offer one's body-person'. This *shen* (body-person) is precisely what is at stake in those religious practices in Angang which *hushen* (protect the body-person), and in medicines which *bushen* (strengthen the body-person).

(43) The child belongs to the patrilineal nation
The notion that patriotism develops from filial obedience is part of the more general notion that all Confucian virtues are based on, and develop from, *xiao*:

Xiao is a beautiful virtue of the Chinese people [*Zhongguo ren de meide*], and all Chinese people emphasise the way of *xiao* [*xiaodao*]. Because *xiao* is the basis of all morality [*yiqie daode de genben*], those who are *xiao* towards their parents will also love their brothers, respect their teachers and elders, be loyal to their country, undertake their public responsibilities, and be honest with their friends. When the country is invaded by enemies, they will go forward bravely [*yonggan xiangqian*], and never retreat. *Xiao* is thus the basis of every virtue: loyalty-patriotism [*zhong*], respectfulness [*jing*], trustworthiness [*xin*], bravery [*yong*], and so on.[7]

This text is accompanied by a photograph of Chiang Kai-shek and his son Chiang Ching-kuo. The text in the last section focused on the relationship of Chiang Kai-shek and his widowed mother; he was *xiao* towards her and *zhong* (patriotic) towards the nation. But a 'father' was also mentioned in that text, Sun Yat-sen, the 'father of the nation' (*guofu*), whose goals Chiang Kai-shek obediently carried out. The implication there and elsewhere is that the fatherless Chiang was 'adopted' by the father of the nation, was nurtured on his ideas, and then dedicated himself to national goals in the way most sons would dedicate themselves to a family.

Following Sun's death, and then Chiang Kai-shek's own death, responsibility for the on-going Nationalist revolution was passed to Chiang's son, Chiang Ching-kuo, who then became president. This Nationalist line of succession is often represented, in a complicated way, as a fulfilment of both patriotism *and* patrilineality. The elder Chiang is represented as the loyal descendant of Sun, and the younger Chiang is similarly represented as the filial child of his father. Even in old age, he was very often associated with young people, as if he were a permanent son. At least until the death of Chiang Ching-kuo (in 1988), the imagery of a patrilineal nation (with leadership passing from Sun to Chiang to Chiang) was explicit. The sense of this may have been heightened by Taiwan's unusual legislative situation, in which representatives elected on the mainland were 'frozen' in government, pending victory over the communists and/or reunification with the homeland, becoming increasingly ancestral with the passing years. They were the elders of a national family built around a dynastic line.

One must be sceptical about the meanings which attach to such portrayals, especially given the direct resistance of many Taiwanese to the Nationalist government. But, stepping away from the texts for a moment, the apparent end of the 'patrilineal line' did provoke genuine emotion in at least one person I knew in Angang. On the night of Chiang Ching-kuo's death in 1988 a middle school teacher came solemnly into my room to tell me the news. She said 'our president has died', and then burst into tears. She added: 'We're a very poor country, and without our president, we're even more pitiful (*kelian*).' However, on the next morning she was more cheerful, and reported having had a dream. In this, President Chiang had visited the middle school in Angang, and had met with the students (befitting his status as a perpetual youth). All she could remember was that the students were very happy and excited (*gaoxing*).

Other people had little to say on the subject, and the most notable immediate effect of the death of Chiang on people in Angang was that television programming was drastically altered, and mostly transmitted in black and white. Relentlessly up-beat variety shows (with their *ke'ai*, 'loveable', performers), now featured a series of renditions of a dirge: 'Beloved Mr. Ching-kuo' (*jingai de Jing-guo xiansheng*). The scenario in one television drama went as follows:

A woman cleans her home, while anxiously awaiting her husband's overdue return. The telephone rings, and she is told to turn on the television in order to learn some important news. She then watches Vice-President Lee (who later became president) announcing Chiang's death; she begins to cry. Eventually her husband arrives, assisted by a daughter. He is in poor health, and has obviously had difficulty making it home. His wife quickly turns off the television to spare him the news, and they try to make him comfortable, giving him medicine. The daughter reaches over to turn on the television, but her mother asks her not to. Eventually, the mother prepares them for a shock, and the television is turned back on. Once again, Vice-president Lee is shown announcing the death of Chiang Ching-kuo, and the family begins to mourn.

At around the same time, students in Angang were taken to a 'public commemoration' (*gongji*) of Chiang at the local auditorium. Incense was offered in front of his photograph as the uniformed students bowed in unison (a reflection of nation-wide services). As others have noted, this form of commemoration (*jinian*), with its echo of ancestor worship, seems rather similar to the worship of Chinese deities.[8] People do very clearly connect the celestial bureaucracy with earthly government, explaining hierarchies of gods with reference to the relationship between president,

6 The Chiang Kai-shek Memorial, Taipei

120   *Angang*

vice-president, etc. Deities are (mostly) men and women who have done extraordinary things, and people also sometimes ascribe extraordinary powers to their earthly leaders. One boy in Angang told me (although his sister disagreed) that all three presidents of the Republic (i.e. Chiang, Chiang and Lee) had special powers. If they visited your store or business then you would be successful, and if they touched your newly born child, then he or she would be exceptionally clever (*congming*). In short, these national leaders were deity-like men.

Return now to the textbooks. In Chinese patrilineality, death is obviously problematic. But here the ideology of kinship becomes part of the rhetoric of the state. The problem of death is transformed into a responsibility to die (for the sake of the national family). The patrilineal leaders of the nation are worshipped as fathers with exceptional powers. At the same time, in the textbooks, families are often (although by no means always) portrayed as being fatherless. To put this more accurately, those texts which most directly deal with the relationship between the family and the state are mostly about families without fathers. It is as if the patrilineal ideal had been more or less transposed to the patrilineal nation. What appears to stand in a relationship to this nation, *in textbooks*, is a matrifocal family. In such families, mothers exert considerable emotional authority over their sons and daughters, in the context of a reciprocal relationship. And, in the textbook version, these mothers often tell their sons to 'go to war'.

(44) Daughters must be patriotic and filial
Most of the texts I have cited appear to be largely confined to 'mothers and sons'. But it would surely be wrong to read these roles literally; in some ways the images themselves, and their various readings, are remarkably fluid. In order to stress this point, I will conclude this survey of texts with the story of Hua Mu-lan,[9] which is an extraordinary, if in some ways predictable, transformation of the stories given above. Hua Mu-lan is a daughter, who is concerned about her ageing father:

Over a thousand years ago, there lived in the north of our country a girl named Hua Mu-lan. She was able, like a boy, to go hunting in the wilds, and she was able, like a girl, to sit quietly, knitting. One year, the borders were invaded by outsiders [*waizu*]. The imperial court, so as to have an army of resistance, sent out an order to all the men of the country, telling them to report at once to the military command. Hua Mu-lan's father received this order, and made preparations to go. Hua Mu-lan said to her father: 'When the country is in peril, everyone must help. But you are already old, and my brother is too young, I should be allowed to represent you in battle.' Her father said: 'You mustn't forget, you're a girl. How could you possibly join the army?' Hearing these words, Hua Mu-lan went to her room and put on men's clothing, and then returned to face her father. She said: 'Father, do you still think I look like a girl?' Her father, seeing Hua Mu-lan in men's clothing, brave and resolute, looking like a handsome youth, was truly happy. He knew that her heart was set, and he could only give his permission.

Having joined the army, in battle Hua Mu-lan was extremely courageous, and able to suffer hardship patiently. When her superiors gave her responsibilities, she carried them out completely. Her colleagues felt that she was an outstanding soldier, and no one knew that she was a girl.

Twelve years later, the war came to an end. The emperor summoned Hua Mu-lan, to praise her wartime bravery, asking if she would stay in the imperial court as an official. Hua Mu-lan said, 'For twelve years I've been away from home, the thing I most want to do is to return home to respectfully support [*fengyang*] my aged parents.' The emperor was moved by her filial heart [*xiaoxin*], and allowed her to go home. Hua Mu-lan returned home to be united [*tuanyuan*] with her parents. Then it was as before, she and her family passed trouble-free [*pingan*] and happy days together.

There are, of course, a number of rather unusual features to this story, including the ending in which a daughter returns home to respectfully *yang* her parents, rather than 'marrying out' and giving *yang* to her parents-in-law. Note however, one very traditional implication: that Mu-lan's *death*, if it had come, would have been relatively unproblematic for her family. She is willing to effectively substitute her life for those of her father and younger brother, and her patriotic commitment is therefore simultaneously a filial sacrifice, which serves to protect the cycle of *yang*.

7
Divining children

Textbook mothers not only give their sons permission to die or 'give up their body-persons' (*xianshen*) for the nation, they also inform them that to do so would be the finest expression of filial obedience. The quandary, however, is that a patriotic death, no matter how honourable, might also bring to an end the flow of blood, food and money within a family. This is not my interpretation, but rather a distinctive line of reasoning within the Nationalist tradition. The argument is that Chinese dedication to the family, because of its power, undermines the nation, as spelt out succinctly by Sun Yat-sen himself: 'for the nation there has never been an instance of the supreme spirit of sacrifice. The unity of the Chinese people has stopped short at the clan and has not extended to the nation' (n.d.:2). Even when school texts concerning patriotic sacrifice are not read literally (as stories of 'dying for the nation'), the problem of competing loyalties remains. For they draw attention to the connexion of children with what I have described as the patrilineal nation. That is, they make important an identification which contends with family loyalties, and which might undermine the cycle of commitment which parents seek to protect.

In this chapter and the next, I want to describe in greater detail some of the ways in which this protection is sought, especially through visits to spirit mediums, and through participation in rituals of various kinds. My point is not that these activities are somehow directed against what is taught to children in school, but rather that they make apparent different sets of identifications and loyalties. As will become clear, women (as mothers) are largely responsible for day-to-day religion, and for much of the private business of family protection. This is often conducted at the altars of *tang ki*, spirit mediums, and the symbolism of these mediums and their rituals may tell us more about the concerns of this book.[1] For mediums are conceptualised not only as 'children', but also as children who wound themselves and bleed, symbolically cutting the flow of patrilineal blood. They are thus (as are some Chinese gods) 'unfilial', a status which gives them certain powers, powers which are then used by mothers to defend children from diverse risks.

(45) Mothers mediate between families and gods
The preparation of food is described as if it were a natural and fundamental duty of mothers and wives in Angang (although men also sometimes cook, and it is not thought unusual for them to do so). As I have mentioned, the rhetoric of maternal responsibility often returns to food-related themes, and in the cycle of *yang* the feeding of children by their mothers is of undoubted importance. One woman told me that after her children began attending school, she considered looking for work outside of the home. Her husband, however, disapproved because it would be unacceptable (*buxing*) if he and the children came home in the evening and there was no food.

But the naturalistic association of women with food preparation is rather complex. Many writers on China have noted, for example, that women are often *not* able to cook when they first marry. The traditional justification for this is that it is a waste of time for parents to teach a daughter, who after all will eventually prepare food for others, how to cook. In Angang as well, daughters are usually not given specific instruction, although in some cases they do watch and perhaps help, learning in an informal way. They more often learn only when they marry and it suddenly becomes a responsibility. I met several recently married women who were unable, or barely able, to cook, and they referred in these cases to the traditional justification (that they had never been taught). I did know one family in which the daughter often prepared the family meals, but in general cooking is not something associated with being a daughter, it is associated with being a wife, and especially with being a mother.

In this context, women also usually prepare the food offerings which are given to the gods, ancestors, and other spirits. Although these offerings form a crucial part of worship, and are thus part of the process of ensuring protection for children (and others), the role of women in preparing them is not commented upon, and appears to be taken for granted. Even when women do not actually cook the food (some items are simply bought), they are almost always responsible for bringing the offering to the altar, setting it out, and taking it away. This is true for offerings to ancestors, and even to the highest gods. For example, during certain rituals in Angang, women bring food for the spirit soldiers of the gods, who are divided into five battalions. They place five bowls of cooked food, along with beer glasses and five pairs of chopsticks, on the altar. When the soldiers have indicated through divination that they have eaten enough, a priest often shouts out: 'A woman! A woman! Take the food away!', because this is a task which women are meant to perform. On the first day of the first lunar month, when special (and personalised) offerings are made to ancestors on the domestic altar, a woman may set out this very important presentation of food and clear it away without her husband (who, after all, is the descendant of these ancestors) even being in the house. A woman, as a daughter-in-law, thus feeds her husband's parents and her husband's ancestors, helping him to fulfil his obligations of *xiao* and *yang*, and also feeds the gods, helping bring security to his household.

Aside from food preparation, there are many other ways in which women have religious responsibilities. While men are more active in special, periodic worship, such as public festivals, women as mothers (and grandmothers)[2] are usually responsible for routine, everyday worship in temples and at domestic altars. One daughter explained to me that she need not worship the ancestors and gods daily, because her mother did so as the representative (*daibiao*) of the entire family. This daily worship by women helps to ensure that children, husbands, and the whole family are kept on good terms with ancestors and gods. Women also often take on routine responsibility for defending the family from bad influences in other small ways. For example, I once saw a man leaving his home in the evening, preparing to collect crabs along the beach. His wife shouted at him: why was he not wearing a charm, a *xianghuo*, to defend him from harm? While he waited in the courtyard, she ran into the family altar, grabbed a *xianghuo*, waved it three times over the incense pot, and brought it out for him to wear.

Sometimes these attempts at protection are made either without the knowledge of, or over the objections of, those who should benefit most from them. The protection itself, thought to come from the gods, is often mediated by *tang ki* (spirit mediums), and then remediated by mothers. For example, *tang ki*, when possessed by a god, are able to curse away evil spirits which might possess children. But a child would never go to a *tang ki* on his or her own initiative. On the contrary, such a step would almost always be taken by a mother or grandmother. In such cases the children are often literally *put* through the motions of worship by these women, either (as infants) being waved up and down in front of the god in the semblance of a bowing motion, or (as children) having their heads dunked down when they are in front of the altar. The important thing is for this respectful motion to happen, and mothers often ensure that it does.

Sons who attend medium sessions or festivals may at times do so grudgingly. On several occasions I saw teenage boys (returning to Angang from school during the holidays) being taken to altars by their mothers, and being told to bow down. They often seemed unhappy about this and especially objected to the more respectful forms of worship (kneeling and making multiple bows). But their mothers would *insist*. I never saw this happen with daughters, but it does with husbands. I attended one *tang ki* session which was held for a small baby, brought by the mother and father. The *tang ki* was possessed and began, as usual, to give a series of instructions, steps that should be taken to improve the health of the child. He told the father to kneel on the ground with incense, but the man objected. His wife intervened, telling him that he *must* do so. Rather angrily, he submitted, and the session continued. I saw a similar disagreement between a husband and wife attending a god's birthday celebration. They were told that everyone should kneel on the ground and bow a certain number of times in front of the deity. The husband objected, saying it was unnecessary, and abruptly left the home of the *tang ki* after a perfunctory nod at the god's image. His wife left with him, but soon returned on her own and anxiously burnt an unusually large offering of spirit money, to compensate for her husband's disrespectful attitude. Some local men disapprove entirely of *tang ki* practices, and their wives go in secret. I should note, however, that many husbands and sons are happy to participate in, and organise, both public and private religious activities. But I wanted to point out the existence of a rhetoric of disapproval, and to note that women often mediate between families (especially children) and the gods.

(46) Mothers are religious experts but are sometimes excluded from rituals
Aside from dealing with everyday religious matters, in some contexts in Angang women are thought of as religious experts. This is because sometimes only elderly women know how certain things are meant to be done. For example, the offerings which are made on domestic altars for Thi Kong during the lunar new year festivities are very complicated, and quite important. Many special kinds of foods, paper images of the gods, and fanciful painted screens, are carefully set out in an elaborate display which fills the entire altar. In Beicun, I saw this being supervised at several homes by an elderly woman who had done it many times over the years. Her decisions were accepted by everyone, and on this specific matter she was

considered more of an authority than the local priests. Sometimes during public rituals the opinions of such women on what should be done will be given more weight than those of male religious experts. Women also often act as the 'interpreters' for divination sessions; they attend often enough to learn to understand the sometimes idiosyncratic ways in which various gods speak.

But this apparent expertise which comes from participation has to be seen in context, because the role of women in Chinese popular religion is, in other ways, quite restricted. All Daoist priests are men, as are all but one of the spirit mediums in Angang. The more public a religious activity, the more likely it is to be male-dominated. For example, temple and festival committees are made up exclusively of men.[3] Sometimes women are excluded from even routine private worship. This exclusion is, in some cases, explained with reference to beliefs about menstrual blood. A group of young sisters explained to me that they personally do not worship very often, because their mother represents the family. But when she is menstruating, they will conduct the domestic worship in her place. Female spirit mediums also do not hold sessions when menstruating, nor are menstruating women meant to participate in rituals, where they might come into contact with images of the gods, thus defiling them.

One man (in his twenties) said he was shocked that women had even discussed this with me. He claimed to have never heard of such restrictions, and was fairly certain that his mother had always offered incense to the gods on virtually every day of the year. But he acknowledged the possibility, and related menstruation to other kinds of 'uncleanness', noting that restrictions on worship are not limited to women. He said that both men and women should use the left hand to offer incense, because the right hand is used to clean oneself after defaecation, and for washing the body (thus touching the genitals). It is the hand for holding a knife, and for killing plants and animals. Everyone must therefore be careful about their 'cleanliness' when they make offerings. But for women, who generally worship much more often than either children or men, the tension between mediation and cleanliness is an abiding concern.

(47) Textbook mothers do not visit *tang ki*

In the last chapter I suggested that the state seems, in some ways, to have taken over the ideals of patrilineality. What remains is sometimes represented as if it were a tension between a matrifocal family and a patrilineal nation, with the school promoting (through virtuous mothers) the option of patriotic sacrifice. If this is a credible account, then the 'opposing' practice, in Angang, would arguably be the promotion by spirit mediums (again through mothers) of the notion of bodily protection. That is, while the virtuous mothers of the school promote *xianshen* ('giving up the body-person'), the mediums and mothers of Angang promote *hushen* ('protecting the body-person'). This is why, in spite of spirit medium practices being conceptually very far removed from schooling, I believe they are relevant to a description of education in Angang (as are the notions about food and money which underlie the cycle of *yang*). Spirit medium practices are not only part of the ordinary knowledge of children in Angang, they also stand in an important relationship to the ideas which students bring back out of the schools.

However, one very important difference between ideas about transfers of food and money, and ideas about spirit mediums, should be stressed. The stories found in Taiwanese school textbooks (e.g., the story of a mother preparing *zongzi* while telling her children about the patriotic poet Qu Yuan) often describe the relationship between mothers and children in terms of feeding, financial obligations and so on. Food transactions, as I have noted, are not always immune to criticism, especially when they reach a certain level of extravagance. But the private level of feeding appears to be seen as relatively unassailable, and the virtue of frugality, as part of the cycle of *yang*, is specifically seen as conducive to national construction and prosperity. Traditional Chinese family reciprocity is seen to be good social welfare, and is openly praised in textbooks.

By contrast, stories are not found (and I suppose would *never* be found) in which mothers take their children to spirit medium altars. From the official viewpoint, *tang ki* (spirit mediums) seem to represent the extreme end of superstitious (as opposed to benign) popular religion, and they are subject to special criticism for exploiting the vulnerable and ill (cf. Weller 1987:155–8). This means that a spirit medium in Taiwan operates in a public atmosphere of official scepticism. There are many people in local communities, especially men, who are prepared also to criticise mediums, whose patrons are largely women. Mediumship is a profession of *knowledge*, and the women who go to *tang ki*, in the context of this prevailing scepticism, are interested in the ability of mediums to provide them with assistance and with the truth. Using a spirit medium, of course, is not necessarily a simple matter of believing what is said, any more than attendance at church is necessarily a matter of 'belief'. But people in Angang do seem to expect certain things from mediums, and across Taiwan there are fairly standard proofs of genuine mediumship.[4] In what follows I will focus on one aspect of this: the connexion between the power of *tang ki* and their conceptualisation as unfilial children.

(48) Children are protected by *tang ki*

One of the unusual things about Angang is that although its population is relatively small, there are quite a few *tang ki* living and working there. I counted ten in Beicun and the neighbouring village alone, although some of these are rarely possessed, whilst others are much more active. By contrast, many villages in Taiwan apparently have no mediums at all. The *tang ki* in Angang also seemingly manage their own careers more than those described elsewhere, i.e., they are not controlled by priests or interpreters. This may have something to do with the absence of 'official' Daoists in the community. The local unofficial priests, called *tou su*, 'Masters of the Way', work alongside but do not control the mediums. Also, the statements of *tang ki* in trance are mostly comprehensible, so interpreters only play a minor role in their affairs. If people are in doubt as to what has been said, the mediums often go back into trance in order to clarify any controversial points.

Most of the *tang ki* practice from their own homes, but they also periodically work in local temples or other public spaces, and in the homes of their clients. Here they are said to be possessed by one or more Buddhist or Daoist gods or 'bright spirits' (*shenming*). When possessed, the *tang ki* speak for these deities, and standers-by are able to request information, assistance and advice on a range of issues: personal health, family matters, financial problems, gambling, etc. Some form of payment is often made, although this usually comes in the form of a small contribution to the expenses of maintaining the altar in the medium's home, which in some cases operate as a kind of minor public temple. All of the *tang ki* in Angang had other sources of income, mostly from fishing, and mediumship is not thought of as a money-making activity. On the contrary, it is thought of as something that is incompatible with success in other spheres of life, and *tang ki* have little direct influence in the community outside of religious matters.

Some people in Angang almost never go to *tang ki* altars, whereas, at the other extreme, some people devotedly come to worship and observe sessions almost every day. Mediums are not the only way of communicating with deities. Many people prefer to simply drop divination blocks in public temples, hoping to receive clear answers from the gods. More serious problems will generally be taken to *tang ki*, however quite minor ones are

Divining children 129

7 An altar in the home of a spirit medium, bearing images of gods, and offerings of food and spirit money

sometimes taken as well. Some examples: a fisherman inexplicably hurts himself with his own equipment, and wants to find out why this happened and how it can be avoided; a couple are placing bets in a lottery, and they come for help in selecting numbers; a son is beginning his military service and his mother brings him to the *tang ki* in order to ask for divine protection. Most villagers only go when a specific problem arises (especially illness, and most especially the illness of a child), but they have more regular contact with *tang ki* through their participation in public rituals.

Several factors influence the choice of a particular *tang ki* when the need for a consultation arises. Perhaps the most important is having a connexion of kinship or close friendship with the medium, which implies a relationship of trust. This also proves economical, as mediums are less likely to charge relatives or friends for services. People are also influenced by the reputation of particular mediums for efficacy, and when they have a special problem they may go out of their way to seek out an especially well-known medium. This overlaps very closely with ideas held about the efficacy of the gods for whom the mediums speak, because people would not say that a *tang ki* was effective, and might even point out how ineffective a medium was in dealing with problems in his or her own life. In theory, the gods have power, and the *tang ki* merely speak for the gods.

(49) One of the most popular gods is a child

In order to give an idea of how *tang ki* operate, here I will describe a session which involved a child-like deity and which, unusually, also involved me. Not very long after my arrival in Angang, I attended two funerals; hearing the very loud mourning music wafting over the village, I went along and asked if I might watch. Both funerals were for people who had led long lives and left many descendants, so they were in fact rather celebratory. The two families seemed happy for me to attend, and before long they were encouraging me to *participate* in the proceedings: offering incense and spirit money to the departed, joining in the entertaining rituals and performances of the Daoist priests, eating meals along with the family, etc.

It was only after the second funeral that I learnt from some villagers that there might be a problem; by attending the funerals (which I had, of course, known to be inauspicious occasions) I had put myself at risk from bad influences. Most people rarely attend non-family funerals, and they carefully close the doors of their homes and shops when coffins are carried through the village to the graveyard (this will be discussed in chapter 8). I began to worry that my curiosity, my desire to learn about Chinese funerals, had led me to be insensitive to the concerns of villagers about spiritual purity and the contamination surrounding death.

One evening, soon after the second funeral, a woman took me to a private home in an alleyway off the main street of one of the villages. This home was different from the others I had so far seen. A large red oven was placed outside in the courtyard. Spirit money could be burnt in this and transmitted to the gods, and inside the home there was an unusually large altar, on which were found a number of statues of various gods. The altar was also crowded with a variety of implements: incense pots, ancestral tablets, flags, flowers, candles, food and a row of sinister looking weapons. The walls and ceiling of the room were blackened with incense smoke. My friend offered incense, first to Thi Kong, and then to the gods on the altar, and instructed me to do the same, and she also set out offerings of fruit. We sat down and talked with another woman in the room, and several other villagers came along and offered incense.

Several moments later, two fishermen came in, joking noisily. They had apparently been drinking, and one of them slumped down in a chair as the various conversations continued. This man then closed his eyes and, a few moments later, his hands began to twitch. His entire body then started to shake, and he suddenly jumped out of the chair and ran up to face the altar, slamming his forehead onto it about six times in rapid succession, making a series of loud crashing noises. After this, he raised his head, still facing the altar, holding onto it with his hands, and began to talk in a child-like high-pitched squeak. The other people in the room stood and approached the altar to hear what was said. I later learnt that he was speaking for San Taizi (the 'Third Prince'), a very popular Chinese deity. This god is usually portrayed as an acrobatic youth; and people sometimes say that he is only three years old. On altars, his image is usually placed near to the incense pot, which he is said to guard, and away from the stern-looking elder gods. The *tang ki* continued to speak, in San Taizi's halting baby-talk, and another fisherman stood to the right of the altar and put questions to him, acting as a kind of assistant. But what the *tang ki* said was mostly comprehensible to the bystanders, and, when it was not, everyone (women, children and men) joined in with their opinion of what had been said. When they had got it right, and had understood, the *tang ki* would bring his forehead crashing down onto the altar with a single resounding thud of approval.

On this occasion it transpired that the main purpose of the session was to enquire about the health of a small child. As is very common, one woman whose children lived at other locations in Taiwan had come to the *tang ki* to find out about their fortunes. The baby girl of one of her daughters was seriously ill, and she asked about this child's situation. Although these questions were quite serious, the atmosphere of most of the session was light-hearted, and there was much laughter. Several topics had been covered when attention unexpectedly turned to me. I could not follow what was being said, and a young girl explained it to me. The child-god San Taizi had evidently noted my arrival in Angang, knew that I was interested in learning about Chinese traditions, and had observed my attendance at a funeral. He knew that I had attended because I was a person with a good heart, but he wanted me to appreciate that funerals could be dangerous. Since I had not known better, he would, this time, protect me from danger, and cleanse me. But I should not attend funerals again. San Taizi furthermore noted that I was writing about what I saw, and said that I must write about it carefully, giving it much thought, because it would be important, and would influence my future. I must write the truth, but I also must be willing to open my heart and mind.

During the session, children were playing outside on the streets of the village, setting off fireworks. Each time a firework exploded outside, the *tang ki* would become very agitated. I was told that San Taizi loved to play with children, and when he heard the fireworks he wanted to end the grown-up discussions and run off to play. At one point, during a loud string of explosions, and in the middle of a sentence, the medium went into a convulsion, and again brought his head crashing onto the altar in a rapid series of thuds. He then appeared to 'come out of it', looking around in surprise, and grimacing in pain as if he had a very serious headache. He was helped into a chair, and people began to tell him what the god had said through him.

After this session, I stopped attending funerals, and this was not the only time people in Angang set out for me the limits of research. I did attend many *tang ki* sessions, although not at that particular altar, and the subject never returned to me in such a direct way. But the pattern at other altars, and at other sessions, is often similar. First, although different *tang ki* have different ways of harming themselves, there is undoubtedly an important connexion between violence and their profession. Second, although different sessions focus on different problems, it is very common for the health and prospects of children to be the main object of divination. And, third, although *tang ki* suggest many solutions for problems, it is common for this to involve some form of 'disciplining' or avoidance: for example, people are told to eat or avoid certain foods and they accept to not move around in specific locations at specific times, just as I agreed to stop going to funerals.

(50) Children 'would be' exemplary mediums

I now want to focus more specifically on the connexions between ideas about spirit mediums and ideas about children. Some of these seem quite clear, whereas others are more speculative, but here I am simply trying to suggest a possible relationship. I will also partly draw on material from outside of Angang, in order to strike a balance between the way in which *tang ki* are generally represented, and the specific personalities and histories of the *tang ki* in Angang.

First, and most obviously, the name. *Ki* means 'to divine', and the expression *tang ki* means, roughly, 'child of divination'. Elliott translates the term as 'divining youth' (1990:147), while Berthier translates the Mandarin equivalent, *jitong* as *enfant de divination* (1987:86). The (Mandarin) term *tong* is sometimes used for boys, but also for children in general (e.g., in *tongnian*, 'childhood'). However, note that the symbolism of mediumship (especially self-mutilation) is potentially 'more meaningful' if the *tong* is assumed to be a son.[5]

In spite of the name, most 'divining children' in Taiwan, and all of them in Angang, are adults, and only exceptionally (e.g. when possessed by a child-deity) do they conduct themselves in an obviously child-like way. Some of the *tang ki* in Taiwan are children, but this is something which provokes condemnation, both official and popular. I have seen it referred to in newspapers as a form of 'child abuse', the suggestion being that child diviners are exploited by adults who encourage them to go into trance and to harm themselves in order to profit from the spectacle. This condemnation in itself is of interest: adults who would allow and even encourage children to be harmed are held in contempt. The practice, however, is not particularly widespread, and the *tang ki* in Angang are adults, mostly with children of their own.

But it is arguably true that children are not only good candidates for mediumship, they are the exemplary candidates. Elliott concluded, in his work with mediums in Singapore, that although anyone of any age could be a *tang ki*, 'youths of under twenty are the most suitable candidates' (1990:46). This leads us to ask whether or not the adults who become 'divining children' might be said to have any connexion with 'childhood'. Most spirit mediums say that they have had an experience which should have resulted in death, e.g., an illness which should have killed them, had they not been saved by the god whom they now serve (cf. Jordan 1985:71–2). There is a sense in which they are therefore living on borrowed time. They were not meant to survive but were allowed to do so, for a special purpose, namely being a medium for communication with the gods. Acceptance of this role allows them to live, but not to live a normal life. Aside from the obvious disruption brought by occasional divine possession, their bodies in particular are subject to supernatural control, for which they suffer. 'Divining children' are thus usually adults who should, in theory, have died young, and who are not expected to live long.

On a more abstract level, *tang ki* share with children certain spiritual and astrological attributes. As Berthier describes it, mediums are people who, like children at birth, lack particular destinies; this makes them especially well-suited to 'correct' (*gai*) the destinies of others (Berthier 1987, 1988:168–80). Also, like those of children, the souls of *tang ki* are thought especially vulnerable to harm. I described in chapter 1 the apparent vulnerability of children to bad influences. This begins before birth, when their volatile souls move about the house, and continues into childhood with their susceptibility to soul-loss, and to 'suffering the frights'. Spirit mediumship also involves a kind of soul-loss. The god who enters the body of the *tang ki* is said to replace the *yang* part of the medium's soul, which wanders around, while the *yin* part is said to be at some risk. This is one of the reasons given for the physical problems of *tang ki* (cf. Elliott 1990:47).

Tang ki are also thought in general more likely than most adults to be aware of contact with the spirit world, an attribute they share with children. They are quite susceptible to seeing, bumping into, and being bumped into by spirits. Such spirits are everywhere, but not everyone sees them, nor can they establish contact with them. In the *kng put*, or 'god-carrying', ritual, which I will describe in chapter 8, adults in pairs of two carry sedan chairs which hold images of the gods. During the ritual the god is said to come (*lai*) into the image, causing the holders to flail about violently and dangerously. On these occasions, many villagers become non-speaking mediums for the gods, but again, this is said to be more likely to happen to some people than to others. The explanation given for this is that people who are able to establish contact have 'light terrestrial stems and branches' (*qing bazi*).[6] This is an astrological calculation, related to the time of birth. *Tang ki*, who make such contacts professionally, are invariably very good at 'god-carrying'; if an image is properly functioning they will be able to get the god to descend into it. Again, Elliott reports that in Singapore having light *bazi* is considered a good qualification for spirit mediumship, adding that: 'such people are expected to lead blameless but unhappy lives, and to die young. They are chosen by the [god] because they can at least be of value to society by lending their bodies for this purpose' (1990:46).

(51) *Tang ki* are sometimes 'childlike'

Aside from name, vulnerability of the soul, and susceptibility to contact with spiritual forces, *tang ki* have certain other traits which might be comparable to those of children. These, however, involve personal attributes,[7] and my comments here are speculative. On the question of the status of *tang ki*, Elliott's ethnography sends an interesting and perhaps confusing signal. At one point he comments that a medium 'must be an honest man of upright character' (1990:47), and that spirit mediumship 'carries considerable prestige' (1990:59). But he also says of *tang ki* that 'their profession is not very highly esteemed. Reputable monks and priests will have nothing to do with them' (1990:44). This kind of apparent contradiction may not, in fact, be far off the mark in terms of popular views of mediumship. In Angang, *tang ki* are, similarly, thought of as 'honest' and yet slightly disreputable. I will try to relate this to similarly ambivalent views of children.

In Angang, children are sometimes said to be very good and honest judges of character; they are able to 'read' strangers and outsiders, and know intuitively how to make judgements about them. For example, I was told by one medium that his granddaughter's acceptance of me had led him to conclude that I must be a good person. This ability is seen to be natural and spontaneous, and *tang ki*, divining children, are thought to have a similar ability (when possessed) to see the truth. Certainly, the ethnography concerning *tang ki* emphasises their talent for judging social situations. Of course, devotees do not say they are seeking the spontaneous wisdom of *tang ki*; what they seek is information (and protection) from the gods. But the *tang ki*'s childish honesty is thought to decrease the possibility that this information will be tampered with. There is a definite sense in which a *lack* of knowledge is an important qualification for a *tang ki*, and this is one reason that children would be ideal mediums. (Note also that mentally disabled persons are sometimes used in divination, e.g. to select numbers for lotteries, because their responses are thought spontaneous.)

The abilities of *tang ki* (as opposed to their techniques) are not seen to be a matter of training. They are, both ideally and almost always in practice, not of a very high educational level. In this sense they are relatively unlearned, like children, but perhaps possessed of similarly intuitive knowledge. One of the most common proofs of genuine mediumship is that illiterate *tang ki* are able to write when possessed (or that *tang ki* with a basic education are suddenly able to write in 'classical Chinese'). The important point (from the perspective of devotees) is, of course, that this ability is not the medium's own, it is from the gods. When mediums come out of trance, they do not claim to know what has happened. On the contrary they look confused and ask bystanders to explain to them what has happened, what knowledge they have transmitted.

Let me give an example. One afternoon, a mother brought her child, who was seriously ill, to the most popular *tang ki* in Beicun. In trance he recommended a number of ritual and practical remedies, and he instructed that an unusually large 'body-person protection charm' (*hushen fu*) should be written for the child. This was to be made in the form of a rather large flag which would be folded up and carried with the body of the child for a specified period of time. The *tang ki*, still possessed, told a priest what to write on the charm, a military-style command which included the term *hushen*, 'protect the body-person'. The medium came out of trance, and watched the charm being made. The man who was to paint the characters on the flag said he was uncertain about *hu*, unable to remember the proper strokes. There followed a general, inconclusive, discussion about the way to write this character, during which the *tang ki*, unpossessed, said that he certainly did not know. A few moments later, however, he was re-possessed, strode dramatically to the altar, and showed the man, using his finger in the incense ash on the altar-top, the way in which *hu* should be written. Later, the son of this *tang ki* told me that while he was disinclined to believe in his father's possessions, he found this ability to write 'ancient' characters (*gudai de zi*) very difficult to explain.[8]

Spirit mediums, like children, are also thought by their devotees (although certainly not by their critics) to be honest and incorruptible in the sense that they cannot use their privileged access to the gods for self-benefit. This attribute is crucial in establishing their credibility. One *tang ki*'s wife told me that her husband's work as a medium had never resulted in any benefits for their family, it was instead a burden. She had many health problems, which he had never succeeded in resolving, indeed she was feeling worse than ever. Furthermore, they were poor, and she felt that this was specifically the intention of the gods for whom her husband spoke. Because they were poor, people would believe.

To sum up (and again this is speculative) *tang ki* are good in some of the ways in which children are good: intuitive judges of character, knowledgeable without education, and incorruptible. But spirit mediums also may be thought of as somewhat bad in a specifically childish way. One of the most striking things about parent–child relationships in Angang was the extent to which they contradicted the passive obedience implied by *xiao*. As I have pointed out, parents seem to expect that children will, by nature, be bad, and that this is something they will, again by nature, grow out of. They speak with pride of their own children as being *tiaopi* (naughty or mischievous), explaining that a child who is *tiaopi* is more likely to become clever, *congming*, as an adult. Parents do not seem to want passively obedient children; instead they want children who are clever enough, and physically resilient enough, to withstand the difficulties of life. This kind of child will survive, and will be able to support them in old age. The child-god mentioned earlier, San Taizi, provides an apt illustration of the cultural ideal of the 'naughty' child who is also exceedingly clever. He is represented as a prankster, but he also has great powers. I'll return to this below, but the point here is to illustrate a particularly childish kind of badness.

Spirit mediums, in their private lives (not necessarily when possessed), also often have reputations as being somewhat naughty in a rather immature but loveable way; they are usually 'characters', but clever ones. At times this is tied specifically to drinking. One of the preceding generation of *tang ki* in Angang was described simultaneously as a man who saved many lives and as a man who drank enormous quantities of rice wine. His son, who as a youth was said to have walked around the streets of the village with a bottle of rice wine in his hand, had also become a *tang ki*. Now he, along with most of the new generation of mediums in Angang, does not drink at all, on the command of the gods.[9] But he is still seen as something of a prankster, an attribute shared by most of the *tang ki*. The mood around spirit medium altars in Angang is definitely one of good-natured, possibly 'childish', joking and teasing.

(52) *Tang ki* (and many important gods) are unfilial children

These are some of the ways in which conceptualisations of *tang ki* and of children *might* be said to have a connexion. But on first observation, and particularly at public rituals, undoubtedly the most striking thing about *tang ki* is not their 'childishness', but rather their violence. All major, and many minor, cases of possession will be accompanied by some violent display. The question of whether this is self-inflicted or god-inflicted is of course crucial. Bodies are convulsed, heads are brought crashing down onto altars, swords are used to cut foreheads and tongues, spiky clubs are driven into the upper back, the face and mouth are pierced with sharp needles, etc. In public rituals, although not always at private sessions, blood is drawn, and this blood is seen as particularly effective in dealing with spiritual problems. In his discussion of the charms used by mediums in Singapore, Elliott notes:

The important point is that before distribution to worshippers they are daubed with the [*tang ki*'s] blood. It is this, rather than the design, that gives them their efficacy, in conjunction with the assumption that directions for their use are received from the [god] himself through his [*tang ki*].[10]   (1990:57)

Of the self-lacerations which produce this blood, however, spirit mediums claim ignorance, because they are only violent when possessed. They claim to not feel pain from the wounds, and note the speed with which they heal.

These violent acts are directly linked to the credibility of *tang ki* in two very important ways. First, people say that someone who was *not* possessed would never, it seems obvious, harm themselves in such a way. One *tang ki* very often pointed out to me the weapons arrayed on the right side of his altar and said that he would usually not even dare to touch them. Only when possessed would he pick them up and use them against himself. Second, as I have been emphasising, and as Jordan notes in his comments on mediumship in Taiwan (1985:82–4), in the Confucian tradition it is highly immoral to allow one's body, which is the property of one's parents, to be harmed, or even to be put at risk of harm. In Angang I never heard this discussed with specific reference to *tang ki*. But the morality of self-protection is such a commonplace as to perhaps not require stating (it is 'ordinary knowledge'). In the case of mediums, only the intervention of the god is felt to permit the breaking of this moral code in such a direct and public way.

This is even more interesting when it is remembered that a large proportion of the work of *tang ki* relates to the protection of children. As noted, mediums help with a range of problems, and in much of this they are helping members of the community to understand and to negotiate what is seen as a kind of spiritual warfare. Much that goes on in the spirit world is explicitly represented as a dramatic and violent conflict between warring forces. But because *children* are seen as particularly vulnerable to contact with these forces, they are very often the main object of the protection which *tang ki* help to provide.[11] This form of protection may seem somewhat strange. Parents (especially mothers), in order to protect their children from spiritual and physical harm, seek the help of 'divining children', who, contrary to filial morality, wound themselves in the course of divination. *Tang ki* are 'childlike' in some ways. However, they are, at least in theory, very *unlike good children*, in that the violence which they commit against their own bodies is unfilial in the extreme.

This is significant because, as I have pointed out, what they profess to know is accepted as the truth partly because of their violence. It might even be suggested that their efficacy actually comes from their unfilial self-laceration. This may seem far-fetched, but if it were true it would certainly not be the only instance in which unfilial behaviour is connected to power in China. Certainly, some of the stories of the gods for whom the spirit mediums speak are suggestive of a relationship. For example, I mentioned the most explicitly childlike deity, San Taizi, the Third Prince. Chinese gods are deified humans, but human beings with extraordinary backgrounds, and San Taizi is no exception. According to Elliott, he: 'was a mighty figure whose birth was miraculous and who developed magical powers and great strength at an early age. He had many quarrels with his father and with the Dragon King's family. In order to save his family from disgrace, he committed suicide' (Elliott 1990:77). In short, he was the epitome of the unfilial son, and even his suicide (to save the family from disgrace) would be seen as disgraceful. San Taizi is in some ways an unusual god, partly because he is represented as a youth. He is also a fairly minor deity. Even people who go out of their way to have statues of him on their altars will point out that he is a 'small' god.

But many of the other gods who are represented in less obviously childlike images, and who are thought more important, are still gods in part 'because of' what happened to them in childhood or adolescence. Guan Di, the very popular god of war, 'had to flee from his home ... after he had broken out from a room in which he had been shut up as a punishment by his parents [and after he] had killed a magistrate who wished to make the daughter of an aged couple his concubine by force' (Elliott 1990:77). Guan Di, a disrespectful son, went on to become a warrior, and died a violent (thus unfilial) death. Perhaps the most popular Chinese deity is Kuan-im, the goddess of mercy. In Angang, as in most of Taiwan, a portrait of Kuan-im hangs over virtually every family altar. But, as Sangren points out, 'In Chinese myth [Kuan-im] is coterminous with Miao-shan, a princess whose father had her killed when she rejected his demand that she marry' (1987:150). Similarly, the enormously popular deity Ma Co is said to have been a young Fujianese woman 'who lived a virtuous and self-sacrificing life, but refused to marry, dying young and childless'; in some versions of her story she is, like San Taizi, a suicide (Feuchtwang 1992:82, also see Schipper 1982:58). These gods (San Taizi, Kuan-im, Guan Di, Ma Co) together account for a large proportion of the worship in Angang and in Taiwan, and yet they are, in some senses, representations of 'unfilial' children.

(53) Children are protected by 'unfilial' divining children
Divine unfilial children are in these cases powerful, as are *tang ki*, unfilial divining children. But I should return here to Ahern's argument that *mortal*

children are also represented as dangerous and powerful (1975:210). From the perspective of a patriline, children are partial outsiders whose loyalties are unformed. They are powerful (as are women) because they are critically needed in order to continue the flow of blood and food. But they are also dangerous because no one can guarantee that they will do what they are meant to do: they might, like San Taizi, be a family disgrace. *Tang ki*, to the extent that they are 'children', may be associated with this powerful ambivalence as well. Because they have, in a sense, given their lives over to a god, they are not fully able to do what they should be doing: giving their lives over to a family. Margery Wolf suggests that this is why someone with weak family ties in a community may be an inappropriate medium. If they only have weak connexions, then the sacrifice of these is meaningless (Wolf 1990: 427–8). (The shedding of their blood would lack resonance.)

This relates back to a more general symbolism. Ahern discusses the attributes of menstrual blood, which is thought to *become* the body of the powerful and dangerous child (Ahern 1975). Spirit mediums are particularly vulnerable to this substance, and pregnant women, in turn, are vulnerable to spirit medium activities, as Elliott describes:

> If the [*tang ki*] has cut himself as part of the performance, he may have great difficulty in stopping the flow of blood if [a menstruating] woman is near him. But a pregnant woman is more likely to damage herself and her unborn child than to cause any harm to the [*tang ki*]. She is thought to be an excellent target for the malice of evil spirits which are bound to be frequenting the outer fringe of the temple area during the [*tang ki*'s] performance. (Elliott 1990:48)

Pregnant and menstruating women are also sometimes blamed for the inability of a spirit medium to attract a god into his body. What I am suggesting is a connexion between the power which 'divining children' have, through unfilial blood-letting, and the power of women, which is associated with the production, through blood, of children.

(54) *Tang ki* influence children's movements

In describing my own attendance at a *tang ki* altar, I noted that I was disciplined by the procedure. I was told not to attend funerals, and although the atmosphere of the session was friendly and casual, this instruction was clearly intended seriously. *Tang ki* often instruct people in similar ways, telling them that they either must or must not make certain movements and do certain things. The special knowledge which *tang ki* provide often relates to a control of movement but, of course, even the seemingly physical disciplines which mediums impose on children and others are moral, and they arguably help to emphasise certain connexions and commitments (i.e., certain directions of loyalty are pointed out).

Divination sessions are not constructed as learning experiences for children, and sometimes the young are specifically kept away from *tang ki* altars. However, their symbolism, the representations they entail, are part of what children in Angang know before they arrive at the school, and part of the environment through which they continue to move. Many children in Angang are periodically taken to *tang ki* by their mothers, and they also overhear or simply walk through the middle of many sessions on their way around the community. They eat candy and food from medium altars, and see the rituals in which *tang ki* lacerate themselves. The displays of *tang ki* at public rituals are especially striking, and every child in Angang would have seen these, and presumably learnt something from them.

But what, exactly, would they learn? The fact that parents bother with rituals of protection perhaps implies the value they place on their descendants. But the rituals are conducted by divining children who are unfilial, cutting the flow of patrilineal blood, and the worship itself focuses on gods who represent, in some ways, the worst kinds of sons and daughters. Furthermore, supplication at *tang ki* altars is usually an activity of women, and it sometimes meets with the disapproval of men, and with official condemnation (as children know). Medium sessions are thus one of the settings in which children might see the seriousness and the stubbornness with which mothers take the protection of the cycle of *yang*.

Margery Wolf, in her discussions of Taiwanese women, has stressed the potential divisiveness of the (often emotional) relationship which Chinese mothers develop with their children, especially with their sons. This relationship, which helps to protect the interests of women, may be a threat to male-dominated families (patrilines), to which the sons should be loyal (M. Wolf 1972). Similarly, the control of mothers over their children may threaten loyalty to the patrilineal nation. If mothers protect their children *too much* (and spirit mediums are part of that process) then there may be a problem when it is time for these children to be given over to the state, when they should be told, even if only metaphorically, to go to war.

Children who are, or who will become, sceptical about the efficacy of 'divining children', will nevertheless go through the motions at a spirit medium altar on the insistence of their mothers. Perhaps, among other things, they acquire there a sense of their own vulnerability to the forces of fate, but also a sense of the vulnerability of their mothers to those same forces. In particular, they might learn the extent to which mothers apparently *rely* on children (this would make what they learn in school about mothers who rely on their sons seem fairly obvious). They might also recognise a rather idiosyncratic chain of protection: unfilial gods, unfilial diviners, anxious mothers, and vulnerable children.

(55) At the centre of 'the way' is a regression to childhood

Feuchtwang (1992) has noted two different ways in which cosmic power is conceptualised in China. In the official version of Confucian orthodoxy, power is harmonious. (As an example, Feuchtwang describes the ordered movements of the official calendar.) This 'harmony' is in marked contrast with the unofficial conceptualisation of power, exemplified by the war-like local gods of popular religion and the rituals held in their honour. In these, power is not seen to be harmonious, it is instead seen as the workings of a command hierarchy. Note, however, that both of these conceptualisations are, in a sense, male-dominated, just as official power in China and the public festivals of local cults are controlled by men.

Historically, spirit mediums have occupied unusual and ambivalent positions with reference to these different spheres. K.C. Chang argues that, in the past, Chinese shamans (very different from the *tang ki* described in this chapter) were closely linked to state power, 'a crucial part of every state court; in fact, scholars of ancient China agree that the king himself was actually head shaman' (1983:45). In contrast to this view of official shamans as crucial to the ancient state, Weller argues that spirit mediums in modern China have been, and still are, seen to be politically dangerous. They are subject to suppression, he argues, because they create 'a great *potential* for dissident interpretation' (1987:158). Certainly, for local communities such as Angang, mediums play an important part in the unorthodox 'command hierarchy' conceptualisation of power, taking key roles in war-like rituals and in the festivals of local gods.

And yet there are many other ways of seeing the role of *tang ki*. When possessed, they seem to acquire authority in a somewhat official, scholarly or Confucian way, self-importantly taking up a *maobi* (writing brush) to write charms in pseudo-classical Chinese. In other ways, they seem a wonderful embodiment of philosophical Daoism: they are unlearned, and yet in their emptiness they know a great deal. What they know, including the writing of characters, that fundamental discipline of scholarship in China, they know without having the discipline to learn it. Meanwhile, their everyday practice is relatively private and dominated by the concerns of women. In this way, and through the symbolism I have described, they are linked to what might be called the sphere of women and children in Chinese religious life,[12] which is arguably an alternative *both* to an official orthodoxy of 'harmony' and to the local orthodoxy of 'commands'.

To the extent that spirit mediums are represented as children, they embody both the danger and the power of their namesakes. They are children who have symbolically broken the patrilineal flow of blood, and their own flowing blood is powerful. In Angang, these 'unfilial children' are patronised mostly by women, and are part of a private religious sphere which might teach children loyalty to their mothers, possibly to a matrifocal ideal. It is easy to think of China as a place where men and old age are respected, and where filial obedience is the virtue on which all others are built. Everything seems to stress the authority and the wisdom associated with men and with age. But, as Schipper notes, even Laozi, the mythical founder of Daoism, whose name means 'old', is represented within Daoist practice as an 'old-infant' (*vieil enfant*), and also as a woman conceiving the 'old-infant' (1982:155–74).[13] And, as Berthier notes, the return to childish, even foetal, 'spontaneity', is a primary goal of Daoism: 'La notion de 'spontanéité' liée au Dao est fondamentale dans la religion chinoise. Caractéristique première du Dao, elle fait l'objet, pour ceux qui veulent l'obtenir d'une ascèse rigoureuse, sous la forme précisément d'une régression vers l'état foetal' (1988:179).

Tang ki are used by women to protect children. What I have said in this chapter would indicate that this relationship has a kind of priority, and I have even suggested that the well-protected matrifocal family is in opposition to the patrilineal nation. If the state suggests that the mother–child cycle of *yang* may honourably be broken, the mediums could be said to suggest that it should not. But, of course, there are potentially many levels of identification for children in Angang, levels *between* their mothers and the nation. One of these is the local community, and here again spirit mediums are an important part of local efforts to produce divine power. In chapter 8 I will turn to one local ritual in which this is said to happen, asking what sense we can make of this spiritual productivity, and of its relevance for children.

8

Dangerous rituals

Mothers in Angang request divine protection at the altars of *tang ki*, 'child diviners'. This activity, well known to children, and something in which they routinely participate, is part of the ongoing relationship between mother and child, one way of defending the cycle of *yang*, and perhaps a way of underlining its importance. As part of a potentially matrifocal sphere within popular religion, it might thus be seen, by extension, as opposed to other spheres of commitment in a child's life. At school, children are exhorted to 'give up their body-persons' for the nation, whilst in the village mothers are helped by *tang ki* to 'protect the body-persons' of these same children. But this formulation is misleading, based on a narrow understanding of how people in Angang conceive of religious protection, and on a restricted view of the range of identifications which children make. For in Angang to be protected by the gods *is* to make sacrifices, including physical sacrifices, and to be protected *is* to express identification with a community beyond the family.

In order to understand this, one must return to the question of divine power. As noted, this is sometimes seen to be produced by forms of collective worship. Deities, in turn, are explicit reflections of the various communities in which they reside. Accumulated incense, the residue of the ritual efforts of these communities, is of great potency. It is redistributed to symbolise the relationships between temples and homes in a region, and dispersed in charms which protect individuals. Gods have strength, but without *human* productive effort, they may diminish in power and literally end up on the scrap heap. Many writers have noted this promotional (and demotional) principle in Chinese popular religion (especially Sangren 1987).

Tang ki are central to the ritual productivity of Angang. Even on the occasions when they seem relatively minor players in major public festivals, they help to establish the efficacy and residency of specific gods in the community.[1] Their involvement in the sphere of mother–child religion must be seen in this overall context. The gods for whom they speak do not simply exist, waiting to be approached by mediums and their clients; rather their existence *requires* ongoing communal productivity. *Tang ki* are part of this process of producing strong gods through dramatic public rituals. These are staged throughout the year, and are an important part of communal life in Angang, something well known to every child.

Identifications are produced, in part, by the practices which make them recognisable. For example, I have suggested that school-children in Angang both enact and learn their filial obligations through a series of family-based transactions in food, money and care. These transactions form a learning environment. Anthropologists also often think of rituals as potentially productive in this way: increasing awareness of, and indeed creating, certain collectivities. But in the case of *tang ki* rituals, the complexity of such a process comes into focus. *Tang ki*, as defenders-of-the-children-of-mothers, draw attention to the emotional identification between mother and child, and to the fragility of the cycle of *yang*. Mediums as producers-of-the-power-of-local-gods draw attention to the identification between children and larger communities, and to the strength which these communities embody.

But, of course, the connexions possibly highlighted in rituals and elsewhere are numerous. This is true whether we focus on *tang ki* rituals, on representations of gods, or indeed on food. For example, a 'single god' such as Ma Co may be worshipped by an individual, or by a family (at a private domestic altar, or in a private *tang ki* session). Ma Co may also be asked to help an occupational group (fishermen), or a local community (e.g., in the competition between temples), and may also be associated with an entire region (Ma Co is often linked to Fujian, or to south China). The groups coalesced by the worship of this god may be very different indeed (although one person might identify with a series of them). A similar compartmentalisation is seen in food transactions. They allude to identifications from the exclusive (the strictly limited family meal at the end of the year), to the more inclusive (the quasi-brotherhood of banquets), to the highly encompassing ('being Chinese' by virtue of eating Chinese food).

Different practices relate to different levels of inclusion and exclusion. Sometimes the boundary they draw seems very distinct, at other times indistinct, and it is arguably in the *contrast* between them that identifications emerge. In other words, what is truly recognisable is the difference between the identifications evoked by different practices. In order to show what I mean by this, I will contrast here two very different kinds of rituals which children in Angang participate in and observe: funerals and the *kng put*. The former is resolutely exclusive, whilst the latter is resolutely inclusive. Funerals cut off, in a dramatic way, a family from the rest of the world. Children who participate are made to act out their connexion with the corpse, and with the family which must deal, in isolation, with this polluting object. The *kng put*, by contrast, brings the energetic community into a family home, and children witness this group of people (the connexions between them) producing divine efficacy. This power then protects them from fire. Both rituals are very dramatic and dangerous: in funerals an exceptionally polluting thing (a corpse and potential ghost) is taken away from the home, whilst in the *kng put* an exceptionally clean thing (a 'bright spirit') is invited to enter the home, and does so with great violence.

(56) A child's family is 'cut off' by death pollution

The process of death, and of turning the dead into ancestors, is said to be very dangerous (*weixian*) for the living.[2] For this reason, a death cuts off a family from the rest of the community, or at least seems to. But in some ways this is misleading. Even those who are not obviously involved in a funeral participate precisely *by staying away*, and by taking special precautions. Children who have never yet been to one will know perfectly well to avoid them, and will be aware of the dangers involved; they will have been told by their parents to stay away, and will have talked amongst themselves about ghosts and other related matters.

It should also be stressed that in the process of 'buying funerals' (*mai zangli*) there is, as people often point out, a clear element of display (regardless of the lack of an immediate public audience for the rites themselves). It is a matter of prestige to buy expensive funerals for one's dead. And it is also true that many villagers (although not children) cautiously approach the survivors at some point, before, during or after the funeral, to leave money in white envelopes (indicating a sad occasion), thus helping to pay for this 'private–public' display. Some people even say that funerals are not dangerous at all, or that any spiritual threat they pose may easily be dealt with by a subsequent visit to a spirit medium. One man dismissed the concerns about death pollution by saying *haoren haoshi*: 'good things happen to good people', meaning that a good person had no reason to fear a funeral.

Still, almost everyone avoids them, and when I was advised not to attend, the advice was given in fairly strong terms. I was told that people would laugh at me for being stupid enough to go; only the 'crazy' (who are thought immune to most spiritual dangers) go along to help. It is thought very dangerous even to cross paths with a funeral procession, and one can become very ill from this. It is bad enough to simply look at the coffin, and as it is carried through the village, doors are closed. People prefer not to utter the name of the dead person, but the very worst thing is to have any contact with the coffin or the body.

Everyone in Angang knows when a funeral is taking place, partly because they will learn quickly of a death, but also because of the considerable noise associated with the ritual itself (cf. Johnson 1988). Very loud, and electronically amplified, mourning music precedes the event (often including a repetitive wailing of 'mother!' [*mama*] or 'father!' [*baba*]), and the rites are punctuated by cacophonous musical interludes. This is taken partly as a warning to stay away, as I was pointedly told (following my earlier participation in two funerals) by devotees of a spirit medium altar which I regularly visited. They were quite concerned that death pollution not find its way, through me, into their system of offerings, and I was told not to even walk past a neighbouring house where a funeral was taking place. Instead I needed to follow a safe, if circuitous, route. Some middle school teachers, hearing funeral music from inside the school compound, also told me that there was a taboo (*jihui*) against going, that it was 'bad for you' (*dui ni bu hao*). Usually only those who must go will attend (immediate relatives, local priests, and hired funeral specialists), but even for these necessary participants, the event is dangerous (*weixian*). This cutting off of the family from the community because of death is in marked contrast to other times. (Recall the daily flow of people through houses in Beicun.)

(57) A child's family are connected to their dead
Given these concerns, people sometimes have little to say on the subject of funerals, but one young man was (hesitantly) willing to talk with me about them. We discussed coffins, which he noted have the auspicious words *fu* (blessings) and *shou* (longevity) written on the ends. During our conversation, he wrote out the characters for 'coffin' (*guancai*), but then crossed them out, saying the term was inauspicious (*bujili*), as is the term for 'death' (*si*). He told me that 'If you say these words on the day of a friend's wedding, he might kill you!'[3] Someone who has gone to a funeral is not meant then to attend *xishi* ('happy events' such as the *manyue* celebrations for children, or weddings) for some time. He said that to go to such events would be to show disrespect for the dead, and could as well bring bad luck to brides and

infants. In 'ancient times' people would mourn for their dead for three years, and even build houses next to the grave in order to show respect. (He told me that now people no longer did so, because they were too busy.)

The doors of the village are closed when a funeral passes, he said, because a ghost (*gui*) is passing by. People do not wish to have contact with this thing which is unclean (*bu ganjing*); and he defined uncleanness as inauspiciousness (*bujili*). His view was that the danger does not, as some suggest, come from the outside evil influences hovering around funerals. The danger comes specifically from the soul (*linghun*) of the dead person, and the possibility it might change (*biancheng*) into a ghost (*gui*). If that person had disliked you, or if you had offended them (*maofan*), then they might come looking for you (*zhaoni*). Close relatives and friends may safely attend funerals, he said, because the dead person would wish them no harm.

The young man related the significance of funeral rites to notions about reincarnation (*lunhui*). When people die, their soul (*linghun*) lives on and becomes another person or animal; if they have been good the reincarnation will be good, and if they have been bad it will be bad. He said funerals are only intended to deal with the transitional period between incarnations, and are an attempt to help the soul to arrive in Heaven (*tiantang*) and to avoid Hell (*diyu*). There is a judgement (*shenpan*) to determine where it will go, and here the merit (*de*) and the good deeds (*shanshi*) of one's ancestors can provide protection (*baoyou*). This is a kind of blessing which they leave to their descendants.

A young woman described for me the purpose of a Buddhist funeral in similar terms. The body, minus the soul, is a corpse (*shiti*), and this is buried. But the soul must be helped to heaven by relatives and friends who chant over it. There is a period of time during which one should wait and not move the body because the soul (*linghun*) remains inside. Sometimes the soul of a dead person hears her relatives crying and the person then comes back to life. But this can be harmful to that soul and in the future it might not be able to make it to heaven. So if a relative has merit (*gongde*), it is better not to cry, and instead to chant and help her to heaven. If the dead person's face is red or goes red rather than white (helped by the chanting), then the spirit is going to heaven. No matter how bad the person has been, it is possible that the chanting will lift her soul to heaven. And no matter how good she has been (how much *gongde* she has), she may still go to hell if no one chants for her.

Some young children (elementary school students) explained the process of death to me as follows. First one's death is announced by special ghosts: *heibei wuchang* (literally 'black-white never-constant'). After this, the spirit goes to heaven or hell depending on whether one has been good or bad (*hao*, *huai*). This fate also may depend on the goodness of one's ancestors. At the funeral itself, a house and servants and money are all burnt so that these things may be used by the dead person in the afterlife. People either stay in heaven eternally or come back as a new person or animal. For most, heaven is a temporary stop, followed by another cycle of life. I asked the children who decides if you go to heaven and they said that a person decides for herself, by doing good or bad things.

Not everyone in Angang would agree with these accounts of death, funerals and the afterlife. (For example, far from encouraging people not to cry, most Daoist funerals involve orchestrated weeping.) But the accounts do highlight two central processes associated with death and funerals: first, that of helping the deceased to cope with what comes next, and, second, that of directing something of the dead person back in a way which can help the living. For example, everyone knows that at funerals the dead person is given money which they may subsequently use to bribe officials in the underworld, thus facilitating their passage. They also know that the placement of the coffin at the end of the funeral is of great concern to the living because good luck (or bad) may be transmitted through the bones of the deceased. In sum, the funeral highlights the exclusion of the family of the dead person from the rest of the community, at the same time as it highlights the inclusive reciprocity of immediate kinship.

(58) Children participate in dangerous rites for the family dead
Although in the past Angang (as a relatively isolated and unprosperous community) was said to have had rather distinctive funerary practices, burials are now conducted by outside professionals. I assume that the rites now performed are therefore similar to those conducted by professionals throughout rural Taiwan. But, as noted, I have few details about funerals in Angang because I was kept away from them by my friends. (By contrast, I was eagerly invited to attend *kng put* rituals on many occasions.) Bear in mind, however, that most villagers are also, almost by definition, not funerary experts, since they only attend them on a very few, unavoidable occasions. For all the elaborate preparations and expenditure involved, there were never more than about thirty relatives watching the two funerals I attended, about half of whom were children (the grandchildren of the deceased). What follows is a schematic outline of what they observe.

In a funeral, there are also clear indications of the positions of people *within* the family. This is done by means of activities (which are undertaken by some participants and not by others), and through clothing (cf. A. Wolf

1970). For example, grandchildren are made to wear white forehead bands with red and purple strips of cloth tied in a knot at the front. Their mothers wear white hoods with red cloth at the crown of the head. The most immediate relatives of the deceased (spouses, eldest sons) wear hoods or bands made of sackcloth. At one of the funerals I attended, a young couple (soon to be married) wore auspicious red: she a full red headpiece, and he a sash over one shoulder.

The main funeral ritual, in which the corpse is removed from the house and placed in the ground, takes up the better part of two days. The location shifts between the home of the deceased, a tent set up as a kind of temple near to the home, and the graveyard. During the funeral, the survivors are put through some unusually complicated procedures (by the standards of most other rituals and celebrations) as instructed by the professionals. They generally do not know what to do, and must be told. They also spend much of the time over the two days watching the funeral troupe (of several men) in a rather humorous musical performance which both describes and assists the progress of the dead person's soul in the underworld.

The proceedings are headed by a Daoist priest (a 'real' one wearing a robe and black cap), who, along with his colleagues, is paid to come from outside Angang. He tells the participants when to offer incense, what to say, and where to stand, and also recites an elaborate series of chants and documents. He and his colleagues perform many songs, which they accompany with drum, gong, reeds and guitar. In the midst of these performances and rites, the mood shifts between grief and jocularity. Crying is an important part of the proceedings. It builds to a high pitch at certain points, and then there is release (sometimes comical). The (local) men sometimes intervene when the crying of the women becomes too intense, perhaps hitting them on the top of the head. There are occasional arguments about protocol, and confusion about what is to happen. But between arguments there is joking and the sharing of betel nuts.

The eldest son is the chief mourner. But at times attention focuses on the grandchildren. For example, after dinner on the first evening of the funeral a story, in comic style, is performed for them, and they are specifically instructed to sit together on two large bamboo mats in the tent to watch. (During this story, at one of the funerals I attended, the children put their hands on their knees and collectively took a nap; no one woke them up.) After this performance, everyone participates in repeatedly walking in single file across a plank which is placed on the ground in the tent, with a pail of water to the right side, and a pail of candles to the left. The mourners cross a number of times, dropping money into the water, a re-enactment of the progress of the soul in the other world, crossing a bridge into re-birth. Each time the group completes a crossing, the priest has a comical exchange with one of the musicians. These provoke laughter, but the crossing itself is said to be dangerous (and I was told not to participate).

Later, but still on the first night (when it is quite dark), a large quantity of spirit money is piled up in an adjacent field; this is then set ablaze (to be transmitted to the newly deceased) as the family walk around it in a circle, hands joined. Then everyone returns to the village, where a large paper house (taller than a man) is on display. This elaborate object is made from thin pieces of wood covered in brightly painted paper. Everyone throws handfuls of spirit money at the house, which contains replicas of useful objects: a car, a television, a refrigerator, a stove, and a motorcycle, as well as human figures. The mourners then eat noodles (symbolising long-life) and the first day of the ritual is then complete.

On the second day of the funeral, more outsiders are involved. Some people come by the house (very briefly) to leave behind money in white envelopes. The men who are to carry the coffin also arrive early in the morning. They are fed before and after their chores, and given money in red envelopes. In Angang theirs is not a job most people would wish to have. Pall-bearers are often retired soldiers, and men who are in some ways not thought to be members of the community (i.e., they were not born in Angang, they do not have local relatives, and some are even Christians). They place the coffin on benches in the courtyard in front of the house, and bowls of rice are set out in a row on top of it. In front of the coffin, the large paper house is placed facing the street, fronted by a temporary altar. At this point, members of the family are instructed by the Daoist to bow, in pairs of two, in front of the altar. They are made to kneel out of respect, and then to crawl to opposite sides of the coffin, until everyone is arrayed around it. At this stage in the ritual, the weeping becomes quite extreme (and I saw one father pull his children away, because they seemed upset).

Then follows the procession to the graveyard through the momentarily deserted streets of the village. This is led by white commemorative banners (e.g., one from the head of the township government), and by a small band made up of students from the middle school, which plays songs such as 'Nearer my God to Thee' and 'Auld Lang Syne'.[4] The band is followed by the paper house, the funeral specialists, the pall-bearers, and the coffin. The eldest son of the deceased carries an incense pot. A red cloth is attached to the coffin, and the family hold onto this, trailing along behind the corpse

152 *Angang*

through the streets of the community. The whole procession is followed by a man carrying on his shoulder a pole which holds baskets of offerings: wine, pork, eggs, spirit money, and a live chicken.

At the graveyard (which is isolated from the village, and next to the ocean), the coffin is lowered into the ground, accompanied by the weeping of the mourners. (This is thought to be a very dangerous moment in the proceedings.) It is put in place very carefully by the Daoist, using a special compass, and under the watchful eye of the chief mourner. The family walk in a circle around the hole in the ground, dropping in handfuls of dirt. After this the pall-bearers move in with shovels to cover the grave, making a mound, and then a rough stone is placed in front of it, along with the incense pot and various offerings. The mourners give coins to the priest, who mixes them with gravel in a pail. This mixture is then redistributed and everyone throws it onto the grave (while retaining the coins), and then eats a boiled egg, throwing the broken shells onto the grave. The paper house is then placed in front of the burial mound. The mourners throw more spirit money into it, and then it is set ablaze, while everyone gathers around in a circle. The family then return to the home, offering incense at the domestic altar both to the gods and to the ancestors. A great quantity of spirit money is burnt, filling the house with smoke. The chief mourner steps into the courtyard with a bowl of water containing medicinal herbs. He tosses this onto the roof of the house. The funeral is over.

A family is isolated from the rest of the community during a funeral; they are actually seen to be dangerous because of their contact with death. This danger relates vividly to the many ideas about ghosts which are a constant feature of children's conversations in Angang, and which are an integral part of Chinese popular culture. The cutting off of the family from the rest of the community by death is in marked contrast to the necessary connexion *within* the family which is stressed by the funeral itself. The funeral underlines the impossibility, for the relatives, of avoiding the contamination of death (even if steps are taken to deal with this). The funeral also underlines the cycle of *yang*. This is clear in the extent to which dead people are shown to depend on the living to provide them with things (money, food), but also in the extent to which the dead are able to transmit good things to the living.

There is an additional feature of funerary practice, rather more abstract, which should be noted here: the way in which the soul of the dead person is fixed in place.[5] I have mentioned several ways in which children come to be 'attached' (e.g., having their souls called back into place, developing loyalties, being told not to roam about in a 'black-white' way, and so on).

After death there is also a very clear, and crucially important, process of 'attachment', because a wandering soul is thought to be a dangerous and polluting thing (as I have already described). This process happens in a variety of ways, and over a period of time extending well beyond the funeral. (And is complicated by the division of the soul into several aspects.) During funerals, the soul is cautiously fixed in the grave, in a flag which is burnt with the paper house, and in a tablet. The latter is eventually reincorporated into a permanent tablet on the domestic altar, the fixed position of the new ancestor.

(59) Gods are invited into children's homes

It would be hard to overstate the contrast between funerals and *kng put*, the rituals which are held in Angang for the gods who reside on family altars. In a funeral, a very unclean thing (a corpse) is disempowered (steps are taken to reduce its polluting capacity), and removed from the home in a process shunned by most of the community. In the *kng put* a very pure thing (a 'bright spirit') is given power, and triumphally brought into a home by a large cross-section of the community. But the two rituals do have similarities, including the forms of commemoration made to spirits, and the calling together of specific groups of people. To participate in a funeral is to be part of a particular web of family connexions. These connexions oblige one to assist the dead through the underworld, a risky procedure. To participate in a *kng put*, which also involves spiritual and physical risk, is to be part of a different web of family and community connexions, part of an association which produces the power of a god.

Here I will describe the *kng put* which is held in private homes (note that a similar ritual is held at public temples). As noted, most households in Angang consist of a married couple and their children, although there are also some stem families (which include the wife and children of one son), and others in which elderly parents periodically live as part of 'meal rotation'. The participants in any given *kng put* may be relatives of the host family, but they equally often are not. One man pointed out to me that usually friends were most helpful on such occasions, while relatives often failed to show up. He took this as further proof that relatives were 'of no use' (*meiyou yong*). It is significant that those who participate must not be limited to the host family (outside help is a requirement), nor are the outside helpers necessarily relatives. Nor, for that matter, are they necessarily co-villagers. People often arrive from neighbouring communities to assist, but one's next-door neighbour may stay away. As a guest, I was asked to help (*bangmang*) with various *kng put*, and given apologies for the trouble (*mafan*) this involved. The ritual thus marks out a community of people who will help, and often the hosts are as surprised as anyone at who turns out to be helpful on any particular occasion.

The ritual, very much a public event, is mounted in order to strengthen an image of a god which is to be used for private interests, and in order to show that this image is powerful. The logic behind this is, needless to say, a complex matter, involving as it does a god, an image, a community, and power. Gods do not equal their representations, and all of the most popular gods may already be worshipped in public temples in the vicinity, where other statues of them are found. But these same gods are also 'invited' (*chia*) into private homes, there to reside in privately owned statues on family altars, and to provide special blessings. In Beicun, about one-third of the households own one or more of these images. They are in some cases inherited, in which case they often come with stories of their supernatural powers. During the Japanese occupation of Taiwan (1895–1945), many such images were reportedly confiscated. People in Angang say that statues were collected, and unsuccessful attempts were made to destroy them. In some cases, villagers were able to recover the statues from the Japanese or to hide them in the hills. In many cases, however, they are newly purchased.

The decision to 'invite' a god in this way often comes through participation in activities at *tang ki* altars, because it is usually only a *tang ki* who is able to confirm the willingness of a god to reside in a particular home. Although most people say that housing an image is not a mark of devotion, *per se* (and too much devotion itself is not necessarily a good thing), it is still seen by some as indicative of a special relationship with a god. There are many gods, and innumerable devotees. In order to be noticed, and then blessed, it may be worthwhile to show in some way (e.g., through housing an image) that a god is especially revered. Few people would say that this works, but many are willing to try it. If they 'invite a god' (*chia sin*) into their home, they are hoping for the same things they hope for in all contacts with benevolent spirits, but they may hope in some way to receive special attention.

The statues, which line the shelves of religious goods stores throughout Taiwan, are purchased in the capital of the county (*xian*). They are carved from wood, brightly painted, covered in imperial-style robes, and decorated with crowns, medallions and weapons. Devotees are particularly interested in their facial expressions, which are held to change, showing the judgement of the gods on events which they witness. When a statue is purchased it is first dealt with ritually by Daoist priests. It must be made more than a piece of wood by having 'eye-opening' (*kai guang*) and 'god-entering' (*ru shen*) ceremonies performed. Once this has happened (in the city), the statue makes a triumphal entry to the village. The host family, along with friends, *tang ki*, and *tou su* (local priests) carry the statue through the village by hand, accompanied by the celebratory noise of firecrackers, drums, gongs and cymbals. The statue is then installed on the domestic altar.

Once an image is in place, it becomes part of routine domestic worship. Daily offerings of incense will be made, along with periodic offerings of spirit money and food. The family, along with the *tang ki* and *tou su*, will then begin to make arrangements for a *kng put* to be held, guided in their decisions by divination and consultation with the lunar calendar. A *kng put* is usually held for the first three years after the purchase of a new statue, but also when one is re-painted, and often simply as a way of honouring and re-invigorating a god represented in an older image. The ritual is thus very common in Angang, so much so that at one point a fisherman told me (only partly in jest) that he had not fished much lately, only helped with *kng put*. On average, the ritual will be held every few weeks.

The Hokkien expression *kng put* roughly means 'to carry the god'.[6] The term *put* is translated by some as Mandarin *fo*, 'buddha', whilst others translate it as Mandarin *shen*, 'deity'. Here it refers to any of the Buddhist or Daoist gods found on altars in Angang. The verb *kng* means 'to carry' (Mandarin *kang*), but more specifically for two or more people to carry something between them. In the ritual, the object carried is a small (about 16 inches tall) image of a god, which is strapped into a child-size chair suspended between two long bamboo poles. The overall structure of the ritual is fairly straightforward. First, throughout the morning and afternoon, people carry the god's image in a sedan chair. Second, at the end of the day, the god, newly strengthened, is said to protect the participants as they walk across fire. Finally, the image of the god, having been given power and proven to be strong, is reinstalled on the family altar.

People in Angang say that the *kng put* is unique to their community, but similar kinds of god-carrying and fire-crossing may be carried out for many reasons and in a variety of places (at temples, private homes, fishing harbours, etc.), and are common features of local religion in Taiwan. Gods are very regularly taken on 'tours of inspection' (*youjing*) in their sedan chairs, and periodically carried over fire in order to be purified and strengthened. For instance, Wang Shih-ch'ing reports that annual fire-walkings are held in Shu-Lin in order 'to *make* the god lively and efficacious' (1974:76, my emphasis). In other words, divine efficacy is seen as a product of such rituals. But the goal is also to attract gods to particular communities, temples, or homes, to 'invite' (*chia*) them to descend.

(60) Children usually do not carry the gods
Early in the morning on the day of the ritual, a sedan chair is brought unceremoniously to the home from the temple where it is kept in storage. Percussion instruments (drum, gong and cymbals) are also collected. Everything breakable must be removed from the home, along with most of the furniture, in order to make room for the chair-carrying and the spectators. The god's statue is removed from the family altar and placed in the courtyard on a table along with its incense holder and other ritual implements, facing away from the house. Well before dawn, the *tou su* and the family stand before this table and make offerings of incense to Thi Kong (Heaven). Once this has been done, they go back inside, waiting for the moment which has been revealed by divination as the proper moment to begin.

At around eight o'clock, there is a flurry of activity in which the host family are assisted by arriving friends and neighbours. The table is removed from the courtyard, and the statue taken back to the altar, where its crown, robe, weapons and medallions are removed. The sedan chair is placed on two stools, with the seat facing the altar, and the image is tied into it with red cloth. As noted, the chair is child-size and wooden, and is slung between two long bamboo poles. It is painted red, with auspicious dragon and fish designs carved into the arms. Although the chair itself is small, the entire contraption is large, heavy and clumsy.[7] Charms (*fu*) in the form of 'imperial decrees' (*fengchi*) are attached to the chair in five positions: on the two shoulders, at the end of the arms, and at the back. These are written out in black ink on small slips of yellow paper by the *tou su*, and they carry messages cursing away evil spirits (e.g., 'Exorcise Sea-demons!' [*zhou shuisha*], 'Please Cleanse and Protect!' [*qing jing han*]), inviting the god to descend, and also invoking the names of the god's soldiers.

The *tou su* wave burning spirit money around the chair, the statue and the room, purifying the ritual space. They then place their implements on the right side of the altar (facing it): a copper bell, a horn and a whip. Next to these are placed two rice bowls. One contains water, in which a charm has been burnt, and a twig of medicinal hibiscus (*furong*). The second bowl contains a mixture of rice and salt (*miyan*), over which a charm has also been burnt. A large piece of red paper is posted on the right wall of the house on which the contributions made by participants will be written. This may be headed in various ways, for example: *Guan Yin Fei Zu*, 'Guan Yin Donor's Group', or *San Taizi Tuhuo Lejuan*, 'Cheerful Contributors to the Ground-fires of The Third Prince.'

When everything is in place, two people lift the sedan chair onto their shoulders, one standing in front, the other in back. The bamboo poles are attached unevenly, and are held in a peculiar fashion: only one pole is placed on the shoulder, while the second swings dangerously free, so that the chair hangs side-ways during the carrying. The typical motion is a swinging back and forth of the chair as if it were being wound up. At the beginning of the carrying, several strings of fire-crackers are set off in the courtyard, and sometimes even inside the house. A few villagers begin a rhythmic pounding of drums and crashing of cymbals which, in the small room, is ear-shattering. This continues through the day, during all of the chair-carrying and fire-crossing, stopping only during rest periods and when the *tang ki* is speaking. The noise is said to frighten away evil spirits, but also to celebrate the deity, broadcasting his or her greatness. The *tou su* stand to the right of the altar and use a whip handle to beat out a rhythm, as they chant an invitation. Occasionally they stop to ring the bell and blow the horn. At other times, they move next to the swaying chair, facing the statue while chanting above the noise, waving burning spirit money over the chair and the carriers.

The drumming and chanting continues as the carriers gently sway back and forth, waiting. In most cases, within several minutes the chair begins to oscillate quite violently, accompanied by an intensification of the surrounding noise. This builds until the carriers are no longer able to hold onto the chair, and it flips over, crashing to the ground or into the walls (sometimes knocking over bystanders on the way). This turning upside down of the chair (and the statue) is the goal, an indication that the god has come (*lai*) into the image. Bystanders often point to the ground during violent moments of the carrying, shouting *tou! tou!* ('Down, down!'). The carriers are not possessed in the manner of *tang ki*, i.e. they do not speak for the god, but they do behave as if they are stunned by contact with a powerful force, and afterwards they claim ignorance of what has happened. When they pick themselves up from the ground, they seem surprised to find themselves there. The first carrying of the chair is held to be especially dangerous, since an evil spirit might come into it, and the first carriers are thus given a small amount of money as compensation for this risk. But all of the chair-holding involves some risk, and is genuinely hard work. The whole event is very athletic, and participants end up with aches and pains, including sore midsections (from twisting back and forth) as well as more serious injuries to the neck and the back of the head, which are repeatedly struck by the flailing bamboo pole. People sometimes say the ritual is held because the god wants exercise (*yundong*), and when there are breaks in the chair-carrying they say it is because the god wants to rest (*xiuxi*). When the chair crashes to the ground, and people bump their heads, onlookers usually laugh. (Compare this with the wounding of spirit mediums, which I have described as 'unfilial', but which is legitimate because it comes from the gods.)

Throughout the day the sedan chair is carried by a succession of two-person teams. Anyone who wishes to do so may carry it, with the exception of those who are 'unclean' (*bu ganjing*) primarily by virtue of menstruation, or recent attendance at a funeral. What is apparently exceptional in the case of Angang is that women are allowed to carry the gods. In the literature this is usually described as a task for men (e.g., Jordan refers to it as 'men's work' (1985:64)); these men are sometimes characterised as soldiers for the god. But in Angang, women carry the chair, as do children. However, women, children and the elderly, generally participate less often (in the carrying itself) than do middle-aged men. People commented that children might be hurt by it (especially because they are good at contacting spirits). In part, those encouraged to carry the most are those adults (men or women) who appear to be most successful in getting the god to descend. Some people try and fail. This is not held to be a matter of faith or virtue, but is instead related to the 'lightness' (*qing*) of one's *bazi* (as noted earlier, an astrological calculation). If the holder's *bazi* are 'light', the god is more likely to descend into the chair. Some people say it is a matter of the cooperation (*hezuo*) of the *bazi* of the two carriers.

Participants in the ritual, regardless of whether or not they hold the chair, are expected to do several things. Upon arrival at the house, they give the host a small contribution (usually about NT$300) for expenses. (The primary expenses are the provision of meals, and payments to the *tang ki* of about NT$1600 and to the *tou su* of about NT$1200.) The donor's name is then written on the red piece of paper on the wall, along with the amount given. The guests also bring incense and spirit money for the god, which they offer individually. In this way, everyone is able to participate and to receive blessings. Some also help with food preparation; two large meals are eaten, and there is a considerable amount of washing, chopping and cooking to be done. Others help by playing the percussion instruments; this must continue through the day, and the chore is shared among the villagers, often among the children and older people who do not carry the chair. As the ritual progresses, a steady stream of visitors arrives at the home, ready to participate in some way. Meanwhile, teams of two continue to carry the chair. When the god arrives, every few minutes, the chair flails about, occasionally flipping over, sending bystanders and carriers and the statue crashing to the floor. People say that the chair does this, and that they become tired from holding it, because the god is heavy (*zhong*). From time to time the *tang ki* are possessed, and people crowd around to hear them speak. Often they simply give instructions to the *tou su*. At other times, villagers are told of affairs in the spirit world (e.g., about arguments between gods) or in the village (e.g., what could be done about an illness).

In mid-morning, the chair-carrying stops so that the *diaoying*, the 'mobilisation of troops', may be carried out. In this part of the ritual, the god's spiritual soldiers are called into five battalions (East, West, South, North and Centre). The soldiers are not physically represented, but their presence is marked in the house by five stacks of spirit money and incense placed on the floor in front of the altar and by a red can which is placed on the altar itself. One of the *tang ki* or *tou su* will call the troops into position, blowing the horn, ringing the bell, and placing the incense at each of the five positions to the accompaniment of drumming. When this is completed, the money is burnt (so that it is transferred to the soldiers), filling the house with a cloud of smoke. This mobilisation is to ensure the protection of the god during the ritual, as well as to protect the house and the participants. When payment is made to the soldiers, it is also made to their horses. Just outside the door a small stack of grass is left for them, along with spirit money, incense and a pail of water.

When the troops have been mobilised, the god-carrying continues for the rest of the morning until, at around noon, it unceremoniously stops. Not everyone who comes to the ritual will stay for the meal which follows. Usually the experts, along with the men who do most of the carrying, will eat at the house. The meal itself is held at several round banquet tables and consists of relatively special foods, but it is not as boisterous as many other banquets, and little alcohol is consumed. People are encouraged to eat, but not usually pressurised in the 'polite' manner. As they finish eating, they leave the table, often returning home for a nap, or they relax in the house or courtyard, visiting with friends and sharing betel nuts.

(61) Children should 'cross the fire'

At around two or three in the afternoon, the *kng put* resumes. Someone may have to be sent through the village to enlist enough helpers to play the instruments and carry the chair. Once the noise begins, however, people return to the house, and by mid-afternoon there are usually more participants watching than in the morning. At some point, the chair will suddenly be thrust backwards out of the house and into the courtyard. After this, most of the carrying will take place outside where it is possible for many more people to watch. It is also possible for the carrying to be more acrobatic, and people come to see the violent seizures of the carriers. During the afternoon, the priests also begin making preparations for the fire-crossing (*guohuo*), assisted by other villagers. There are two major variations in the fire-crossing. In the first, and simpler, case, seven pots of coal or spirit money will be arranged in the courtyard for villagers to step over. In the more complicated and dangerous version, one large fire of wood and coal is built at some distance from the house, either in a disused field or on the beach.

In both cases, late in the afternoon the *tang ki* is possessed and organises the participants into a procession. Although it might be thought that walking on fire would be a dramatic, if not chaotic event, it is in some ways carefully ordered. The procession is led by the *tang ki*, followed by the sedan chair and its carriers. The chair is usually also accompanied by the *tou su*, who continue to chant at the image, cracking the whip, ringing the bell, and blowing the horn. *Tang ki* will usually wound themselves at this stage in the ritual, cutting their foreheads or tongues with a sword or hitting their backs with a spiky club. Sometimes there are several *tang ki*, possessed by their respective gods. Visitors may bring their own household gods as guests, and these are carried by their owners near to the sedan chair. Behind them, the remaining villagers take off their shoes and form a line. In the case where seven small fires have been placed in pots in the courtyard, the villagers simply step over the pots. As three passes are made through the seven fires, the line of participants winds back upon itself. After the third pass, the villagers step over another fire at the entrance of the home, and then return inside. I was told that this was 'walking through the seven star-fires with the god',[8] the star-fires representing the 'seven stars of the big dipper', *beidou qixing*.

The more complicated option, employing one large fire, is thought more dangerous. A pile of wood, coal and spirit money is placed in the middle of a nearby plot of land, or on the beach. This is set ablaze well before it is walked through so that by the time of the crossing it has become a pile of burning coals. The fire is surrounded by four markers which are constructed by the *tou su* out of bamboo and red paper, and on which are written the names of important local deities. The bamboo poles are sometimes dotted with blood from the spirit mediums. Next to these are pails of water and hibiscus in which protective charms are burnt; this water is subsequently splashed on the feet of participants to insure against wounds. Again, the *tang ki* organises a procession, which goes from the house to the fire. The medium then strides through the coals followed by the bare-footed villagers. Infants are carried by adults (or their siblings), but children are encouraged to cross on their own, and are told that the fire cannot burn. I asked the children, why should you walk through it? They said: 'we don't know'. But they did say that shoes should be taken off before crossing, and that it cannot burn. People also say that only those with a *reason* to fear ghosts would be at risk in this activity. One woman said you should look at yourself (*kan ziji*), because if you are not clean (*qingjie*), then you may be hurt.

Note that these fires are specifically a collective product: an accumulation of wood, coal or spirit money brought to the ritual by individual participants (as instructed beforehand). So, as with practices involving accumulated incense, fire (*huo*) is central to the effectiveness of the ritual, *and* it is a product of collective efforts. People are cleansed by passing through this fire, as are the gods. But gods themselves are already thought 'bright' (*ming*), and clean. That is why people who are unclean (e.g., after a funeral) are meant to stay away from them. Villagers are cleansed of bad influences by participating in the *kng put*, but those who are not already relatively clean should not join in. One woman in Angang became very upset when she learned that she had missed a fire-crossing at the home of her next-door neighbour. She was helping to prepare the food, and had somehow missed it. She went to a spirit medium to ask how such a thing could happen. The god said that she was not meant to go through the seven fires, it would not have been good for her, and so she had been kept from learning of it.

Once the fire-crossing is complete, the procession returns to the house, crossing over a stack of burning spirit money at the threshold. The *tang ki* stands in front of the altar and delivers a final message from the god. After this, many villagers go home. The image is then removed from the chair, put back into robes, and placed in position on the altar. A generative fire, the residue of the ritual, is placed under the altar and the god. Attention then returns to the god's soldiers, who must be paid for the work they have done, and who must be called back in. Five bowls of food, and one of rice, along with five sets of chopsticks and five beer glasses, are placed on the altar for the battalions. The *tou su* offers this to the soldiers, speaking to them in comradely fashion, while filling their glasses. After a suitable interval of a few minutes, the *tou su* asks if the soldiers have had enough to eat. He then drops divination blocks to obtain a reply: yes, no or laughter. Eventually, perhaps after a pause for more eating, the yes response arrives, and the

162   *Angang*

money and incense placed in front of the altar is burnt to the noise of drumming, filling the house again with heat, smoke and noise. As this progresses, fewer and fewer people are about. The pans of ash are cleared away, the bowls of food are removed from the altar, and the house is restored to normality. The *tou su* handles the final ritual detail, often unobserved in the darkened courtyard of the house. He burns the stack of incense money which has been left for the soldier's horses, and tosses their grass into a nearby deershed. He then takes the horses' pail of water, chanting as he splashes it around the door of the house, telling the horses to go away as he throws the water onto the courtyard. Tables are then set up and the evening meal is held.

(62) Children are protected by a communal ritual; the ritual produces an aspect of a god

In most cases, villagers outside of the host family will not again worship in front of the image they have honoured in the *kng put* (or will do so only exceptionally). But they still anticipate that the god may help them in some way, and it is specifically the fire-crossing part of the ritual which generates the widest participation. In particular, those who are thought to be at greatest risk from harm are encouraged to not miss this opportunity to receive divine help. Parents send their children to cross the fire, infants are carried across the coals, and I have also seen spirit mediums lead the sick and the elderly by the hand through the flames. This activity is what makes participation worthwhile. The ritual is held to have been a success if fire-crossing reveals that the god is powerful, but this is a production as much as a revelation. For as one man noted, without a *kng put* the power of the god fades away, until there is nothing left. If villagers walk across the fire without injury, then it is clear that the owners of the statue possess an object with a use. But this usefulness in protecting from fire is clearly linked to the violent chair-carrying which precedes it.

Discussion of a *kng put* usually lasts for several days, often focusing on the degree of participation, and the relative 'bustle' of the event. Much is also made of the aches and pains related to the violent chair-carrying, and to the *absence* of injury from the fire-crossing. One woman (a mother of four) smiled as she proudly showed me bruises on her arms and legs, which she said came from wrestling against one of her neighbours (a man) while holding the chair. A young woman (aged about twenty) told me that while she was carrying the chair (very violently) she had no feeling (*meiyou ganjue*). But then afterwards she felt quite sore. Another woman told me her stomach muscles hurt from all the twisting; this was caused by pushing against her son, who was pushing the chair in another direction. She also commented that she particularly enjoyed the occasions when a *kng put* was held for San Taizi, and he was carried in his very small sedan chair: this threw her about quite violently, and she was hurt by it. But her wounds were healed when another god instructed her to eat candy from his altar.

It is as if people give of themselves physically in order to be physically protected. But, more to the point, this contribution is made collectively, just as two people at a time carry the chair (and their astrological *cooperation* helps attract the god into the chair in the first place). Usually this work of protection is undertaken by those who are strong, and the benefit is aimed at those who are weak (including children and the elderly). It is equally important that *many* people should attend, in spite of the private nature of the event (and this is one of the things that is good about Angang, that people will help). This suggests that while there are private images, there are no private gods, for the strength of the gods is connected to the activities of groups of people.

But what, more precisely, produces divine power? Obviously, the ritual is very 'physical'. In Chinese popular religion, seemingly 'physical' worship (so-called ritualism) is often combined with monetary sacrifice. That is, people bow in front of the gods, but they also spend money in providing gods with things (spirit money, food) and entertainments (operas). Although they themselves often invest in religious activities, people in Angang are ambivalent about this, and critical of those who try to buy favours from the gods. In the case of the *kng put*, people in Angang, who are not in a position to compete with wealthier Taiwanese in attracting the attention of gods through expenditure, make use of a ritual which relies primarily on human effort.

But the fact of labour-intensive rituals raises more general questions about physical obligations and productivity. One of the reasons protection is a focus of ritual concern, as I have stressed, is that children are seen to represent the future of families in very practical terms. They must be biologically, economically and ritually productive if their parents are to have a peaceful old age and after-life. Doing anything to bring one's body-person (*shen*) into risk is unfilial. Of course, children are usually protected by adults in the *kng put*; i.e. the adults usually carry the chair, the children simply walk through the fire and are not said to be at risk: the fire 'cannot burn'. But remember that the adults in the dangerous ritual are also sons and daughters, even if their parents are dead. However, to the extent that these adult-children are at risk, the dangers are felt justified by the protection which the ritual as a whole brings. There is a shift from danger to safe-keeping, and an implicit recognition that for the sake of protection in general, some individual concerns about filial obligations must be overlooked. (Recall the exhortation of the school, that children should 'give up their body-persons' [*xianshen*] for the nation, overlooking family-based anxieties.) This means, as well, that the *kng put* implies the necessity of broader identifications, of moving beyond the confines of the family, and into membership of a wider community which works for collective benefit.

Note, however, that the work put into the ritual is not so much a production as a *re*-production of a symbol which already exists. By the time anyone in Angang thinks of holding a *kng put*, the gods exist through the ritual productivity of the entire historical community of their devotees. What the ritual does call together is a segment of this historical community. Another way of saying this is that the ritual produces an 'aspect' of a god, one which is relevant to the context in which the image is owned and used. Gods are powerful in context, and a household's own statue of a god, through the ritual, embodies the productivity of the community on whom the family can depend. But this community (as a series of recognised connexions) is only momentarily pulled together, and then disbands.

Compare this with the difficulty of specifying, once and for all, the essence of a particular deity. A Chinese god (*shenming*) such as Ma Co may be described in a number of ways (cf. Feuchtwang 1992:180–98). For example, there are stories, and versions of them, which most believers (although not all) relate if asked 'who is Ma Co?' They might begin by saying 'Ma Co was a young woman from Fujian ...', and continue from there. There are also paintings and drawings of this god. These are standardised enough that people recognise certain of them as being 'of Ma Co'. There are also statues which are meant to represent the deity. These are found in temples and private homes, and people offer incense in front of them, saying that they are 'worshipping Ma Co'. These statues are not the god, and yet some are thought more powerful than others, and people go out of their way (even make very long pilgrimages) to worship in front of them. Some of the statues do not look the same, because, again, there are strikingly different portrayals of Ma Co (and of other gods). Is there one Ma Co? Yes, in the sense that we might say there is one of any god, no matter how many different stories, representations, or even 'misrepresentations' are found of her. And it would have to be acknowledged as well that there are many perspectives on these various representations. As seen through their stories and images, Chinese gods are both singular and metamorphic.

But recall that these volatile deities do not simply exist, they are produced. People in Angang describe the *kng put* ritual as something done for a god, to 'make him/her able to be effective' (*ho i e-lieng*). This could also be described as 'producing a god', although the god (as story, as image) already exists, or as 'producing divine power'. But also, in the context of this book, with its emphasis on learning, we might say that what is being produced is a particular way of *seeing* the god. The rituals underline an 'aspect' of the deity. But because every deity is seen as the product of sets of social relationships, the rituals also underline an 'aspect' of the participants themselves, namely the shifting world of identifications in which they live.

9

Conclusion

In the late afternoon, people in Beicun often sit along the sea-wall which was built to protect their community from typhoons. Elderly men and women sometimes gather there, facing the calm water, their fingers and lips stained red with betel-nut juice. From the sea-wall they look across the Pacific, watching fishing boats pull in and out of the harbour to the south of the village. Below them, on the coral reef, children splash in small pools of water, playing with bits of seaweed, or gathering rocks and shells. Sometimes the children take up sticks in order to engage in a kind of dramatic warfare on the beach. A woman appears on the sea-wall, surveying the scene below her, and calls her children to dinner: *ciaq png*!

As evening sets in, the breeze from the ocean becomes cooler. Looking back at Beicun from the sea-wall, the narrow rows of grey houses begin to merge with the steep hill behind them. The roof of the Ma Co temple, with its auspicious dragons curling up towards the sky, is the most colourful thing in sight, but this is also soon lost in shadow. Then the sounds of evening begin to filter through: villagers laugh as they share food and wine; a woman sings a Taiwanese folk-song through a scratchy-sounding amplifier; a melodramatic opera booms out from a television; a *tou su* pounds on an altar as he chants an invitation to a god; a motor-scooter arrives with a roar from the next village. A child, talking with friends on the sea-wall, would hear these sounds, and, obviously, any number of things might go through her head at such a moment: a history lesson, a grandmotherly scolding, the sound of waves, and so on. And, of course, even when talking to this child it is difficult to imagine what she thinks, and how she thinks it, while sitting there. In this book, as I said at the outset, I have only tried to outline some of the ways in which her attention might be drawn as she goes about her life in Angang.

This, in itself, is an unusual thing for an anthropologist of China to attempt, it is unfamiliar ground. However, anyone who knows the literature might well have observed a shift in the text towards increasingly familiar territory. At the end of chapter 8, I discussed adult-centred Chinese popular religion in a way which may seem to have had increasingly little to do with children, and almost nothing whatever to do with education. However, I hope to have shown the relevance of familiar themes from the anthropology of China to questions about childhood and learning, and also the relevance of questions about childhood and learning to those more familiar themes. Recall that everyone in Angang remains, in certain senses, a child for life, and notions of childhood are therefore relevant to them all. By extension, the actions of adults (e.g., in the protective rituals of local religion) must be seen in the context of their on-going childhood, and of their concerns for their own descendants. What these descendants learn in school is also set against a background of life in a community, including symbolic and practical transactions of many kinds. In order to understand school-based morality, we must see how it is made to appear commonsensical, as something known before it is taught. And in order to investigate the practical impact of education, we must understand school-based competition, something partly driven by the cycle of *yang*.

An intricate learning environment
Children in Angang learn against a background of representations related to childhood. These include very general Chinese notions about persons and the life-cycle which sometimes appear to be somewhat contradictory, or at least to lead in different directions. For example, the souls of children are said to be vulnerable, easily frightened away. As children come to appreciate, much of the religious activity of their parents is directed towards protecting them from this and other kinds of harm. What is most obviously celebrated during childhood is survival, and the reasons for this seem compelling. And yet, in spite of the apparent vulnerability of children, certain representations suggest that they also possess a kind of dangerous power. They are as likely to be 'toughened up' as protected. Other, 'Confucian', representations meanwhile emphasise quite different things: the link between studying and being a child, and between learning and being a person.

What children in Angang learn is, of course, also influenced by the nature of the community in which they live. This is a place where people are closely interconnected, both in the sense of having many local relatives and friends, and in the sense of living at close quarters. In both senses, this connectedness is seen to protect children and other residents from the dangers of physical, social and spiritual isolation. Against this background, children in Angang begin to observe and participate in schooling, in religion, and in the everyday life of the community. This is an ongoing process of encountering images, concepts and practices. In the school, for instance, they read texts of motherhood, and of virtuous mothers and their sons. What they learn about women in school is, in many ways, commonsensical, 'ordinary knowledge'. And yet the mothers represented in textbooks teach their children more, and protect them less, than do women in Angang. The virtuous mothers of textbooks encourage their children to dedicate themselves to the nation, to move beyond the family. Meanwhile, in the community, family loyalty is underlined time and again through transactions in money, food and care. The cycle of *yang* is enacted through the earliest celebrations of survival, the lunar new year gifts of red-enveloped cash, everyday family meals, the consumption of expensive medicinal foods, private visits to *tang ki* altars, public rituals to ensure 'the absence of problems' (*pieng-an*) and so on. If the relationship of a child to her parents and to her family seems obvious by the time she arrives in school, this obviousness must be seen in light of these practices.

Learning, identification and 'roads'

Accounts of learning consistently come up against an apparent disjunction, as if there were two sides to the question. On the one hand, the social organisation (or non-organisation) of teaching or cultural transmission, i.e., the 'social' aspect of learning, gives rise to certain kinds of sociological questions. How are traditions reproduced over time? How are claims to knowledge validated? On the other hand, psychological questions about learning are also of obvious importance, even when they seem beyond the grasp of traditional anthropological methods. How do persons acquire and develop specific concepts and notions?

In practice, however, these 'two sides' of the question of learning are not very easily distinguished, and this is an issue which cognitive anthropology tries to address. I have suggested that one important point of intersection is found in the process of 'drawing attention to'. Ostensive behaviour is, as Sperber and Wilson (1986) argue, a central feature of human cognition, especially in the context of interpersonal communication. In other words, it stands between persons, as a feature of human relationships, *and* acts directly on the 'individual' production of mental representations. Here I have applied this notion to a whole range of 'widely distributed representations' (such as rituals). I began by noting the obvious: that children in

Angang, as they grow up, have their attention drawn by representations to various things. I further suggested that this ostensive feature of learning might have important implications for identity. A child is pointed in certain directions or, to use the Chinese idiom, 'roads', which lead to certain relationships, or to ways of living within relationships.

This process could be conceptualised in different, although closely interconnected, ways. First, a representation might draw attention to a particular existing relationship, i.e. lead to the identification *of* a connexion (noticing it). Second, a representation might *produce* a relationship, lead to an identification *with* someone or something (the development of an attachment). Third, a whole set of representations and representational practices, might be said to *be* the relationship. Because, for example, to do certain things is to be a child. But notice that these three interconnected ways of conceptualising the same process have very different analytical consequences. For the first is primarily about cognitive issues (what people notice), while the second relates to human emotions (of attachment). The third is arguably not about ostension at all: the significant thing is to do something, rather than to notice that you are doing it.

My fieldwork was not of the (experimental) sort which could properly address questions of cognition, and in the end my account is perhaps most relevant to the third of these perspectives. But here I will note several of the issues raised by my use of an ostensive model of learning and identification. Obviously, one of the most important of these is the extent to which various learning processes may be said to be conscious or unconscious. Does the model of 'drawing attention to' lose its sense if people are not conscious of what their attention is drawn to? (Remember that Bourdieu's model of habitus stresses unconscious learning.) For example, when a child attends a *tang ki* session, does she there explicitly become more conscious of her relationship to her mother? Many children in Angang certainly know the debt they owe to their parents, and this they talk about, but where and when did they become conscious of it? I have no direct evidence that this kind of explicit awareness comes from the practices I have described (e.g., direct statements that participation in a ritual, or reading a text, made someone *notice* an identification).

This kind of evidence would, I believe, be hard to come by, and the difficulty relates to a second issue: the repetition of similar representations, or of similar themes between representations. A child going to a *tang ki* altar, even for the first time, would already know a great deal about her relationship to her mother (it is experienced in many different ways). For this reason, what would be most striking or noticeable about a visit to a *tang ki* would probably be something else, e.g., the medium's self-laceration. (However, as I have suggested, this violence itself is highly instructional.) What also arguably happens in the context of repetition is an accumulative *re*-learning of various relationships, even if this is largely unconscious or latent. One point I made at the beginning of the book should be seen in this context. There I said that children seem to already know what they learn in school about morality, it is 'ordinary knowledge'. But to be taught what you already know is still to be taught something, because (as analyses of ritual and formal language often stress) repetition is not the same as non-repetition. In context, repetition might imply increased emphasis, increased naturalisation, increased obviousness: 'ordinary knowledge' might become more 'ordinary'. Also, as I hope to have shown, what children are taught in school is often *not* what they already know, because there are significant, if subtle, differences between the morality of the school and the morality of the community. In this sense, schooling is less repetitive than it perhaps seems.

A further issue which arises here is that of belief or the level of commitment to various representations. Many of my accounts have come from children. That is, they are based on what children told me they believe to be true, and what they act as if they believe to be true. But it is also rather easy to find in Angang people who are sceptical about many of the 'beliefs' I have outlined: those who do not believe in the effectiveness of *tang ki*, or the danger of funeral pollution, or the vulnerability of children's souls and so on. It should however be stressed that even someone (child or adult) who does not hold a particular belief must still process it in some way. As I noted in the introduction, cultural acquisition is not simply about absorbing whatever is there. But it is also surely impossible to *not* produce some version of what is out there to be learnt; even rejecting a belief involves paying attention to it.

The composition of identity

But now I must say again that I am only presenting a partial view of a complex process. For instance, I have stressed three levels of identification: the national, the familial and the local. It is certainly true that in Angang something approximating these levels is of significance to all children. And yet, the closer one looks, the less clear these objects of identification become, because they are also clusters of representations. What, for example, is the 'nation' in this case? The Republic of China as defined by the KMT and the school? The China construed from ancient cultural traditions? And what of the 'family' as an object of identification? Is it the family of mothers and their children, or of patrilines, or both? Is it made up of the relatives who are 'of no use' in *kng put* rituals? Identification with these relatives (many of whom are neighbours) overlaps with 'local' identity. And yet the local communities celebrated in popular religion often have very indistinct boundaries. What is the work of composing an identification around such ill-defined material?

And what is salient (for this is a related issue) in various practices and representations? For instance, it is one thing to say, from the outside, that the story of Hua Mu-lan (the daughter who goes to war in place of her father and younger brother) 'is about' filial obedience and patriotic sacrifice. But it is another thing to show the salience for a particular reader of this aspect of the story. Someone reading it might have her attention drawn to knitting, might literally be thinking of yarn rather than the nation. (The knitting of women, it should be said, is not at all irrelevant to the issues raised in this book.) But what is it that makes something seem salient or relevant to a particular person?[1]

Consider this question from the perspective of gender. Images of what it is to be a daughter, and what it is to be a son, are dramatically different, so much so that to conflate them under 'childhood' as I have done is arguably misleading. The activities and the life-courses of men and women in Angang are dramatically different. However, most children encounter quite similar representations as they grow up. This does not, of course, mean that they *notice* the same things about these representations, nor that they identify with them (e.g., with characters in stories) in the same way. Gender is only one of the more obvious factors influencing the development by children of their own singular representations of the world.

In short, 'drawing attention to' is an open-ended process. On the one hand are complex representations which have many readings. On the other hand are complex identifications which lead in many directions. I have presented a partial description of childhood in Angang, the going back and forth between different ways of learning, and have noted that in this process certain identifications are both highlighted and constructed. I would argue that this kind of description is worthwhile, but it obviously does not begin to capture the complexity of childhood experience in Angang. For instance, sensory experience would arguably be interwoven with identification and attachment, as an indistinguishable part of what it means to be a child in Angang. Here I end with several notes on one young girl. In the afternoon, she is given a taste of acrid betel nut as a joke. She makes a face, and runs into the courtyard, spitting it out. Her parents laugh, and from the corner her grandfather smiles sympathetically and says *o-peq*, 'black-white'. She pulls on the red string around her neck from which hangs a protective charm, and then runs to a neighbour's house. Here a 'happy event' is being celebrated, and she is told to help roll rice flour into balls. Half of these are red, half are white (later they will be placed in sugary water), and the flour sticks to her fingers. Women squat on the kitchen floor around her, laughing. In the front room, a television drones on. That night she walks through her grandfather's sitting room; he is a *tang ki*, and her eyes sting from the smoke of incense and spirit money burnt by devotees. She falls asleep in a side-room as he speaks for the gods.

PART 3
EPILOGUE

10

Notes on childhood in northeastern China

The preceding chapters have been based on my fieldwork in Angang, although some reference has also been made to research conducted by others in Taiwan, Singapore, Hong Kong and mainland China. Depending on one's perspective, attempts to compare material from these places in order to say something about 'China' may be fascinating, dangerously misleading, or both. Obviously, there are cultural continuities throughout mainland China, and beyond it, among people who identify themselves as Han Chinese. (There are, for that matter, some fascinating continuities with Japan and Korea.) But there are also profound differences: in economy, history, religion, language, food, ritual and so on. As one woman told me, it is 'one place, one way of doing things' (*yige difang, yige xiguan*). And because the notion of the fundamental unity of China has political implications, attempts to gloss over these differences are both misleading and naive.

In this epilogue I will briefly outline several notions related to childhood in farming communities in northeastern China (Dongbei). However, in doing this, and in showing some apparent similarities, it is not my intention to *stress* continuity. Given the circumstances of life in Angang and life in rural Dongbei, to do so would be absurd. My account of Angang centred on families, local religion and national education, three spheres which dominate the lives of children there. But in Dongbei the legal and moral status of families differs greatly from those of families in Angang, as does the accessibility and the content of formal education. And while in Angang religion is a highly visible part of everyday life, in Dongbei it is often a private, and sometimes secret, matter. In short, to be a child in these two places is to experience a different world. Continuities are found, for example in notions of family-based reciprocity, but Angang and Dongbei remain, in important ways, dramatically unalike.¹ To properly compare them would be to write a very different book. Here I selectively cite material which may help to illuminate notions discussed in previous chapters, and which may perhaps reinforce my argument. But this is not an attempt to describe childhood in Dongbei, much less 'Chinese childhood', and it should be read cautiously.

Most of the material comes from villages in the southern part of the three-province Dongbei region, where the residents are primarily farmers (*nongmin*) engaged in the cultivation of maize, or of fruit orchards. Collectivisation was taken to an extreme in this area, but now villagers have their own land, and farm for profit. With few exceptions, they have many immediate relatives in the vicinity, but the villages themselves are multi-surname communities. Because of the system of household registration (*hukou*), it is difficult to move away. There are elementary schools in these villages, which most children attend, but few are able to study beyond this level. They then work in the fields and orchards, or seek other employment nearby (e.g., as factory or construction workers), usually on the basis of family or work unit (*danwei*) connexions.

The farmhouses in the area are much more self-contained than the homes of fishermen in Angang. Outside gates mark off most compounds, and they are separated from each other by plots of land where grain, fruit and vegetables are grown. Winters in Dongbei are bitterly cold, and domestic social life often centres on the *kang*, the brick bed which is heated from a wood-burning kitchen stove. The inside walls of many homes are covered with old newspapers (usually the *People's Daily*) as additional insulation, and many walls also bear images of Chairman Mao, along with other Communist memorabilia. There are no temples nearby (only in the mountains and the cities), and families do not have domestic altars. However, many traditional festivals are celebrated. During the lunar new year, almost every home displays a paper representation of the 'god of wealth' (*caishen*), and most families make some form of offering to their ancestors.

(1) Children easily see the ancestors, and grab their own destinies

Several people in Dongbei told me that children should not be present during ancestor worship. One young woman said this is because their eyes are very powerful or sensitive (*lingmin*), and they are thus likely to see the ancestors eating the offerings. A child might then say something which could be heard by the ancestors. This would anger them, and might lead to trouble for the child. One woman told me that her three-year-old nephew had been present when offerings were made, and had started to say something about 'the people eating over there'; his mother quickly bundled him away. This ability to see spirits is not widespread among adults.

Children are also thought capable of 'divining' in other ways. On the celebrations marking their first birthdays they are placed on a *kang* (brick bed) and given objects, one of which they are meant to grab. The various items on the *kang*, e.g., books, scales, rocks, steamed rice-buns, etc., symbolise various destinies such as scholar, trader, labourer, and useless 'rice-pot'. The object they grab reveals their future. This is usually treated simply as an old tradition, and one which is funny to watch, rather than as an instance of serious divination. However, many people say it is 'accurate' (*biaozhun*), because the child 'does not understand things' (*bu dongshi*), and simply grabs.

(2) Children should be protected from harm
Many parents take steps to protect their children from physical and spiritual harm. Sometimes these are fairly simple. For example, if the weather is fine and clear on the seventh day of the lunar new year, it is said that children will have 'the absence of problems' (*pingan*), which one woman defined as 'not having illness' (*meiyou bing*). However, on this day children are also instructed to eat noodles (symbolising long-life and *shunli*, 'smooth going'), so that they will be protected regardless of the weather. (There are similar days at the beginning of the year for the elderly, for animals, etc.)

If a child has many illnesses, or is in some other way *buhao yang*, 'not easy to raise', then he or she may be given to foster parents. This is thought to increase their chances of survival, a turn in fortunes which relates to a change of name. For example, it is felt especially wise to foster a sickly child to someone surnamed Wang, because this surname sounds like the first character in *wangsheng*, which means 'full of life, vigorous'. Another auspicious surname for foster parents, one which also emphasises survival, is Liu, because this suggests that the child will 'be retained', *luixialai*.

Some of the steps taken to safeguard children involve spirits. For example, many young girls now wear red marks in the middle of their foreheads. I was told that this was in imitation of the goddess Guan Yin and that it was done to ensure 'heavenly protection' (*tianshang baohu*). Images of this goddess are increasingly found in private homes, and offerings are also now made (usually discretely) to many other deities. For example, in fishing communities along the coast, offerings are made to Haishen Niangniang (a sea goddess); these are made on the sixteenth day of the first lunar month specifically in order to protect children, to ensure that they have 'peace' and 'the absence of problems'.

Sickly children are also sometimes taken to spirit mediums, although this is apparently not very common. In this region female mediums are usually referred to as *wupo* ('old-woman sorcerer'), while male mediums are called *tiao dashenr de* ('spirit-dancer'). I was told that these experts are called on primarily to cure illnesses (*zhibing*), especially those which doctors cannot heal (*yisheng zhibuliao de bing*). I was told of the following case. A four-year-old boy was crying incessantly, and his grandmother felt this must be due to some evil (*fanxie*). She took him to a medium, who revealed that the child's difficulties were provoked by an unhappy ancestor. In order to protect the child from further harm, his mother was instructed to approach one-hundred homes, and to collect from each a piece of string. These were to be wound together into one large string, which was then placed around the neck of the child 'in order to cure his illness' (*weile zhibing*).

(3) A child's survival is celebrated

Various celebrations are held to mark the passage of time since a child's birth. In different communities and families these are held at different

8 A sister and brother in front of their grandparent's farmhouse

moments, but generally after twelve days, one month, one-hundred days and one year. For example, many families commemorate 'one-hundred days' (*baitianr*), which is said to symbolise long-life; the event is sometimes even called 'one-hundred years' (*baisui*). It was explained to me that on this day the infant truly becomes part of a family, because it is now felt unlikely to die. For *baitianr*, and 'one-year' celebrations, guests are invited (*qingke*), and banquets held. Visitors (friends, relatives and 'comrades' of the parents) bring money in red envelopes (*hongbao*) for the child. In some communities, the 'twelve-day' celebrations are specifically for the mother's side, while the 'full-month' is primarily for the father's side. For example, during the 'full-month' event the paternal grandparents 'hang a thread' (*guaxian*) with money around the child's neck. The thread represents long-life (*shou*), while the money represents prosperity (*facai*).

Several people observed that with increased prosperity, and with restrictive birth control policies, these events had become increasingly widespread and popular. Most couples in the countryside are restricted to one child (or two, if the first is a girl). With only one child, they said, the cause for celebration (and perhaps for anxiety about survival?) seemed clear. It is also very commonly said that the one-child policy has changed the way in which children are raised, and has lead to an increase in coddling. One young father said: 'the children around here are emperors' (*women zhebianr de haizi dang huangdi*). Of course these children are important, I was told, because when you are elderly 'society won't be bothered' about you (*shehui bu guan*). If you are sixty, and have no rice to eat (*meiyou fan chi*), and no children to *yang* you, then what would you do? To have children too late in life, when you were likely to die before they made a return, was said to be a waste of energy (*feijin*).

(4) Children are mischievous, and they are 'toughened up'

Parents routinely complain that their children are mischievous (*tiaopi*), or that they are 'not at all well-behaved' (*yidianr laoshi meiyou*). But children are often seemingly allowed or even encouraged to be this way, e.g. they are not scolded for being bad, and parents sometimes express the opinion that mischievousness is a good thing. Children who are *tiaopi* are thought more likely to eventually become clever (*congming*). One woman said that this connexion was scientific (*kexue*): rowdy children, she noted, have more brain activity.

It sometimes appears that parents and other adults are actually training children to be clever, resilient or tough. Even infants are subjected to fairly constant teasing. I sat with one grandmother on a number of occasions when she was playing with her daughter's son (he was about eleven months old). She would tease him, saying in convincing mock-anger: 'Go away, I don't want you!' The child would then *pretend* to cry, in a little whimper. Then grandmother and grandson would stop, and give each other a smile. She told me this shows that he 'understands things' (*dongshi*). On several other occasions, I saw a group of adult relatives playing with another boy, a two-year-old, on a *kang*. They would tease him, and dare him to hit some adult. His grandmother said to him: 'Do you dare to hit me?' (*ni gan da wo?*) The boy then lightly slapped her face, and she only smiled in reply. Later a neighbour told him to hit his own mother, which he did; she had no reaction. (Note that this teasing and playful hitting happens in a joking and friendly manner amongst close friends and relatives; a great deal of attention and physical affection is given to these same youngsters.)

Parents are clearly concerned about the health and survival of their children, but in some ways do not appear to coddle them. For example, very young children are allowed to set off fireworks, especially during the lunar new year festivities. I will give one example of this, which also relates to mischievousness and teasing. During the lunar new year, several children were running in and out of a house, entertaining themselves while their fathers sat inside at the banquet table. One of the children, an eight-year-old boy, was in a bad mood and was acting, by general agreement, very *tiaopi* (mischievous). He went so far as to kick out at an elderly man who was trying to humour him (and was not reprimanded for doing so). Then, without asking, he helped himself (in full view) to several firecrackers which were left over from the new year's eve display. He went outside to set these off, and one exploded in his hand. Screaming, he rushed back into the house.

Almost immediately the adults in attendance (including his mother) began to mock him, and to laugh. Several people did simultaneously look to see how badly he was hurt; his mother examined his hand, which was red and swollen, and undoubtedly painful. The men (outside of his hearing) said to themselves that there was 'no problem' (*meiyou shi*), i.e. that he was not seriously injured. But to the child they showed no sympathy, only ridicule. After some time the boy stopped crying. The men then treated him (still mocking, but not aggressively) as an adult. He was made to sit at the table with them (where they were still eating and drinking), something which children are usually not meant to do when guests are present. He was given beer to drink, and soon became tipsy. The men teased him, pulling out more fireworks for him to detonate, if he dared.

(5) Children receive red envelopes

As part of the lunar new year festivities, children are given *yasuiqian*, money in red envelopes, by parents and other adults. This follows a show of respect (usually a simple bow). The people I asked had no explanation for the term *yasuiqian* ('anchor-the-year money'), nor did they expand on the significance of the practice. One man did say that parents give *yasuiqian* to children in order to show that they love (*tong'ai*) them; whereas children give gifts to their parents, or bow in front of them, to show that they respect and honour (*zongjing*) them.

(6) A child's relationships are enacted with food

Respect for senior generations is meant to be shown in many ways, especially in public. Children almost always do not eat with their parents if guests are at hand. They eat later, often at tables to the side, or simply standing. This is because they would not dare (*bugan*) to presume equality by publicly sharing food with their elders. However, when I asked one

9 The *manzhousui* celebration for a boy. The item he grabs is said to represent his future career

young man if this was a sign of respect, he said it was simply the custom (*xiguan*). I asked him at what age he would be allowed to eat at the table with his father and he said, with a smile, that it would never happen.

The idea that food symbolises many things, and underlines many relationships, is a fundamental aspect of social life in Dongbei. To give only one example, on new year's eve dumplings (*jiaozi*) are privately shared by the family, and with the ancestors who have been greeted (*jie*) that night upon their annual return. The dumplings symbolise, in their circularity, reunion and completeness (*tuanyuan*). A coin is placed in one of these, and the person who finds this dumpling is thus predicted to 'have prosperity' for the coming year.

Similarly meaningful foods, and ways of sharing food, abound. I noted that in Angang when people want to eat or drink less at banquets they often say *yi-su* (Hokkien 'meaning'), and then take, for example, a small but 'meaningful' sip of rice wine. In Dongbei, when people are felt to be eating too little in public situations, they are sometimes told that it is 'not enough to show the meaning' (*bugou yisi*). Many of the polite words used with guests in formal eating situations are very similar to those used in Angang and, again, these are well known to children. In Dongbei a five-year-old girl shared her snack with me, saying I should 'not be polite' (*bu keqi*), that I should 'take it for myself' (*ziji na*), that I should 'eat an extra bite' (*zai chi yi kou*), etc.

(7) A child must 'listen to the elders'

Parents have considerable control over important decisions in the lives of children and young people, including those about education, marriage and careers. For example, I knew of one farming family in which the youngest son, aged about twenty, lived and worked with his parents, and planned to settle with them (it is traditional for the youngest son to do so). At one point he brought home a girlfriend for inspection as a potential wife. The young woman stayed in the village for two days, and sat in silent, red-faced embarrassment as her potential in-laws ate meals, visited with relatives and played *majiang*. When she left, the youngest son was teased mercilessly by his relatives about this 'wife' (*xifu*). They said she was not nearly as pretty (*piaoliang*) as the other women in the family, and that she didn't seem strong enough to work (*ganhuo*).

Only one uncle came to his defence, saying he thought it unnecessary to 'be so extremely choosy' (*tiao de name lihai!*). But without parental approval it was out of the question for the young man to marry. I asked his aunt whether his mother's or father's opinion was more important; she said it was all the same, but that he must 'listen to the elders' (*tinglao*). In this case, the fact that he was to live with his parents increased their influence. But it is also widely said that the great expense now associated with marriage makes the approval and support of parents all the more important, regardless of future living arrangements. I mentioned above that the survival of a couple's 'one child' is taken quite seriously, the implication being that parents rely more on this sole descendant. However, it is also said that children are now more dependent on their parents than were previous generations. This is because parents must underwrite and also arrange (in a world of complex bureaucracy) housing, marriage, education and employment.

(8) A debt of yang is earned in childhood

The reciprocal obligations of *yang* are explicitly acknowledged in Dongbei. One young man from the countryside explained it thus: 'We must return our parents' money (*huan fumu de qian*). When we are small, our parents *yang* us, when they are old, we *yang* them.' This repayment is taken for granted; it is, as one man said, something one 'cannot fail to do' (*buneng buzuo*). If you do not support your parents, then other people will look down upon you (*qiaobuqi*, 'not see you'). However, many people now say that the young are increasingly failing to care for the old.[2] For example, I was told that many young couples spend so much money on their 'emperor'-like children that they neglect to care for the elderly (*yanglao*). One afternoon, I sat with a woman and her eldest son, who was married and living in the same village. The two households shared many economic interests and there were some tensions over money matters. On this day they were joking with each other, when she turned to me. She pointed at her son, asking 'Is he any good (*hao*)?' I said that I didn't know. 'Oh, he's no good', she said, 'he doesn't *yang* me (*ta bu yang wo*). He makes plenty of money, but doesn't give me a thing!'

The obligation to *yang*, at least in theory, arises from having received *yang*, not from parenthood as such. For example, I met one elderly woman whose mother had died when she was eleven. While her father went out to work, she was left at home to raise the children, and to cook for them, as if she were their mother. This, she says, her brothers have never forgotten, and now they care for her (in the way they might have cared for their mother). She specifically mentioned three things they provide. First, they regularly give her food (including rice). Second, they give money, especially to deal with medical expenses. Third, their sons (her nephews) are regularly instructed to visit her, sometimes every day, as a sign of affection.

(9) Couples hope to 'have a son quickly'; but all children 'are useful'
In the middle of the marriage ceremonies in some communities, a small boy (two or three years old) is brought in and placed on the *kang* (bed) where the new couple will sleep. This activity is called 'pressing the *kang*' (*yakang*), and 'a girl is of no use for it' (*yongbushang nuhair*). The purpose of 'pressing the *kang*' is to ensure that in the future the couple will have a son (*weile jianglai neng sheng nanhai*). The newlyweds also eat dates (*zao*) and chestnuts (*lizi*), because together these words sound similar to *zao li zi* 'to have a son quickly'. One woman, the mother of two daughters, told me it was no good not having sons, because without them you 'have no family' (*meiyou jia*).

However, many adults now say that sons and daughters are the same (*dou yiyang*); all children, one woman declared, are 'useful' (*dou youyong*). Nor should it be assumed that the preference for sons over daughters means that *women* lack power or prestige. One young married man said to me, with exasperation, that the women had control of the men, *qi guan ye*. Many people feel that with the one-child policy it is necessary for a married couple to support both sets of parents-in-law, and this inevitably changes the perspective on daughters. Certainly, most of the girls and young women with whom I spoke said they intended to provide support for their parents in old age. One young woman even said that if her future husband refused to do this she would divorce him. It remains more common for a newly-wed couple to settle with or near the groom's parents, rather than the bride's. However, when the woman's family (*niangjia*) is able to provide better living conditions (e.g., to arrange hard-to-come-by housing) then the couple may live with them. Parents without sons may also arrange uxorilocal marriages, in which the sons-in-law are called *yang lao xu*, i.e. '*yang*-the-elderly sons-in-law'. In short, both sons and daughters are fully implicated in the cycle of family reciprocity.

(10) Children recite poetry; but traditions are 'not discussed'
Finally, two comments on learning. Many children in Dongbei are now encouraged, *by their parents*, to memorise and recite classical Chinese poetry. For example, pre-school children sometimes recite Tang dynasty poetry for the entertainment of guests. (This is especially common in towns and cities, but also in the countryside among those with some education.) Schools also emphasise memorisation and recitation. The meaning of the

verses is often not clear to the children (the language is classical). However, as they come to learn, many of the ancient verses relate in some way to filial obedience, to loyalty, to human emotions and to hospitality. One teacher referred to this practice as teaching through poetry, *shijiao*. The memorisation of poetry is of course part of the Chinese classical and literate tradition.

However, as in Angang, I would argue that children in Dongbei learn much of what they know about morality not from direct teaching, but rather from their involvement in cycles of reciprocity. These cycles are not necessarily spoken about or analysed; they are lived, as is the custom or habit (*xiguan*). Here I will give a final example. On *qingmingjie* (the day of 'tomb-sweeping' to commemorate the dead), I visited a farmer. As we stood outside, he explained to me at length the virtues of his milk-cow, a very large and rather beautiful animal. Every morning he milked her, he said, and then rode by bicycle in the darkness for over an hour to the market. This subject interested him greatly, and we dwelt on it. Later I thought I might venture to ask about traditions, but he dismissively said 'oh, we don't emphasise traditions' (*women bu jiangjiu chuantong*). The term *jiangjiu*, 'emphasise', is quite interesting. Its usual meaning is 'to stress', or 'to be particular about' (e.g., 'they are very particular about what they eat', *tamen hen jiangjiu cai*). But *jiang* itself means 'to speak', while *jiu* means 'to examine or study'. *Jiangjiu chuantong* thus could also, by extension, mean 'to speak about the whys and wherefores of traditions', i.e., to analyse in an anthropological way. And while this elderly farmer was saying to me that his family did not emphasise (or have much to say about) traditions, his son was placing yellow paper, representing money, in a basket, and setting off on his bicycle for the ancestral graves, where he would make the respectful offerings.

Notes

Introduction
1. The last word in this saying is not found in Bodman (1958). However, the pronunciation is very similar to *cheq*, 'book', and the expression is apparently a play on words: to *thak cheq* is to read or study. Children translated it into Mandarin as *yue du yue taoyan*, 'The more you study the more you're sick of it', or *yue du yue dai*: 'The more you study, the more you're stupid!' Along similar lines, Potter and Potter recount a conversation held with a teacher about education during the Cultural Revolution. She said students told her that 'if you study too much you make your brain mad' (1990:88).
2. Young people in Taiwan often make such offerings while specifically requesting help with examinations, and the girl later told me that she burnt her textbooks for 'good luck'.
3. For details of legends about the Stove God see Chard (1990).
4. Chang means 'common' or 'ordinary', and is also used in expressions of frequency, such as *jingchang*, 'constant, frequent'. *Shi* means 'knowledge', 'to know', or 'to recognise'.
5. Chinese characters are combinations of strokes, and many obviously 'contain' other characters (e.g., a 'grass' radical is found in many characters for plants). The origin of these combinations sometimes relates to sound or to meaning, and in many cases the original logic of the combination is difficult to trace. As Karlgren points out, the unravelling of this history is also complicated by various commentators over the centuries who have given 'farfetched, scholastic, often very amusing explanations' of characters (Karlgren 1923:2). The actual etymologies of *zi* are a matter for linguists, but most students, as they learn to read and write, also engage in a kind of folk linguistics about the meanings of various combinations of strokes. Teachers often emphasise, as a memory device, the separate components of a word, and students may also recall strokes with private memory devices unrelated to etymology or public meaning. For an accessible and thought-provoking introduction to some related issues, see Lindqvist (1989).
6. See Morris (1987) for a survey of issues related to religion as a category. Also see Feuchtwang on Chinese religion (1975:61–82, 1991:139–61).

7. Might this be due to a Western, largely functionalist, folk model of education?
8. Ironically, some sociologists have also adopted a so-called ethnographic approach which appears to privilege what takes place inside of schools, e.g., in playground 'culture' (Woods & Hammersley 1993).
9. Two other recent contributions to the anthropology of learning are Lambek (1993) and Astuti (in press). For a review of developments in 'the anthropology of teaching and learning', and a discussion of the formal/informal distinction, also see Pelissier (1991).
10. Akinnaso criticises this type of description (referring especially to papers in Middleton (1970)), on the grounds that it involves 'focusing on discontinuities and ignoring possible similarities'. It may also contribute to the comparison of two things which do not necessarily bear comparison: formal, school-based learning in literate societies with informal, practical learning in non-literate societies (Akinnaso 1992:70–2).
11. More precisely, two 'opposed modes of inculcation', inculcation being defined as 'the imposition of the cultural arbitrary'.
12. My interest in this issue was originally inspired by reading Wittgenstein's discussion of ostension (1953).
13. Sperber and Wilson note that 'When a representation is stored not as a basic factual assumption but by being embedded under an expression of attitude, it is often processed in a self-conscious, non-spontaneous way. This is true of representations used in problem-solving tasks of the kind familiar from experimental psychology. It is true of speculatively held opinions, religious beliefs or scientific hypotheses. The largely conscious reasoning processes which these indirectly held representations undergo are of great intrinsic interest, but we see it as a mistake to extrapolate from them to the spontaneous and essentially unconscious inference processes used in most ordinary thinking, and in particular in ordinary verbal comprehension' (Sperber & Wilson 1986:75). See also Boyer 1993.
14. For discussions of an important part of this heritage see Baker and Feuchtwang (1991).
15. For one highly personal account of this, see Gao (1987).
16. Given the problematic nature of anthropology in China, and the obligations of researchers to their informants, some writers may have been disinclined to suggest that local people, in their religious practice, were actually undermining *contemporary* official power in some way. However, see Ahern (1981b) and Feuchtwang (1974).

1 Two roads
1. Discussions of child-related themes are found throughout the anthropology of China. A few recent and diverse examples include Gates (1993:251–74), Jankowiak (1993:223–57) Potter & Potter (1990:225–50), and Berthier (1988). See also M. Wolf (1968, 1970, 1972).
2. Or 'caught the frights'. Note that the corresponding ritual (see below) is also transcribed as *siu kia*, but that the meaning of the latter is different, '*gathering* the frights'.
3. Schipper notes that among the minor exorcisms and individual purifications

performed by Daoists, 'Le cas le plus courant est celui de la guérison des "frayeurs enfantines". Que l'enfant ait eu un traumatisme réel, causant une perte subite de ses forces vitales, ou qu'une indisposition générale se manifeste chez lui dont les causes sont attribueés à une possession démoniaque quelconque, la première chose à faire est de l'amener chez le Maître' (1982:103). Also see Topley (1974) and Berthier (1988:237–40). See Harrell (1979) and Cohen (1988) on Chinese ideas about the soul.
4. 'Les enfants sont des proies faciles pour les influences pernicieuses, car leurs énergies sont encore faibles et peu stables. L'adulte, par contre, peut connaître la plénitude de ses forces et n'a nul besoin de protection ou de purification, s'il prend garde à ne pas gaspiller son capital de puissance vitale' (Schipper 1982:103).
5. There is some evidence for this 'fatalism', in that a given fate or destiny (*yunqi*, *mingyun*) is held to largely determine the course of a person's life-events, including catastrophes such as accidental death. But people also take steps to intervene with pre-determined fates (e.g., by 'changing destiny', *gaiyun*), and are quite optimistic about their ability to do so.
6. I use the translation 'body-person' for the Chinese term *shen*, following Mark Elvin (1989). Also see Feuchtwang on the inappropriateness of distinguishing belief and performance in Chinese religion (1992:7–16).
7. That is, children eventually encounter the ideas around *siu kia*, but this is as likely as not to be through hearing of the condition of another child.
8. Berthier discusses these stages in greater detail (1988:227–58), and Thompson (1990) describes the life-cycle (see below).
9. The *manyue* celebration is also linked to Chinese naming practices, as discussed by R. Watson with reference to rural Hong Kong (1986). I will turn to this in the next section.
10. Again, see Berthier (1988:227–58).
11. The *qixian* (seven fairies), or *qixiannu* (seven fairy maidens), are said to be the servants of Huang Mu Niang Niang, the wife of the Emperor of Heaven, and are often asked to protect children. They are associated with the seven stars of the 'Weaving Maiden' constellation, which, on the seventh day of the seventh lunar month crosses celestial paths with the 'Shepherd'.
12. *Shenghuo yu lunli*, 6:27.

2 Ghosts are not connexions

1. See the monographs by Feuchtwang (1992) and Sangren (1987) on the significance of 'locality' in popular religion. Sangren's analysis is influenced by Skinner's important work on Chinese 'marketing communities' (1977).
2. For a detailed history of the relationship between aborigines, Chinese settlers and various regimes, see Shepherd (1993), which provides an excellent background to the complex political history of the 'Taiwan frontier'. Given that my book addresses the question of identity, material on relations between the Han Chinese residents of Angang and aboriginal communities would obviously have been of great interest. However, Angang is unusually isolated, and people in the *xiang* normally have little, if any, contact with aborigines. Nor do they often refer to them in conversation (although see the discussion on religion below).

3. See Thompson (1984) on industrialisation in rural Taiwan, and Gallin & Gallin (1974) on rural–urban migration.
4. At the time of the fieldwork, the township administration was developing plans to expand tourism, which was seen as one of the few alternatives to fishing.
5. However, the uncertainty of fishing incomes is said to be partly offset by the retirement benefits available through the fishermen's association.
6. This may be typical of Chinese fishing communities (Wang Sun-hsing 1974). Lineages, as such, are usually not very elaborated even in Taiwanese farming communities (Thompson 1984). For a review of the literature on Chinese lineages, see J. Watson (1982b).
7. More specifically, while it is common for friends and relatives to do business together, and to try to profit from others, it is seen as wrong to profit from one's own friends and relatives. For example, relatives give each other 'introductions' into factories, and they work together on boats. But actually *selling* something to a relative or friend, and taking money for it, is very problematic. In a community where everyone is known, a local person running a shop might risk having to give everything away. In fact, most of the 'outside' shopkeepers in Angang have been in the community for many years, have many friends, and give some things away. But the pressure for them to do so is less than it would be for a 'local' (*bendi*) person, especially one with many relatives.
8. In Mandarin: *Jin zhu zhe chi, jin mo zhe hei.*
9. The Mandarin expression *heibai* ('black-white') has the same meaning as Hokkien *o-peq*. But in Angang the term *luan* is more often used in Mandarin to express 'disorder'.
10. Ghosts or demons (*gui*) of various kinds are discussed in most accounts of Chinese religion; see especially Weller's more detailed discussion of the 'ghost festival' (1987).
11. These spirits are said to be sent by the King of Hell (Yan Luo Wang) to grab the souls of people who have outlived their predetermined time of death. They are also called 'soul-nabbing envoys', *gouhun shizhe*.
12. I have been told that similar ghost stories are told about schools in the rest of Taiwan, and in Hong Kong.
13. Cf. the discussion in chapter 1 concerning the morality of 'physical' action.
14. In Mandarin: *bu pa san geng ban ye gui qiao men.*
15. One young woman told me the following 'success story', (which is arguably also a kind of 'protection story') to explain why people *should* worship (*yinggai baibai*): 'A man from Angang was preparing to take an examination in [another part of Taiwan]. When he sat down and looked at the examination, he realised that he didn't understand it and could not write any answers. But before he went to take the exam he had been to worship Kuan-im, The Earth God, and so on [popular deities]. And so he just wrote, and somehow the gods passed the exam for him.' There is some ambivalence among villagers about asking the gods for help in acquiring wealth or achieving success. People make such requests all the time, but it is seen by some as slightly improper or selfish, whereas requests for health, protection or 'peace' are relatively unproblematic.
16. Note the possible connexion to some of the ideas given in chapter 1 about childhood; what is truly desired is for *nothing* (extraordinary) to happen to a child. Also see the discussion below on names.

17. Christian missionaries in Taiwan are said to have had more success in aboriginal communities than among the Chinese.
18. *Fengshui* is sometimes used to help a child come into existence in the first place. I was told (although I knew of no cases) that if a couple were unable to have a son they might ask an expert in *fengshui* to correct the position of their bed.
19. These are usually the stories of particular deities. Cf. Jordan and Overmyer (1986), for an account of spirit-writing cults in Taiwan, in which texts are, by contrast, a central concern.
20. Watching such a performance would not necessarily be a way of directly 'learning about religion', because the operas are not necessarily religious (although sometimes they do involve gods or god-like characters). But my point here is about children's participation and non-participation in religious activities; they are often kept away by their parents.
21. I have also seen an incident which provoked a similar response, in which a girl had placed her own sister at risk.
22. I will discuss later the possibility that moral instruction is something that takes place in private.

3 The proper way of being a person
1. *Guoyu* 9:55–6.
2. There was no comment or particular reaction by the family to this moral, although the mother had expressed (on other occasions) her belief that dreams could indeed be a way of receiving messages from spirits. Villagers sometimes say, however, that people can make tragic errors if they *misinterpret* dreams, or use the wrong means to deal with spiritual problems. I suspect that most of them would have agreed with the docu-drama moral, but with a slightly different logic: the woman was certainly wrong to stab her husband, but this does not mean that dreams are simply made up by people.
3. The term *mixin*, commonly translated as 'superstition', is used, especially in the PRC, to describe beliefs in ghosts, etc. It more precisely means 'to be lost/confused in one's beliefs'. To *xin* something is to believe it, while *mi*, 'confused, lost', is used in combinations such as *milu* 'to lose the road'.
4. Although there are three elementary schools in Angang, none are in Beicun.
5. Cf. Anderson's discussion of nationalism. He stresses the 'pilgrimage' aspect of education, the process of binding together those who attend school as they move through educational sites (Anderson 1983).
6. Many families, although mostly not those from the countryside, now set their sights overseas. But expectations in Angang are modest. During my fieldwork I met the *first* young person from Angang to ever attend Taiwan's leading university, located in Taipei, and this was seen as a major achievement.
7. *Hongbao* are an important part of commercial, political, social and religious life in Taiwan, sometimes with negative, sometimes with positive connotations.
8. In Mandarin: *bujin jiaoshou shuben zhi shi, haiyao jiaodao zuoren de daoli.*
9. And yet, as everyone would know, most *liumang* are closely connected within 'sworn brotherhoods'. Such associations, however, in addition to being anti-authoritarian (illegal), are potentially anti-family, because they involve sworn loyalty, in a kinship-based idiom, to a non-kin group.

10. Sometimes the single term *guai* is used to mean well-behaved, e.g., 'this child is very *guai*'. But *guai* can also mean 'perverse, obstinate, cunning, etc', and the meaning is only established in context.
11. The stereotype is that parents attach more importance to the careers of their sons, but I knew of a number of families where considerable importance was attached to the academic standing of daughters. In some cases, although not always, these were families without sons.

4 Textbook mothers and frugal children

1. Even most of the supplementary texts which students sometimes buy and read are simply explanations and elaborations of school-system textbooks.
2. Note also that in Hokkien a scholar is a 'book-reading person' (*thak-cheq-lang*), and teachers may be referred to as 'book-teachers' (*ka-cheq-e*). Also see Thompson's (1990) discussion of the centrality of literacy in Chinese conceptualisations of the person.
3. This might be related to the traditional view that the relationship between fathers and children should be rather distant, with occasional displays of paternal 'severity' (*yan*), whilst the stereotypical relationship with mothers is meant to be warmer, and more emotional (see below). It may also reflect the fact that the legend-histories of several important Nationalist heroes (from Yue Fei to Hu Shi to Chiang Kai-shek) emphasise the sacrifices of their mothers. Fathers are present in a number of texts, but high emotion seems mostly reserved for stories involving mothers.
4. Taught in National Language class, during the fifth year of elementary school (*Guoyu* 10:43–4).
5. National Language, fifth year of elementary school (*Guoyu* 10:47–8).
6. Taught in National Literature, first year of middle school (*Guowen* 2:69–74).
7. Taught in National Literature, during the first year of middle school (*Gouwen* 1:13–7).
8. Note also the much less common expression *cifu*, 'affectionate father', arguably a father who acts in the motherly way.
9. I mentioned before that they sometimes try to keep private those matters which might arouse jealousy, but I do not see how this would apply to the disciplining of children.
10. Hu Shi's response is a play on the words (for 'chilly' and 'mother'). He says, *Niang shenme! Laozi dou bu laozi ya!*, which is glossed in the accompanying notes as *Ti niang zuo shenme! Laozi dou buneng guan wo le ya!* ('What is this talk of mothers? Even father can't control me!')
11. Taught in Life and Ethics, during the fourth year of elementary school (*Shenghuo yu Lunli* 2:41–51).
12. As I will discuss, children are given money (sometimes substantial amounts) by adults at the lunar new year.

5 Red envelopes and the cycle of *yang*

1. Partly because so-called real money and real economic transactions are also symbolic and moral (cf. Parry & Bloch 1989). But also because the symbolic

transactions in question are often substantive (involving food which is eaten and money which is spent).
2. This *yang*, by the way, has nothing to do with '*yin* and *yang*'. For an account of obligations to the elderly in mainland China, see Davis-Friedmann (1991).
3. *Guoyu* 10:45–6. The term *lijie* means 'etiquette, formality, courtesy, protocol'. *Li*, 'rites and ceremonies', is central to Confucian doctrine.
4. The term *guo* means 'to pass or cross through space or time'. It is sometimes translated as 'spend', e.g., 'to spend the night' (*guoye*), or 'celebrate', e.g., 'celebrate the new year' (*guonian*). It is also used as a complement following a verb, e.g., *kanguo*, 'to have looked at'.
5. For an account of adoption in China, and the complicated strategies by which family continuity is maintained, see Wolf and Huang (1980).
6. The term *qin* means 'related by blood or marriage'.
7. His wife had the same surname as, but was not related to, his foster father.
8. See Ahern (1973) for a discussion of the connexion between the inheritance of property and the maintenance of ancestor worship.
9. Traditionally, parents would, in any case, expect nothing from a daughter. But now it would usually be expected that an only child (boy or girl) would provide support in some way.
10. These are sometimes described as payments to replace the work the daughter might have done for her own family, had she not 'married out'.
11. See, for example, Chang 1977, J. Watson 1987, Thompson 1988, Anderson 1980.
12. However, I did receive contradictory accounts of the way in which *lubian* should be used, and some people seemed surprised I had been told that women eat it. Anderson, in his discussion of food in China, reports that 'the male genitalia of deer are believed to be especially strengthening to the human equivalent, doubtless because one male deer can service approximately seventy does during rut season' (1980:193).
13. See Anderson and Anderson 1977:372–3 on 'role overkill' in Chinese banquets.
14. To what extent might incense be seen as a kind of 'food' offering? The Chinese term for it is 'fragrant' (*xiang*), the same word used to describe good-smelling food. A deity consumes this 'fragrance', and similarly consumes the 'fragrance' of a food offering.
15. It is interesting to compare the evidence from Angang with that provided by Ortner concerning Sherpa notions of food, hospitality and obligation. Ortner notes that while a Sherpa host tries very hard to not let a guest leave with an 'empty mouth', the guest tries to resist receiving food, with the obligation this would imply (1978:81). Ortner argues that Sherpa families resist exchange of all kinds and 'the social bonds such exchange might produce', just as they resist the breakup of nuclear families through marriage (1978:68).
16. In saying this I am thinking of Parry's argument concerning Mauss's *The Gift*. He argues that 'while Mauss is generally represented as telling us how *in fact* the gift is *never* free, what I think he is really telling us is how *we* have acquired a *theory* that it should be' (1986:458).
17. This is also reported by the Hsus for northern China (1977:307) and the Andersons for the south (1977:360).

6 Going forward bravely

1. The Confucian notion of *zhong* originally meant 'loyalty' to a leader, but is now commonly taken to mean loyalty to a nation (*zhongai guojia*), i.e. patriotism.
2. *Renren chi zongzi*, National Language (*Guoyu* 4:23–4).
3. There are popular versions of the story in which Qu Yuan's body is miraculously recovered, intact, from inside a fish.
4. The text which follows is about dragon boat races, to which a girl is taken by her father. The meaning of the races is not discussed, and the father's only comment is that the attitude of the losing crews typifies the 'athletic spirit'; *Guoyu* 4:35–6.
5. *Gudai de xianmu*, fifth year of elementary school, National Language, *Guoyu* 10:47–8.
6. *Xiaoshun: xiaoqin baoguo*, taught in Life and Ethics, *Shenghuo yu Lunli* 2:23–50, fourth year of elementary school.
7. *Xiaoshun*, taught in sixth year of elementary school, 'Life and Ethics', *Shenghuo yu Lunli* 6:24–31.
8. See Wakeman (1988) for a discussion of the burial and mourning of Chiang Kai-shek and Mao Zedong.
9. 'Mu-lan Joins the Army', fourth year of elementary school, National Language, *Guoyu*: 8:27–9.

7 Diving children

1. There are many discussions of Chinese spirit mediums in the anthropological literature. These include Elliott (1990), Jordan (1985), Kleinman (1980), M. Wolf (1990, 1992), and Berthier (1987, 1988). An account of Korean shamanism, very interesting for comparison (especially with M. Wolf 1992) is found in Kendall (1988).
2. Women often make offerings for their grandchildren. Here I conflate this into 'motherhood', partly for the sake of simplicity, but also because the offerings are seen as attempts to protect one's children's children. That is, they are an extension of being a mother.
3. I should note that in Angang women appear to be comparatively active in public religion. For example, they are allowed to carry images of gods, something which in many locations is strictly forbidden.
4. The 'job qualifications' for mediums are summarised in M. Wolf (1990:425).
5. The etymology of *tong* is fascinating, and might potentially explain something about its use to refer to mediums. However, so far as I know, this etymology is not apparent in modern usage. According to Wieger, a *tong* is 'a boy, a lad under fifteen years, who became a slave for a great crime committed by his parents'; he also comments that 'those slaves were forced to live unmarried; hence the extended meanings, a bachelor, a spinster, a virgin' (1940:249, 282). According to Karlgren: 'a menial, servant; boy or girl under 15 y. of age; young, virgin, undefiled' (1923:325).
6. The *bazi* and their connection to mediumship are fully discussed in Berthier (1987).
7. The relationship between mediumship and personality is discussed in Kleinman (1980) and M. Wolf (1992).

8. The character *hu* is used in several common modern terms (e.g., *hushi*, nurse) but is fairly complicated to write. Most charms written by mediums contain some legible characters, but also much more esoteric scribblings which are said to be divine and/or 'ancient'.
9. This professionalisation may be an attempt to fend off criticisms; the *tang ki* say that the gods do not want them to drink, because people may not believe what they say when drunk.
10. See also Elliott (1990:88).
11. In many cases they are even nominally adopted by the gods represented by *tang ki* (cf. Elliott 1990:83 on the registration of 'dedicated children' in spirit medium cults). See also Berthier (1988) for a description of the cult of Chen Jinggu, which specifically focuses on the protection of mothers, children and mediums.
12. Cf. Sangren's discussion (1983) of the 'counterculture embodied in the worship of female deities'.
13. *Lao* means 'old', and *zi* means 'son'.

8 Dangerous rituals

1. Seaman (1978) discusses the relationship between divination and the promotion of the gods; this is further discussed in Feuchtwang (1992, chapter 5).
2. Much has been written about this. See especially J. Watson's account of how death pollution is rechannelled into fertility (1982a) and his discussion of Cantonese funeral specialists (1988); also see Ahern (1973), and the volume edited by Watson & Rawski (1988).
3. On auspicious occasions such as weddings, and during the entire lunar new year period, there is a taboo against saying inauspicious things.
4. These students are not thought to be at risk from participating. They are only at the home briefly, walk in front of the coffin and mourners to the graveyard, and leave immediately upon arrival there.
5. This was not drawn to my attention by people in Angang, but rather by an anonymous reader. I am very grateful for this help.
6. *Kng put* is the most common name for the ritual. However, it was sometimes also referred to as *mng sin*, 'asking [questions of] the god', or *chia sin*, 'inviting the god'. One person grandly referred to it (in Mandarin) as *shenming zuo jin jiaozi*, 'the bright spirit sits in the golden chair'; in Hokkien *ce kio*, 'sitting in the sedan chair', or *ce kimkio*, 'sitting in the golden sedan chair'.
7. Various kinds of sedan chairs are used in Taiwan for ritual purposes. Some are designed to be carried by four people; in Angang these are not used for *kng put*, although on occasion they are used to carry the large images found in temples. In some locations in Taiwan (although not in Angang) sedan chairs are sometimes used as divination tools; the ends of the poles scrawl out characters in the incense ash on altars, which are then interpreted as messages from the gods (Jordan 1985:57–9, 64–7).
8. In Mandarin *gen shenming guo qi xinghuo*.

9 Conclusion

1. Note that 'relevance' is used in a technical sense by Sperber and Wilson (1986).

They suggest that something communicated is, by definition, guaranteed to have 'relevance'.

10 Notes on childhood in northeastern China

1. There are, however, some very general similarities between Taiwan and northeastern China. Both are Chinese 'frontiers' (cf. Shepherd 1993, esp. chapter 12), and have been, in recent centuries, the destination for Han migrants (e.g., to Taiwan from Fujian, to northeastern China from Shandong). Taiwan and northeastern China were also both occupied by the Japanese in this century, a fact which often dominates the childhood memories of elderly people in both locations.
2. Cf. Davis-Friedmann 1991.

Glossary

This list excludes the words and expressions quoted from school textbooks, and those in the Epilogue, *all* of which are given in Mandarin, and which are translated in the body of the text. Other Mandarin terms are given below in *pinyin*, but without diacritics, and are listed in roman alpabetical order (i.e., not by syllables). Hokkien terms are transliterated according to Bodman (1958), but given without diacritics, and are indicated below with the symbol [H].

ai chiou [H]: to love (enjoy) to laugh
an cuan [H]: security, defence

bangmang: to help
bangyang: example, pattern
bangzhu: to assist
baoda: respond to, repay (e.g. care)
baoguo: commit oneself to the nation; repay the nation
baoshou: conservative
baoyou: protection
bazi: terrestrial stems and branches (astrological calculation)
beidou qixing: the big-dipper
bendi: local, native
biancheng: change, be transformed
bou chai [H]: to not have food (polite expression)
bu: to strengthen, supplement
bu gan: to not dare
bu ganjing: unclean
bu tai liaojie: to not really understand
buhaokan: not good to watch
buhui shao: it can't burn
bujili: inauspicious
bushen: to strengthen the body-person
bushou: to not accept
buxing: not acceptable

buyao: invigorating tonic
buyao keqi: 'don't be polite'
buyao langfei: 'don't be wasteful!'
buxiban: supplementary school

caichan: wealth, estate
Cau Kun [H]: the Stove God
ce kimkio [H]: 'to sit in the golden sedan chair' (ritual)
ce kio [H]: 'to sit in the sedan chair' (ritual)
chai [H]: food, 'dishes'
changshi: ordinary knowledge, common sense
chenggong: succeed
chengren: adults
chengshou: mature, fully cooked
cheq [H]: book
chia [H]: to invite
chia lang-kheq [H]: invite guests
chia sin [H]: to invite a god
chong'ai: over-indulgent
chujia: to marry out (said of a woman)
chunpo: pure, simple, sincere
chuxi: new year's eve
ci'ai: loving
ciaq [H]: eat
ciaq-pa be [H]: are you full?
ciaq pieng-an [H]: eat security/peace
ciaq-png [H]: eat
ciaq-png be [H]: have you eaten yet
cifu: affectionate father
cimu: loving mother
congming: clever
cun: village

daibiao: to represent
dao: way, road, doctrine
daode: morality
Daojiao: Daoism ('the way')
daoli: reason ('the proper way')
de: merit
diaoying: mobilise the troops (ritual)
diyiming: first place, 'number one name'
diyu: hell
dou chi yidian: eat more of everything
dou xiongdi: all brothers
dou yiyang: all the same
dui ni bu hao: bad for you
dui shenti hao: good for the health
duli: independence

e gui: hungry ghost

fa cai: to strike it rich
feng: crazy
fengchi: imperial decree (charm)
fengshui: 'winds and waters', geomancy
fengyang: respectfully support (one's parents)
fo: Buddha
fojiao: Buddhism
fu: blessings
fu: a charm
furong: hibiscus

gai: to correct
gaiyun: 'to change destinies' (ritual)
ganbei: 'bottoms up'
gaoxing: happy and excited
gaozhong: high school
gege: elder brother
gongde: merit
gongji: public commemoration
gongmin: citizen
guai: good, perverse, obstinate
guaiguai: good (of a child), 'goody-goody'
Guan Di: the god of war
Guan Yin: the goddess of mercy (Hokkien Kuan-im)
guancai: coffin
guanxi: connexion, relationship
gudai de zi: ancient characters
gui: ghost
guo shengri: 'pass through' a birthday
guofu: father of the nation
guohun shizhe: 'soul-nabbing envoys' (ghosts)
guohuo: cross the fire
guojie: cross the street
guoli: national calendar (Gregorian/solar)
guonian: 'pass through' the new year
guomin xiaoxue: national elementary school
guomin zhongxue: national middle school
guonian: passing of the year, the lunar new year
guoye: spend the night
guoyu: national language (Mandarin)

hao: good
haoren bu pa gui: 'good people don't fear ghosts'
haoren haoshi: 'good things happen to good people'
haoshi, huaishi: good and bad affairs

hao xiongdi: 'good brothers', ghosts
haoxue, haojiao: easy to learn and teach
haowan: fun
heibai: 'black-white', mixed-up
heibai wuchang: the ghosts who announce death
hezuo: cooperation
ho i e-lieng [H]: 'make him/her able to be effective'
hongbao: red envelope (with money as gift or bribe)
honggui: red turtle buns
hou [H]: good, alright
hou-ciaq [H]: good to eat
hou-khua [H]: good to look at
hu: to protect
Huang Mu Niang Niang: wife of Emperor of Heaven
huai: rotten, bad
huairen: bad person
huaishi: bad things
huo: fire
hushen: to protect the body-person
hushen fu: body-person protection charm
hushi: nurse

i-su [H]: meaning

jiachang bianfan: regular family meal
jiang tai duo: to talk too much
jiao: to teach
jiaoshi: teacher, 'teaching master'
jiaoyu: education
jiaoyubu: ministry of education
jiejie: elder sister
jihui: taboo
jili: auspicious
jilie: agitated
jingfeng san: frights powder
jinian: commemorate
jitong: spirit medium, 'divining child' (*Hokkien tang ki*)
jiugui: 'wine ghost', alcoholic

ka-cheq-e [H]: teacher, 'book-teacher'
kai guang: eye-opening (ceremony)
kai wanxiao: to make a joke
kan ziji: to examine oneself
kanbudong: to watch without understanding
kang: to carry
kao: to lean on, depend on
ke'ai: loveable, cute

kelian: pitiful
kheq-thia [H]: central or 'guest' room of house
kheq-khi [H]: the air of a guest
ki [H]: to divine
kng [H]: to carry
kng put [H]: god-carrying (ritual)
Kuan-im [H]: the goddess of mercy

lai: to come
laiwang: come-go (to have a relationship)
langfei: to waste, literally 'a wave of expenditure'
lang-kheq [H]: a guest
lao: old, experienced
laoshi: teacher, 'venerable master'
lau-ziat [H]: bustling, 'hot and noisy'
linghun: soul
liumang: gangster, 'drifting rascal'
liushui: flowing water
lu thak lu cheq: the more you study, the more it makes you crazy
luan: disorder, chaos
luanjiang: chaotic talk
luanpao: wander aimlessly
luanxiang: mixed-up thinking
lubian: deer penis
lucao: deer grass
lunhui: reincarnation
lurongjiu: deer-antler wine

m kheq-khi [H]: don't be polite
Ma Co [H]: goddess who protects fishermen
mafan: trouble, bother
mai taitai: to 'buy a wife'
mai zangli: to 'purchase a funeral'
manyisui: 'full-year' (celebration)
manyue: 'full-month' (celebration)
manzhousui: 'full-annual-cycle' (celebration)
maobi: writing brush
maofan: to offend
meihualu: 'plum blossom' deer
meiyou ganjue: to have no feeling
meiyou guanxi: it doesn't matter, 'there is no connexion'
meiyou shi: not having things happen
meiyou yong: useless
mianzi: 'face'
milu: to lose the road
ming: bright
mingyun: destiny

mixin: superstition
miyan: rice and salt combination
mng sin [H]: to ask the god, divination
mogui: demon

ni pa si: 'you're afraid of death'
ni yao da tamen: 'you should hit them'
niannian youyu: 'year after year of abundance'
nongjia zidi dushu nan: 'rarely do the sons of farmers study'
nongli: agricultural calendar
nu'er ye shi haizi: 'a daughter is also a child'

o-peq [H]: 'black-white', mixed-up
o-peq kong [H]: 'black-white talk'

pa leng: fear the cold
pai, paipai [H]: to worship
pang: fat
peiyang laodong de jingshen: foster the labouring spirit
pengyou: friend
phai: [H] bad
phai-lang [H]: bad person
pieng-an [H]: security, absence of problems
pingdeng: equal
png-thang [H]: rice pot, 'useless person'
put [H]: deity ('buddha')

qi: energy, breath
qiguai: strange
qin: related by blood or marriage
qixian: Seven Fairies
qiang: strong
qing: light
qing bazi: 'light bazi' (astrological calculation)
qing jing han: 'please cleanse and protect' (charm)
qinggao: morally lofty and upright
qingjie: clean
qingsong: relaxed
qinqi: relative
qiu pingan: to request security
qiuxue: to seek learning
quwan: to go out for fun

re: hot (used for foods)
renshi: to know, recognise
renzi: to recognise characters, to read
rongxing: to tolerate punishment/torture
ru shen: god-entering (ceremony)

San Taizi: Third Prince (deity)
shandiren: 'mountain people', aborigines
shanshi: good deeds
shao: to burn
shao keben: to burn textbooks
shen: body-person
shen: deity, spirit
shen xiang: god's image
sheng: to be born
shenming: deity, 'bright spirit'
shenming zuo jin jiaozi: 'the god sits in the golden sedan chair'
shenpan: judgement
shiti: corpse
shou: long-life
shouku: 'take bitterness', to withstand hardship
shoumian: long-life noodles
shoutao: eternal-life peaches
si: death
sia zi [H]: to write Chinese characters
siu kia [H]: to suffer the frights, to receive the frights
siu kia [H]: to gather the frights
songzao: to see off the Stove God
suanmingren: fortune teller
ta bu hui xiang: he's not thinking
taipingyang: ocean of great peace, the Pacific
tang ki [H]: spirit medium, 'divining child'
tangyuan: red and white sweet rice ball soup
tiaopi: naughty, mischievous
Thai Sin [H]: Placenta God
Thi Kong [H]: Emperor of Heaven
thak cheq [H]: read books, study
thak-cheq-lang [H]: scholar
tiantang: heaven
tili: physical strength
tong: child, boy
tongnian: childhood
tou [H]: way, road, doctrine
tou [H]: down, fall down
tou su [H]: 'masters of the way', local Daoist priests

weixian: dangerous
wen: culture
wenshen: to ask the gods, divination
women shoubuliao: we can't stand it
wusuowei: beside the point

xifangren: westerners
xian: county

xiang: incense, fragrance
xiang: rural township
xianggongsuo: rural township government office
xianghuo: 'fragrant fire', charm
xiangzhang: township head
xianshen: dedicate oneself, 'give up the body-person'
xiansheng: teacher, mister, 'born earlier'
xiao: filial obedience
xiaodao: the way of filial obedience
xiaogui: 'little ghost', i.e., child
xiaoshun: filially obedient
xiaoxin: 'little hearted', i.e., cautious
xiaoxue: elementary school
xinyi: kindly feelings, feelings of the heart
xinku: bitter, difficult
xishi: happy events
xiuxi: to rest
xue: to learn
xuesheng: student, 'new to learning'

ya: to press, suppress, extort
yan: strict, severe
yanfu: strict father
yang: to support, nurture
yang haizi: to raise children
yang hua: to grow flowers
yang zhu: to raise pigs
yange: severe
yangfu: foster father
yanghuo: to support
yangmu: foster mother
yao: medicine
yasuiqian: new year's gift of money to children
yijiaren: all from one family
yinggai baibai: should worship
yinggai zuode: something which should be done
yizi: foster son
yonggong: hard-working
you daoli: to be reasonable
you guanxi: to have a connexion
youjing: a tour of inspection
yu: extra, abundance
yu: to cultivate
yu miao: to cultivate seedlings
yueli: lunar calendar
yundong: exercise
yunqi: fate

zhang da: to grow up
zhaogu: to look after (someone)
zhaoni: to come looking for you
zhengqi: striving
zhong: loyalty/patriotism
zhong: heavy
zhongai guojia: love of the nation
zhongxue: middle school
zhongyao: Chinese medicine
zhou shuisha: 'exorcise sea-demons'
zhuanke: junior college
zhuanqian: money-making
zhuanxin: to concentrate
zi: character
zi: son, descendants, seed
ziyou: independent
zongzi: food eaten for Dragon Boat festival
zou ma guan hua: viewing the flowers from horseback
zun shi zhong dao: respect the teacher and respect his way
zuofan: to cook, 'do the rice'
zuoren: being a person, conduct
zuoren de daoli: the proper way of being a person

References

Textbooks
The textbooks cited are the editions used for the school year 1988–9, published in Taipei by Guoli Bianyiguan.

Guomin Xiaoxue, *Guoyu*
Guomin Zhongxue, *Guowen*
Guomin Xiaoxue, *Shenghuo yu Lunli*

Other works
Ahern, Emily Martin 1973 *The cult of the dead in a Chinese village.* Stanford: Stanford University Press.
  1975 The power and pollution of Chinese women. In Margery Wolf & Roxane Witke (eds.) *Women in Chinese society.* Stanford: Stanford University Press.
  1981a *Chinese ritual and politics.* Cambridge: Cambridge University Press.
  1981b The Thai Ti Kong Festival. In Emily Ahern & Hill Gates (eds.) *The anthropology of Taiwanese society.* Stanford: Stanford University Press.
Akinnaso, F. Niyi 1992 Schooling, language and knowledge in literate and nonliterate societies. *Comparative studies in society and history* 34:68–109.
Anderson, Benedict 1983 *Imagined communities: reflections on the origin and spread of nationalism.* London: Verso.
Anderson, Eugene N. 1980 *The food of China.* New Haven, Yale University Press.
Anderson, Eugene N. and Anderson, Marja L. 1977 Modern China: South. In K. C. Chang (ed.) *Food in Chinese culture.* New Haven: Yale University Press.
Astuti, Rita (1995) *People of the sea: identity and descent among the Vezo of Madagascar.* Cambridge: Cambridge University Press.
Baker, Hugh and Feuchtwang, Stephan (eds.) 1991 *An old state in new settings.* JASO Occasional Papers No. 8. Oxford: JASO.
Bernstein, Basil 1975 *Class, codes and control.* Volume 3, second edition. London: Routledge & Kegan Paul.
Berthier, Brigitte 1987 Enfant de divination, voyageur du destin. *L'Homme* 101, 27(1):86–100.
  1988 *La dame-du-bord-de-l'eau.* Nanterre: Société d'Ethnologie.

Bloch, Maurice 1989 From cognition to ideology. In *Ritual, history and power: selected papers in anthropology*. London School of Economics Monographs on Social Anthropology No. 58. London: Athlone Press.
  1991 Language, anthropology and cognitive science. *Man* 26:183–98.
  1993 The uses of schooling and literacy in a Zafimaniry village. In Brian Street (ed.) *Cross-cultural approaches to literacy*. Cambridge: Cambridge University Press.
Bodman, Nicholas 1958 *Spoken Amoy Hokkien*. Kuala Lumpur: Charles Grenier & Co.
Borofsky, Robert 1987 *Making history: Pukapukan and anthropological constructions of knowledge*. Cambridge: Cambridge University Press.
Bourdieu, Pierre 1977 *Outline of a theory of practice*. Cambridge: Cambridge University Press.
Bourdieu, Pierre and Passeron, Jean-Claude 1990 *Reproduction in education, society and culture*. Second edition. London: Sage Publications. (First English edition 1977.)
Boyer, Pascal (ed.) 1993 *Cognitive aspects of religious symbolism*. Cambridge: Cambridge University Press.
Chang, K.C. 1977 *Food in Chinese culture: anthropological and historical perspectives*. New Haven: Yale University Press.
  1983 *Art, myth, and ritual: the path to political authority in ancient China*. Cambridge: Cambridge University Press.
Chard, Robert 1990 Folktales on the God of the Stove. *Chinese studies [Hanxue Yanjiu]* 8(1):149–82. Taipei.
Cohen, Myron L. 1988 Souls and salvation: conflicting themes in Chinese popular religion. In James L. Watson & Evelyn S. Rawski (eds.) *Death ritual in late imperial and modern China*. Berkeley: University of California Press.
Davis-Friedmann, Deborah 1991 *Long lives: Chinese elderly and the communist revolution* (expanded edition). Stanford: Stanford University Press.
Durkheim, Emile 1972 The social bases of education. In *Selected Writings* (Anthony Giddens ed.), pp. 203–18. Cambridge: Cambridge University Press.
Eastman, Lloyd et al. 1991 *The Nationalist era in China: 1927–1949*. Cambridge: Cambridge University Press.
Eickelman, Dale 1992 Mass higher education and the religious imagination in contemporary Arab societies. *American ethnologist* 19(4):643–55.
Elliott, Alan J.A. 1990 *Chinese spirit-medium cults in Singapore*. London: Athlone Press. (Originally published 1955.)
Elvin, Mark 1989 Tales of *shen* and *xin*: body-person and heart-mind in China during the last 150 years. In Michel Feher et al. (eds.) *Fragments for a history of the human body*. New York: Zone Books.
Feuchtwang, Stephan 1974 City temples in Taipei under three regimes. In Mark Elvin & G. William Skinner (eds.) *The Chinese city between two worlds*. Stanford: Stanford University Press.
  1975 Investigating religion. In Maurice Bloch (ed.) *Marxist analyses and social anthropology*. London: Tavistock.
  1991 A Chinese religion exists. In Hugh Baker & Stephan Feuchtwang (eds.) *An old state in new settings*. Oxford: JASO.

1992 *The imperial metaphor: popular religion in China.* London: Routledge.
Firth, Raymond 1970 Education in Tikopia. In John Middleton (ed.) *From child to adult.* Garden City, New York: The Natural History Press.
Gallin, Bernard and Gallin, Rita S. 1974 The integration of village migrants in Taipei. In Mark Evlin and G. William Skinner (eds.) *The Chinese city between two worlds.* Stanford: Stanford University Press.
Gao, Yuan 1987 *Born Red: a chronicle of the Cultural Revolution.* Stanford: Stanford University Press.
Gates, Hill 1993 Cultural support for birth limitation among urban capital-owning women. In Deborah Davis and Stevan Harrell (eds.) *Chinese families in the post-Mao era.* Berkeley: University of California Press.
Godelier, Maurice 1986 *The making of great men.* Cambridge: Cambridge University Press.
Granet, Marcel 1975 *The religion of the Chinese people.* New York: Harper & Row. (First published 1922.)
Harrell, Stevan 1979 The concept of soul in Chinese folk religion. *Journal of Asian studies* 38:519–28.
Hsieh, Jih-chang 1985 Meal rotation. In Hsieh Jih-chang & Chuang Ying-chang (eds.) *The Chinese family and its ritual behavior.* Taipei: Institute of Ethnology, Academia Sinica.
Hsu, Vera Y. N. and Hsu, Francis L. K. 1977 Modern China: North. In K. C. Chang (ed.) *Food in Chinese culture.* New Haven: Yale University Press.
Jankowiak, William R. 1993 *Sex, death and hierarchy in a Chinese city: an anthropological account.* New York: Columbia University Press.
Johnson, Elizabeth L. 1988 Grieving for the dead, grieving for the living: funeral laments of Hakka women. In James L. Watson & Evelyn S. Rawski (eds.) *Death ritual in late imperial and modern China.* Berkeley: University of California Press.
Jordan, David K. 1985 *Gods, ghosts and ancestors: folk religion in a Taiwanese village* (Second edition). Taipei: Cave Books. (First edition published in 1972 by University of California Press, Berkeley.)
Jordan, David K. and Daniel L. Overmeyer 1986 *The flying phoenix: aspects of Chinese sectarianism in Taiwan.* Princeton: Princeton University Press.
Judd, Ellen R. 1989 Niangjia: Chinese women and their natal families. In *Journal of Asian studies* 48(3):525–44.
Karlgren, Bernhard 1923 *Analytic dictionary of Chinese and Sino-Japanese.* Paris.
Kendall, Laurel 1988 *The life and hard times of a Korean shaman.* Honolulu: University of Hawaii Press.
Kleinman, Arthur 1980 *Patients and healers in the context of culture: an exploration of the borderland between anthropology, medicine, and psychiatry.* Berkeley: University of California Press.
Lambek, Michael 1993 *Knowledge and practice in Mayotte: local discourses of Islam, sorcery and spirit possession.* Toronto: University of Toronto Press.
Lave, Jean 1988 *Cognition in practice.* Cambridge: Cambridge University Press.
Lave, Jean and Etienne Wenger 1991 *Situated learning: legitimate peripheral participation.* Cambridge: Cambridge University Press.
Lindquivst, Cecilia 1989 *China: Empire of the written symbol.* London: Harvill.

Martin, Roberta 1975 The socialization of children in China and on Taiwan: an analysis of elementary school textbooks. *China quarterly* 62:242–62.
Meyer, Jeffrey E. 1988 Teaching morals in Taiwan schools: the message of the textbooks. *China quarterly* 114:267–84.
Middleton, John (ed.) 1970 *From child to adult*. Garden City, New York: The Natural History Press.
Morris, Brian 1987 *Anthropological studies of religion: an introductory text*. Cambridge: Cambridge University Press.
Ortner, Sherry 1978 *Sherpas through their rituals*. Cambridge: Cambridge University Press.
Parry, Jonathan 1986 The gift, the Indian gift, the 'Indian gift'. *Man* 21:453–73.
Parry, Jonathan and Bloch, Maurice (eds.) 1989 *Money and the morality of exchange*. Cambridge: Cambridge University Press.
Pelissier, Catherine 1991 The anthropology of teaching and learning. *Annual reviews in anthropology* 20:75–95.
Potter, Sulamith Heins and Potter, Jack M. 1990 *China's peasants: the anthropology of a revolution*. Cambridge: Cambridge University Press.
Sangren, P. Steven 1983 Female gender in Chinese religious symbols: Kuan Yin, Ma Tsu and the 'Eternal Mother'. *Signs* 9:4–25.
  1987 *History and magical power in a Chinese community*. Stanford: Stanford University Press.
  1991 Dialectics of alienation: individuals and collectivities in Chinese religion. *Man* 26:67–86.
Schipper, Kristofer 1982 *Le Corps Taoiste*. Paris: Fayard.
Seaman, Gary 1978 *Temple organization in a Chinese village*. Asian Folklore and Social Life Monographs, vol. 101. Taipei: Orient Cultural Service.
Shepherd, John Robert 1993 *Statecraft and political economy on the Taiwan frontier 1600–1800*. Stanford: Stanford University Press.
Skinner, G. William 1977 *The city in late imperial China*. Stanford: Stanford University Press.
Sperber, Dan 1985 Anthropology and psychology: towards an epidemiology of representations. *Man* 20:73–89.
Sperber, Dan and Wilson, Deirdre 1986 *Relevance: communication and cognition*. Oxford: Blackwell.
Stafford, Charles 1992 Good sons and virtuous mothers: kinship and Chinese nationalism in Taiwan. *Man* 27:363–78.
Sun Yat-sen n.d. *San Min Chu I: The three principles of the people; with two supplementary chapters by Chiang Kai-shek* (F.W. Price trans.) Taipei: China Publishing Company.
Thompson, Stuart 1984 Taiwan: rural society. *China quarterly* 99:553–68.
  1988 Death, food and fertility. In James L. Watson & Evelyn S. Rawski (eds.) *Death ritual in late imperial and modern China*. Berkeley: University of California Press.
  1990 Metaphors the Chinese age by. In Paul Spencer (ed.) *Anthropology and the riddle of the sphinx: paradoxes of change in the life course*. London: Routledge.
Topley, Marjorie 1974 Cosmic antagonism: a mother–child syndrome. In Arthur Wolf (ed.) *Religion and ritual in Chinese society*. Stanford: Stanford University Press.

Toren, Christina 1990 *Making sense of hierarchy: cognition as social process in Fiji*. London School of Economics Monographs on Social Anthropology No. 61. London: Athlone.
  1993 Making history: the significance of childhood cognition for a comparative anthropology of mind. *Man* 28:461–78.
Wakeman, Frederic, Jr. 1988 Mao's remains. In James L. Watson & Evelyn S. Rawski (eds.) *Death ritual in late imperial and modern China*. Berkeley: University of California Press.
Wang, Shih-ch'ing 1974 Religious organisation in the history of a Taiwanese town. In Arthur Wolf (ed.) *Religion and ritual in Chinese society*. Stanford: Stanford University Press.
Wang, Sun-hsing 1974 Taiwanese architecture and the supernatural. In Arthur Wolf (ed.) *Religion and ritual in Chinese society*. Stanford: Stanford University Press.
Watson, James L. 1982a Of flesh and bones: the management of death pollution in Cantonese society. In Maurice Bloch and Jonathan Parry (eds.) *Death and the regeneration of life*. Cambridge: Cambridge University Press.
  1982b Chinese kinship reconsidered: anthropological perspectives on historical research. *China quarterly* 92:589–622.
  1987 From the common pot: feasting with equals in Chinese society. *Anthropos* 82:389–401.
  1988 Funeral specialists in Cantonese society: pollution, performance, and social hierarchy. In James L. Watson & Evelyn S. Rawski (eds.) *Death ritual in late imperial China*. Berkeley: University of California Press.
Watson, James L. and Rawski, Evelyn S. 1988 *Death ritual in late imperial and modern China*. Berkeley: University of California Press.
Watson, Rubie S. 1986 The named and the nameless: gender and person in Chinese society. *American ethnologist* 13(4):619–31.
Weller, Robert P. 1987 *Unities and diversities in Chinese religion*. Houndmills: Macmillan.
Wieger, L. 1940 *Chinese characters: their origin, etymology, history, classification and signification*. Peking: Editions Henri Vetch.
Willis, Paul 1977 *Learning to labour*. Farnborough: Saxon House.
Wilson, Richard W. 1970 *Learning to be Chinese: the political socialization of children in Taiwan*. Cambridge, Mass.: MIT Press.
Wittgenstein, Ludwig 1953 *Philosophical investigations*. Oxford: Basil Blackwell.
Wolf, Arthur P. 1970 Chinese kinship and mourning dress. In Maurice Freedman (ed.) *Family and kinship in Chinese society*. Stanford: Stanford University Press.
Wolf, Arthur and Huang Chieh-shan 1980 *Marriage and adoption in China, 1845–1945*. Stanford: Stanford University Press.
Wolf, Margery 1968 *The house of Lim: a study of a Chinese farm family*. New York: Appleton-Century-Crofts.
  1970 Child training and the Chinese family. In Maurice Freedman (ed.) *Family and kinship in Chinese society*. Stanford: Stanford University Press.
  1972 *Women and the family in rural Taiwan*. Stanford: Stanford University Press.
  1990 The woman who didn't become a shaman. *American ethnologist* 17(3):419–30. (Reprinted in M. Wolf 1992.)

1992 *A thrice-told tale: feminism, postmodernism, and ethnographic responsibility.* Stanford: Stanford University Press.
Woods, Peter and Hammersley, Martyn (eds.) 1993 *Gender and ethnicity in schools: ethnographic accounts.* London: Routledge.

Index

aborigines, 37. 46, 188 n.2
Ahern, Emily, 22–4, 92, 104, 140–1
Akinnaso, F. Niyi, 8, 187 n.10
ancestors, 29, 85–6, 87-8, 97, 118, 124, 148, 153, 176–7, 185
ancestral tablets, 153
Angang
  economy of, 37–9, 41
  identification with, 39–42, 110, 163
  movement of persons in, 33–7, 42–8, 56, 110, 147

bad influences, 42–3, 72–3
banquets, 95, 100–2, 107–8, 159
bazi (astrological calculation), 134, 158
Berthier, Brigitte, 134, 143
birth, 22–4
blood, 24, 122–3, 137–40
'body-person', 21, 115–17, 126-7, 136, 163–4
bones, 29
Borofsky, Robert, 9
Bourdieu, Pierre, 9–11
breast-feeding, 98
Buddhism, 148
buxiban (revision schools), 4, 5, 61

calendars, 3, 50
calligraphy, *see* Chinese language
Chang, K.C., 142
charms, 105, 124, 156
Chiang Ching-kuo, 117–20
Chiang Kai-shek, 37, 115–17, 117–20
childhood
  representations of, 17–18, 130–2, 137–9
children
  health of, 20–1, 75–6, 97–100
  mischievousness of, 52–4, 136–7, 179–80
  protection of, 45–7, 50–1, 71–2, 122–3, 130–2, 161–2, 177–8
  punishment of, 51–4, 75
  raising of, 80–1
  survival of, 24–6
  teasing of, 51–2, 96, 180
China
  anthropology of, 12–15
  childhood in mainland, 175–85
Chinese (language)
  calligraphy, 7–8, 61, 135–6
  dialects, xiii–xiv, 59
  expressions related to learning, 6–8
  teaching of, 72–3, 186 n.5
  use in divination, 135–6, 142
  use in fortune-telling, 48
clothing, 100
coffins, 96, 147
cognition, 10–12, 168–70
Confucianism, 12–13, 27–8, 61, 81–2, 114, 117, 138
consumerism, 61
crying, 51–2, 148–9, 150

Daoism, 12, 142–3
daughters, 3–4, 87, 89–92, 120–1, 123, 184, 191 n.11
death, 21
deer-antler wine, 93, 98–9
deer penis, 98
destinies, 134
discipline, 51–4, 65–6
disorder, 35, 43–5
divination, 46, 129–30
  in mainland China, 178
  see also tang ki
Dragon Boat Festival, 113–14
'drawing attention to', 11–12, 15–16, 17–18, 79, 99–100, 141–2, 145, 168–70

211

Index

dumplings, 182

economy, 37–9, 41
education
    anthropology of, 8–10
    Chinese, 6–8, 12–16, 69–70
    competitiveness of, 5–6, 67–8
    embeddedness of, 3–16
    expenses of, 39, 86
    political implications of, 10
    sociology of, 8–10
Elliott, Alan J.A., 133–40
examinations, 66, 67, 69, 186 n.2, 189 n.15

festivals, 145
Feuchtwang, Stephen, 14–15, 92, 109, 139, 142
filial obedience, 4–6, 28–9, 60–1, 73–4, 76–8, 81–3, 89–92, 109, 114–17, 137–9
firecrackers, 19–22, 132, 180
fire-crossing, 155–6, 159–62
Firth, Raymond, 9–10
fishing, 37–9, 46–7
food, 25, 95–111
    and 'connexions', 107–8
    in relation to 'face', 100
    in religion, 123–4, 161–2
    symbolism of, 95–7, 104, 181–2
fortune-tellers, 48, 109
fostering, 86–8, 177
friendship, 40–1, 153–4
'frights' (condition), 18–19, 134
frugality, 76–8, 92–4
funerals, 29, 102, 130–2, 146–53

gambling, 4, 42–3
gangsters, 63–4
gender, xiv, 26–8, 71, 171
geomancy, 47–8, 149, 152
ghosts, 18, 35, 44–5, 54, 97, 102–3, 110, 148
gods, 104–6, 128
    statues of, 154–5
Granet, Marcel, 13
Guan Di, 139

hongbao (red envelopes), 62, 66, 83–5, 179, 181
Hu Shi, 74–6
Hua Mu-lan, 120–1, 171
humour, 41

identification, 12–16, 33–4, 59–60, 70, 112–13, 123, 144–6, 166–72
incense, 106, 144
inheritance, 89
instruction, 34
isolation, 35

Japanese occupation, 93, 154
Jordan, David, 138, 158

kng put (ritual), 21–2, 134, 153–65
knowledge
    transmission of, 9
    lack of, 48–50
Kuan-im (goddess), 46–7, 139

language, *see* Chinese
learning
    in relation to personhood, 26–8, 56–8
    ways of, 3–6, 8–10
    see also education
life-cycle, 18–30
lunar new year, 83–5, 125–6, 180, 181

Ma Co (goddess), 46–7, 49, 139, 145, 164
manyue (ritual), 24–6
marriage, 28, 40, 82, 88–9, 91, 109, 182–3, 184
martyrdom, 112–21
meal-rotation, 96
medicinal foods, 97–100
Mengzi (Mencius), 72–3
merit, 148
military service, 26, 84, 90
mobilisation of troops (ritual), 159
money, 76–8, 80, 83–5, 88–9, 95, 104–6, 110–11
morality, 4–6, 55, 56–8, 70
motherhood, 69–78, 96, 100, 113–14, 114–17, 123–8
mourning dress, 149–50

naming, 26–8, 48
nationalism, 13, 112–21, 122
nurturance, *see* yang

one-child policy, 179, 184
o-peq ('black-white'), 43–4
opera, 49
Ortner, Sherry, 192 n.15
ostension, *see* 'drawing attention to'
Ou-Yang Xiu, 73

pallbearers, 151
paper houses (for funerals), 149, 151, 152
Parry, Jonathan, 192 n.15
patrilineality, 24, 39–40, 108, 117–20, 140, 141
patriotism, 78, 112–21, 113–21, 126–7, 193 n.1
poetry, 184–5
politeness, 84, 100–2, 102–4, 107–8, 182
pollution (spiritual), 22–4, 126, 130–2, 146, 158, 161

posture, 62
Potter, Jack and Sulamith, 186 n.1
priests, *see* tou su
pregnancy, 22, 98, 139–40
privacy, 75

qingmingjie (tomb-sweeping festival), 185
Qu Yuan, 113

'red envelopes', *see hongbao*
reincarnation, 148
religion, 12–16, 45–51, 104–6, 122–43, 144–65
  expenses of, 158
  role of women in, 123–8
representations, xiv, 10–12, 17–18, 27, 167–8
revision schools, *see buxiban*
rice, 108
'roads', 15–16, 60–1
role models, 63–5

San Taizi (god), 130–2, 137, 139
Sangren, P. Steven, 14, 139
Schipper, Kristofer, 19, 143, 187 n.3
schools, 44, 56, 74
sedan chairs, 155, 156
self-cultivation, 27
self-reliance, 107–8
sensations, 171–2
Seven Fairies, 25
Shepherd, John Robert, 188 n.2
socialisation, 17–18
souls, 18–19, 22–24, 134, 148, 152–3
Sperber, Dan, 12
Sperber, Dan, and Wilson, Deirdre, 11–12, 168, 187 n.13
spirit mediums, *see tang ki*
spirit soldiers, 156, 159, 161–2
Stove God, 4

suicide, 113–14
Sun Yat-sen, 117, 122

Taipei, 60–1
Taiwan, 37
  in relation to China, xiii, 117–20, 175–6, 195 n.1
tang ki (spirit mediums), 18–19, 50, 105–6, 122–3, 123–5, 126–43, 144–6, 155, 160–2
teachers, 6–7, 61–6, 94, 109, 118, 147
television, 58–9, 64, 97–8, 118
textbooks, 3–4, 28–9, 56–8, 69–78, 112–21, 127
texts, religious, 48
Thompson, Stuart, 27, 61, 108
tou su (priests), 50, 128, 155, 161–2
travel, 45–7

uxorilocal marriage, 91

violence, 137–8

Wang Mian, 73–4
Wang Shih-ch'ing, 155–6
waste, 92–4
  see also frugality
Watson, Rubie, 26–8
Weller, Robert, 142
white envelopes, 146
Wittgenstein, Ludwig, 187 n.12
Wolf, Margery, xiv, 140, 141
work-units, 176

yang (nurturance), 71–2, 78, 79–111, 141, 152
  and schooling 108–10
  in mainland China, 179, 183–4
Yi Guan Dao (sect), 50–1
Yue Fei, 114–15

Cambridge Studies in Social and Cultural Anthropology

Editors: *Ernest Gellner, Jack Goody, Stephen Gudeman, Michael Herzfeld, Jonathan Parry*

11 Rethinking Symbolism*
    DAN SPERBER. Translated by Alice L. Morton
15 World Conqueror and World Renouncer: A Study of Buddhism and Polity in Thailand against a Historical Background*
    S. J. TAMBIAH
16 Outline of a Theory of Practice*
    PIERRE BOURDIEU. Translated by Richard Nice
17 Production and Reproduction: A Comparative Study of the Domestic Domain*
    JACK GOODY
27 Day of Shining Red: An Essay and Understanding Ritual*
    GILBERT LEWIS
28 Hunters, Pastoralists and Ranchers: Reindeer Economies and their Transformations*
    TIM INGOLD
32 Muslim Society*
    ERNEST GELLNER
36 Dravidian Kinship
    THOMAS R. TRAUTMANN
39 The Fish-People: Linguistic Exogamy and Tukanoan Identity in Northwest Amazonia
    JEAN E. JACKSON
41 Ecology and Exchange in the Andes
    Edited by DAVID LEHMANN
42 Traders without Trade: Responses to Trade in Two Dyula Communities
    ROBERT LAUNAY
45 Actions, Norms and Representations: Foundations of Anthropological Inquiry*
    LADISLAV HOLY and MILAN STUCKLIK
46 Structural Models in Anthropology*
    PER HAGE and FRANK HARARY
47 Servants of the Goddess: The Priests of a South Indian Temple
    C. J. FULLER
49 The Buddhist Saints of the Forest and the Cult of Amulets: A Study in Charisma, Hagiography, Sectarianism, and Millennial Buddhism*
    S. J. TAMBIAH
51 Individual and Society in Guiana: A Comparative Study of Amerindian Social Organizations*
    PETER RIVIERE

53 Inequality among Brothers: Class and Kinship in South China
    RUBIE S. WATSON
54 On Anthropological Knowledge
    DAN SPERBER
55 Tales of the Yanomami: Daily Life in the Venezuelan Forest*
    JACQUES LIZOT. Translated by Ernest Simon
56 The Making of Great Men: Male Domination and Power among the New Guinea Baruya*
    MAURICE GODELIER. Translated by Ruper Swyer
57 Age Class Systems: Social Institutions and Politics Based on Age*
    BERNARDO BERNARDI. Translated by David I. Kertzer
58 Strategies and Norms in a Changing Matrilineal Society: Descent, Sucesssion and Inheritance among the Toka of Zambia
    LADISLAV HOLY
59 Native Lords of Quito in the Age of the Incas: The Political Economy of North-Andean Chiefdoms
    FRANK SALOMON
60 Culture and Class in Anthropology and History: A Newfoundland Illustration*
    GERALD SIDER
61 From Blessing to Violence: History and Ideology in the Circumcision Ritual of the Merina of Madagascar*
    MAURICE BLOCH
62 The Huli Response to Illness
    STEPHEN FRANKEL
63 Social Inequality in a Northern Portuguese Hamlet: Land, Late Marriage, and Bastardy, 1870–1978
    BRIAN JUAN O'NEILL
64 Cosmologies in the Making: A Generative Approach to Cultural Variation in Inner New Guinea*
    FREDRIK BARTH
65 Kinship and Class in the West Indies: A Genealogical Study of Jamaica and Guyana*
    RAYMOND T. SMITH
66 The Making of the Basque Nation
    MARIANNE HEIBERG
67 Out of Time: History and Evolution in Anthropological Discourse
    NICHOLAS THOMAS
68 Tradition as Truth and Communication
    PASCAL BOYER
69 The Abandoned Narcotic: Kava and Cultural Instability in Melanesia
    RON BRUNTON
70 The Anthropology of Numbers*
    THOMAS CRUMP
71 Stealing People's Names: History and Politics in a Sepik River Cosmology
    SIMON J. HARRISON
72 The Bedouin of Cyrenaica: Studies in Personal and Corporate Power
    EMRYS L. PETERS. Edited by Jack Goody and Emanuel Marx

73 Bartered Brides: Politics, Gender and Marriage in an Afghan Tribal Society
    NANCY TAPPER
74 Property, Production and Family in Neckerhausen*
    DAVID WARREN SABEAN
75 Fifteen Generations of Bretons: Kinship and Society in Lower Brittany, 1720–1980
    MARTINE SEGALEN. Translated by J. A. Underwood
76 Honor and Grace in Anthropology
    Edited by J. G. PERISTIANY and JULIAN PITT-RIVERS
77 The Making of the Modern Greek Family: Marriage and Exchange in Nineteenth-Century Athens
    PAUL SANT CASSIA and CONSTANTINA BADA
78 Religion and Custom in a Muslim Society: The Berti of Sudan
    LADISLAV HOLY
79 Quiet Days in Burgundy: A Study of Local Politics
    MARC ABÉLÈS. Translated by Anella McDermott
80 Sacred Void: Spatial Images of Work and Ritual among the Giriama of Kenya
    DAVID PARKIN
81 A Place of their Own: Family Farming in Eastern Finland
    RAY ABRAHAMS
82 Power, Prayer and Production: The Jola of Casamance, Senegal
    OLGA F. LINARES
83 Identity through History: Living Stories in a Solomon Island Society
    GEOFFREY M. WHITE
84 Monk, Householder and Tantric Priest: Newar Buddhism and its Hierarchy of Ritual
    DAVID GELLNER
85 Hunters and Herders of Southern Africa: A Comparative Ethnography of the Khiosan Peoples*
    ALAN BARNARD
86 Belonging in the Two Berlins: Kin, State, Nation*
    JOHN BORNEMAN
87 Power and Religiosity in a Post-Colonial Setting: Sinhala Catholics in Contemporary Sri Lanka
    R. L. STIRRAT
88 Dialogues with the Dead: The Discussion of Mortality among the Sora of Eastern India
    PIERS VITEBSKY
89 South Coast New Guinea Cultures: A Regional Comparison*
    BRUCE M. KNAUFT
90 Pathology and Identity: The Work of Mother Earth in Trinidad
    ROLAND LITTLEWOOD
91 The Cultural Relations of Classification: An Analysis of Nuaulu Animal Categories from Central Seram
    ROY ELLEN
92 Cinema and the Urban Poor in South India
    SARA DICKEY

93 In the Society of Nature: A Native Ecology in Amazonia
   PHILIPPE DESCOLA
94 Spirit Possession and Personhood among the Kel Ewey Tuareg
   SUSAN J. RASMUSSEN
95 People of the Sea: Identity and Descent among the Vezo of Madagascar
   RITA ASTUTI
96 Social Reproduction and History in Melanesia: Mortuary Ritual, Gift Exchange, and Custom in the Tonga Islands*
   ROBERT FOSTER

* available in paperback

Printed in the United Kingdom
by Lightning Source UK Ltd.
110715UKS00003B/121-132